Trade Unions

Kevin Hawkins

Hutchinson

London Melbourne Sydney Auckland Johannesburg

Hutchinson & Co. (Publishers) Ltd
An imprint of the Hutchinson Publishing Group
24 Highbury Crescent, London N5 1RX

Hutchinson Group (Australia) Pty Ltd
30–32 Cremorne Street, Richmond South, Victoria 3121
PO Box 151, Broadway, New South Wales 2007

Hutchinson Group (NZ) Ltd
32–34 View Road, PO Box 40–086, Glenfield, Auckland 10

Hutchinson Group (SA) (Pty) Ltd
PO Box 337, Bergvlei 2012, South Africa

First published 1981

Set in Times

Printed in Great Britain by The Anchor Press Ltd
and bound by Wm Brendon & Son Ltd
both of Tiptree, Essex

British Library Cataloguing in Publication Data
Hawkins, Kevin
Trade unions.
1. Trade-unions – Great Britain
I. Title
331.88′0941 HD6664

ISBN 0 09 144310 5 cased
0 09 144311 3 paper

Contents

Tables

Figures

Preface

The past thirty years have seen a fundamental change in the popular perception of trade unions in Britain. In the immediate post-war period the unions were described as 'the bulwark of industrial peace and lawfulness'.[1]* Today, however, such a statement would be greeted with derisive laughter. In the intervening years British trade unions have acquired an international reputation for overmightiness and irresponsibility. If bad industrial relations lie at the heart of Britain's economic problems, as popular theology asserts, then the trade unions are widely regarded as the principal culprits. Opinion polls suggest that an overwhelming majority of ordinary people, many of whom themselves belong to a trade union, believe that the unions have aquired 'too much' power and have used it in a variety of damaging ways. Controlled for the most part by a handful of political extremists and militants, they have blackmailed managers into conceding inflationary wage increases, inflicted massive disruption on a defenceless public, brought once mighty industries and firms to their knees and cocooned their members in a web of inefficient working practices. If British industry is losing ground to foreign competitors and British living standards are steadily falling behind those of Western Europe, the blame lies mainly if not exclusively with the 'new barons' of the trade union movement and their acolytes on the shop floor.

This view of British trade unionism, assiduously propagated day in and day out through the mass media, cannot be dismissed out of hand. Governments have won and lost office on the voters' assessment of their competence in handling 'the union problem'. Anyone who wishes to understand the development of British society since the second world war must therefore come to grips with the role of the trade unions. *Trade Unions* has been written with this need in mind. It does not offer a comprehensive analysis of every facet of trade union activity but rather seeks to examine the more popular

*Superior figures refer to the Notes on pages 245–53.

assumptions and beliefs surrounding this activity. I hope, therefore, that it will stimulate the student's interest in the subject and encourage him to read the more specialist literature which is increasingly available. Up to the 1960s, industrial relations was regarded in most academic circles as a rather obscure, esoteric field of study. This perception in turn reflected a belief in the existence of an industrial relations *system* which was quite separate and distinct from the rest of British society. Without entering into the long debate over the conceptual relevance of the 'systems' approach, it can simply be said that the separation which existed twenty years ago has now virtually disappeared. The widespread preoccupation with the relative decline of the British economy and the continuing search for an effective 'cure' has brought the conduct of industrial relations to the forefront of British politics. The need for a cool appraisal of the role of trade unions in industrial relations has consequently never been greater.

The structure of the book is self-explanatory. After outlining the history and traditions of the British trade union movement, I discuss the role that the law and the voluntary principle have played in shaping its current outlook. I then analyse the reasons why, despite the adverse public image of the unions, trade union membership has increased substantially over the past decade. The structural characteristics of the trade unions and their external relationships are also considered. The next major theme for analysis is the structure of power within trade unions and the relationship between union officials and union members. This leads logically to an in-depth consideration of the nature and pattern of union activity in the workplace and the challenge which this presents to managerial authority. The principal union activity, however, is collective bargaining – the structure, development and conduct of which are then discussed, together with the attempts of successive governments to regulate the level of pay settlements. The concluding chapter seeks to draw together the major themes in the analysis and focuses attention on the effects of trade union activity. Some contemporary ideas for changing the bargaining system are discussed and the book ends with a brief discussion of the role which the unions are likely to play in British society during the last two decades of the twentieth century.

Two additional points should be made at the outset. First, this book is primarily concerned with the role of trade unions in industrial relations; it is not a study of their political activities or of their relationship with the Labour Party. Second, it is concerned exclusively with trade union activity in Britain. No attempt has been made to compare British trade unions with those of, say, West Germany or the USA for the simple reason that any comparisons would have to be detailed and comprehensive if they were to mean anything at all. There is no space in an introductory text of this kind for detailed comparative analyses and superficial comparisons are more likely to mislead than assist the student. My main purpose is to stimulate interest in and convey some information about the trade union movement that has emerged in Britain over the past century and will remain a prominent feature of British society in the foreseeable future.

In conclusion I should like to thank the publishers for giving me the privilege of writing a book which replaces the standard introductory text of the late Allan Flanders. I should also like to thank Jo Baxter and Lucy Mathieson for typing out the manuscript.

University of Bradford Management Centre
February 1980

Abbreviations

ACAS	Advisory, Conciliation and Arbitration Service
ACTSS	Association of Clerical, Technical and Supervisory Staffs
AEU	Amalgamated Engineering Union
APEX	Association of Professional, Executive, Clerical and Computer Staffs
ASBSBSW	Amalgamated Society of Boilermakers, Shipwrights, Blacksmiths and Structural Workers
ASE	Amalgamated Society of Engineers
ASLEF	Associated Society of Locomotive Engineers and Firemen
ASTMS	Association of Scientific, Technical and Managerial Staffs
ASW	Amalgamated Society of Woodworkers
AUEW	Amalgamated Union of Engineering Workers
BIFU	Banking, Insurance and Finance Union
CAC	Central Arbitration Committee
CBI	Confederation of British Industries
CIR	Commission on Industrial Relations
COHSE	Confederation of Health Service Employees
COSA	Colliery Overmen and Shotfirers' Association
DATA	Draughtsmen's and Allied Technicians' Association
DE	Department of Employment
EEC	European Economic Community
EETPU	Electrical, Electronic, Telecommunication and Plumbing Union
EPA	Employment Protection Act, 1975
ETU	Electrical Trades Union
GMWU	General and Municipal Workers' Union
GNP	Gross National Product
IMF	International Monetary Fund
MFGB	Miners' Federation of Great Britain

NALGO	National and Local Government Officers' Association
NAS	National Association of Schoolmasters
NATSOPA	National Society of Operative Printers and Assistants
NBPI	National Board for Prices and Incomes
NEC	National Executive Committee
NGA	National Graphical Association
NIRC	National Industrial Relations Court
NUM	National Union of Mineworkers
NUPE	National Union of Public Employees
NUR	National Union of Railwaymen
NUT	National Union of Teachers
NUVB	National Union of Vehicle Builders
ORC	Opinion Research Centre
SBA	Sole Bargaining Agency
TASS	Technical and Supervisory Section (of the AUEW)
TGWU	Transport and General Workers' Union
T&GWU	Tailors' and Garment Workers' Union
TSSA	Transport Salaried Staffs Association
TUC	Trades Union Congress
TULRA	Trade Union and Labour Relations Act, 1974
UCATT	Union of Construction, Allied Trades and Technicians
UKAPE	United Kingdom Association of Professional Engineers
UPW	Union of Post Office Workers
USDAW	Union of Shop, Distributive and Allied Workers.

1 History and tradition

It is often said that British trade unions are hidebound by tradition. It would be very surprising, however, if tradition did not exert *some* influence over their policies, rules and structures. Many of the unions currently affiliated to the TUC can trace their origins back well over a century to the formative decades of British industrialism. More importantly, whatever their age they have all expanded their membership and won recognition from employers almost entirely by their own efforts. Unlike their counterparts in the USA and in several other western countries, they owe little to the assistance of the state. Most Victorian trade unionists practised the doctrine of self-help as vigorously as Samuel Smiles preached it. Suspicious of outsiders in general and of lawyers in particular, they bequeathed to their twentieth-century successors a determination to defend their traditions against all encroachment, whether by employers, governments or other trade unionists.

It follows that the current pattern of trade union organization and behaviour cannot be properly understood without some knowledge of the history and traditions of the movement. The intention here is not to embark on a detailed narrative but to focus on the objectives, methods and structures of British trade unions as they emerged in the late Victorian era and evolved in the first half of the present century.

Norms and beliefs

At the root of trade unionism lies the belief that the terms and conditions of employment which apply to the vast majority of the labour force can only be improved through collective action. As the Webbs observed:

In unorganised trades the individual workman, applying for a job, accepts or refuses the terms offered by the employer, without communication with his fellow-workmen, and without any other consideration but the exigencies of

> his own position. For the sale of his labour he makes, with the employer, a strictly individual bargain. But if a group of workmen concert together, and send representatives to conduct the bargaining on behalf of the whole body, the position is at once changed. Instead of the employer making a series of separate contracts with isolated individuals, he meets with a collective will and settles, in a single agreement the principles upon which, for the time being, all workmen of a particular group, or class, or grade will be engaged.[1]

These principles together constituted what the Webbs called the 'common rule', which in turn embodied a set of collectively agreed norms or standards (such as rates of pay and hours of work) under which a defined group of workers were to be employed. The extension of common rules across each trade and industry was seen by the Webbs as a method of restricting competition in labour markets. In circumstances where the supply of labour exceeded the demand, the absence of a common rule would encourage individual workers to undercut each other in competing for the available jobs. Where, by contrast, demand exceeded supply, employers would bid against each other for scarce labour unless collectively they agreed to follow the common rule.

The Webbs emphasized, however, that each occupation or trade would tend to generate its own distinctive body of common rules which would in turn reflect the divergent beliefs and normative standards of different trade unions. Three sets of beliefs or 'doctrines' were distinguished by the Webbs. The first of these was the *doctrine of vested interests,* which assumed that the terms and conditions of employment customarily enjoyed by a given workgroup 'ought under no circumstances to be interfered with for the worse'.[2] This doctrine was particularly influential with groups of craftsmen, each of whom tended to regard their own particular set of skills as their personal property, to be defended against confiscation or encroachment from whatever quarter it might come. The Webbs saw this doctrine as the underlying cause both of demarcation disputes between craftsmen's unions and of resistance to technological change and new working methods. Resistance to innovation was particularly widespread in the late Victorian era as more manufacturing trades moved into the factory stage of production and their dependence on traditional craft skills declined. In the engineering industry, for example, a protracted national strike occurred in 1897 as a result of the employers' refusal to accept the Amalgamated Society of Engineers' demand that new machines should remain the preserve of skilled men.[3] The strike failed but the issue which had caused it remained unresolved for many years.

The second doctrine distinguished by the Webbs was that of *supply and demand.* In contrast to the notion of vested interests which the Webbs regarded as a legacy of the eighteenth century, the doctrine of supply and demand was seen as very much in tune with the norms of mid Victorian society. When, after 1800, the state abandoned its traditional role of fixing terms and conditions of employment by law, self-help was the only course of action open to dissatisfied workers:

> Working men were told, by friends and foes alike, that they could no longer be regarded as citizens entitled to legal protection of their established expectations; that labour was a commodity like any other; and their real position was that of sellers in a market, entitled to do the best they could for themselves within the limits of the law of the land, but to no better terms than they could, by the ordinary arts of bargaining, extract from those with whom they dealt. . . . It followed that the only criterion of justice of any claim was ability to enforce it, and that the only way by which the workmen could secure better conditions of employment was by strengthening their strategic position against the employer.[4]

Stated in these terms the doctrine appears to have been a prescription for conflict. In practice, however, it gave rise to a more co-operative approach to wage determination. Since it assumed that rising profits justified rising wages, it underlined the mutual dependence of product prices and wage costs. In coal mining and the iron and steel industry, the response of employers and unions was to negotiate a series of sliding scale agreements which tied wage rates to the selling price of the product.

Such agreements, however, were not appropriate to those industries in which price fluctuations were relatively modest and costs other than wages were important.[5] The real significance of the supply and demand doctrine was that, in the final analysis, it not only underlined the need for effective combination on *both* sides of the labour market but also indicated the likelihood of a tacit conspiracy between employers and unions against the rest of the community. As the Webbs noted:

> The workmen, finding themselves individually powerless to stand out for better terms, combine in order to strengthen themselves against the employers. The employers, on their side, combine to protect themselves against the workmen. Finally both parties, discovering no other way of maintaining the price of their product, upon which both wages and profits are deemed to depend, unite their forces in order to exact better terms from the community for the trade as a whole, and incidentally to protect themselves against what they choose to consider the unfair competition of a few individuals among them.[6]

In this sense it could be said that a trade union motivated by the doctrine of supply and demand would ultimately behave like a labour *cartel,* and would evoke a parallel response from the employers with whom it negotiated.[7]

Viewed from the perspective of the ordinary worker, however, the principal drawback of tying wages too closely to prices and profits was that when the latter fell they dragged the former down with them. The growing resistance of trade unions to reductions in wage rates from about 1890 onwards, therefore, prompted the Webbs to speak of the emergence of a third doctrine – that of a *living wage.* The rapid growth of trade unionism among certain groups of semi-skilled and unskilled workers – a development popularly (though somewhat erroneously) known as the 'New Unionism' – was ascribed to the demand for a better standard of living. Such groups had no vested interests to protect nor were they in a position to exploit the laws of supply and demand. Yet their spontaneous protest against low wages and bad working conditions carried trade unionism into industries and occupations which it had hitherto shunned. The doctrine of a living wage, the Webbs argued, gave no guarantee that any particular individual would be employed at any particular trade, but rather offered the prospect that as long as the worker was in employment he could expect to receive a wage which was enough to ensure that he enjoyed 'an efficient and vigorous working life'.[8]

The doctrine of a living wage was, even before 1914, a powerful – if not always the dominant – normative influence on many trade unionists. Over the next few decades, however, it strengthened its hold. Thus when established collective bargaining arrangements, maintained and operated by the officials of trade unions and employers' associations, failed to ensure that wages kept pace with the rapid rise in the cost of living during the first world war, workgroups exerted pressure on individual employers and secured additional increases. By 1920 it was widely accepted that 'a wage sufficient to afford a man an adequate and decent livelihood must be regarded as a first charge on industry'.[9] The depth of feeling on this issue accounts for the bitter conflict which arose during the 1920s when employers in hard-pressed export industries (notably coal, cotton and engineering) were compelled to cut their wage costs. But while heavy and prolonged unemployment probably restrained employee expectations, it is worth noting that, taking the inter-war period as a whole, average wages fell less rapidly than the cost of living. After 1945 the unemployment constraint disappeared and the demand for a living wage developed into an expectation of annual improvement.

The Webbs noted one practical objection to the living wage doctrine – namely that while different occupations and workgroups had widely divergent requirements and expectations, the doctrine itself implied a growing tendency towards the fixing of standard terms and conditions of employment for all groups. Left to themselves, however, employers and trade unions would negotiate terms which reflected a combination of market forces and vested interests. The best-organized groups would therefore tend to achieve the highest living wage and those groups which lacked both organization and bargaining power would remain at or below subsistence level. The Webbs came to the conclusion, therefore, that as the demand for a living wage grew, so the state would inevitably find itself cast in the role of arbitrator 'between the workman who claims more and the employer who offers less than is consistent with the welfare of other sections'.[10] In short, they envisaged that as expectations advanced, so the negotiation of private wage agreements would gradually give way to a general system of fixing wages by statutory enactment.

While the Webbs' three doctrines or sets of assumptions have changed and developed since the 1890s, they are still clearly discernible in current patterns of trade union and workgroup behaviour. The doctrine of vested interests, for example, emerges not so much in the form of demarcation disputes (which are far less common now than in the Webbs' day), as in the protracted resistance of certain well-organized groups of skilled workers to the introduction of new technology. Technological innovation is opposed not simply because it often reduces job opportunities but also because it tends to 'deskill' jobs and thus reduces their status in the occupational hierarchy. Similarly, some unions and workgroups still evince a strong belief in exploiting market forces. In recent years the public sector in particular has seen several major disputes in which the union's argument has stressed the strategic importance of the service provided or the goods produced and the need to remunerate employees accordingly. The argument has usually been effective where the union has demonstrated that inadequate rewards have led to staff shortages and the point has been driven home by industrial action. In the private sector, unions have been quick to claim higher wages for their members if they believe that the employer's ability to pay, measured by the productivity of the workforce or the profitability of the firm, has improved significantly.

Finally, the concept of a living wage still determines the bargaining objectives of unions who represent large groups of low-paid workers, especially in the public sector. In general, however, what sum of money constitutes a living wage is determined not by some absolute standard of material well-being but by factors such as the rate of increase in the cost of living, the 'going rate' for wage settlements across the economy as a whole and the level of employee expectations. The Webbs were obviously mistaken in their belief that the state itself would define what a living wage should be for different workgroups, yet in so far as their analysis pointed to a growing involvement by the state in the process of wage determination it has been validated by the experience of the past thirty years.

Objectives and methods

Traditionally the rule book of every trade union has contained some reference to the objectives of the organization. Normally they include the improvement of the members' terms and conditions of employment. Occasionally they include specific legislative goals – the enactment of laws which will also in some way improve their members' position. In general, however, formal statements of objectives have never thrown much light on what a trade union actually does. In the words of the Webbs:

> We must not look to the formal rules or rhetorical preambles for a scientific or complete account of trade union action. Drafted originally by enthusiastic pioneers, copied and recopied by successive revising committees, the printed constitutions of working-class associations represent rather the aspirations than the everyday actions of the members.[11]

It was for this reason that the Webbs devoted much more space to an analysis of trade union *methods* – they sought to infer what a union was from what it actually did.

Historically the oldest trade union method is that of 'mutual insurance'. Many of the older unions, composed entirely of craftsmen, began their life in the early and mid Victorian years as 'friendly societies' whose principal function was to provide their members with certain financial benefits in the event of unemployment, sickness or some other calamity befalling them. The provision of friendly benefits – sick pay, accident benefits, superannuation allowances – gave these societies ultimate control over their members since expulsion from the organization brought severe financial penalties. The provision of unemployment pay, however, fulfilled an even more important function. In times of depression, with many craftsmen seeking work, there would be a natural tendency for them to compete against each other by offering their services at successively lower prices. It was to combat this threat that friendly societies provided unemployment pay:

The main object of the individual member may be to provide against the personal distress which would otherwise be caused to himself and his family by the stoppage of his weekly income. But the object of the union, from the collective point of view, is to prevent him from accepting employment, under stress of starvation, on terms which, in the common judgement of the trade, would be injurious to its interests.[12]

Despite the fact that the friendly society functions of trade unions have long since been usurped by the state, the provision of unemployment pay reflects the continuing rationale of trade unionism – the subordination of the interests of the individual to those of the group to which he or she belongs.

The method of mutual insurance sprang directly from the doctrine of vested interests. For the craftsman, defending the customary 'rate for the job' was no less important than protecting any other part of his property from encroachment. The doctrine of supply and demand, by contrast, encouraged trade unionists to adopt the method of 'collective bargaining'. Workmen succeeded in compelling their employer to negotiate terms and conditions of employment with their representatives wherever they managed to organize themselves in a collective body and marshal whatever bargaining power they possessed. In an era of small employment units and local product specialization, however, both employers and trade unions quickly realized the advantages of negotiating on a *district* basis rather than factory-by-factory. From a trade union point of view, a collective agreement imposed common rules or standard terms and conditions on all workmen in a given workplace:

The starving man gets his job at the same piecework rate as the workman who could afford to stand out for his usual earnings. The superior craftsman retains all his advantages over his fellows, but without allowing his superiority to be made the means of reducing the weekly wage of the ordinary worker.[13]

But if the neutralization of individual differences was a legitimate objective within the workplace, why could the same objective not be pursued between several workplaces in one district, or even between all the districts within one industry? If common rules could be applied at local level, why not at national level where they would apply to the trade as a whole?

The logic of concentrating the process of collective rule-making at a level above the workplace was not lost on many employers. In so far as it fixed one standard wage rate for a given trade within a particular district, collective bargaining ensured the equalization of one major cost factor. In Phelps Brown's words:

> Not a few (employers) reached the conclusion that it was a positive advantage to them to have a floor put under price competition in this way. Those who had little love for the union were still willing to meet it to negotiate a rate, because of all union activities this interfered with them least. . . . It was never a main function of the unions to conduct negotiations between the workpeople of one plant and their employer. Such negotiations raise more issues and touch more sensitive nerves than district bargaining. Because this has to cover many firms at once, it can deal only with a short list of common factors and cannot enter into the detail of the conditions of work firm by firm.[14]

It was therefore in the interests of the individual employer to combine with his fellows in order to present a common front in wage negotiations. It was also in his interests to negotiate with a union which was capable of ensuring that its members observed whatever agreements it concluded on their behalf. The development of stable bargaining relationships, first at district and eventually at industry level, required comprehensive organization on both sides of the labour market. It was this requirement which led the Webbs to deny that collective bargaining was voluntary in nature. On the contrary, they argued that in effect it ultimately compelled workers and employers to become members of their respective combinations.

The Webbs saw two major deficiencies in the method of collective bargaining. First, there were still many trades and districts in which the common rule could not be enforced because of poor organization on one side or the other. Second, even where the organization on both sides was comprehensive there was still no guarantee that the contents of a collective agreement would be 'conducive to the welfare of the community'.[15] Consequently, the Webbs believed that the method of *legal enactment* was not only superior in some respects to collective bargaining but would eventually displace it as the principal method of rule-making. If the common rules of a given trade or industry could be embodied in an Act of Parliament, not only would they apply to all districts regardless of differing levels of organization but would also be virtually immune from the vicissitudes of the business cycle.

The main stumbling block to the development of legal enactment as a rule-making method, however, was the lack of an appropriate institutional framework at both national and local level. As the Webbs pointed out, if the trade union movement as a whole was to succeed in persuading Parliament to enact legislation on the scale envisaged, at least three conditions would have to be fulfilled. First, the movement as a whole would need to develop a common programme based on a real sense of unity. Second, there would need to be a strong central organization which was capable of formulating such a programme and bringing sustained pressure to bear on Parliament to enact it. Third, the central organization would have to be based on a network of local institutions which represented all the various trade unions in a given district.

Unfortunately, as the Webbs admitted, there was never the slightest chance that any of these conditions would be met. At local level there was no identity of interest or outlook between representatives of the various trades and occupations. The only institutions which could in theory have acted as a common forum at this level – the local trades council – was regarded with acute suspicion by union officials and denounced by the Webbs as akin to an 'unorganized public meeting'. Lack of unity at local or district level was inevitably reproduced at national level. The Trades Union Congress was 'utterly unable to formulate any consistent or practical policy' and its Parliamentary Committee (subsequently renamed the General Council) had long since abandoned any claim to the intellectual leadership of the trade union movement.[16] These organizational weaknesses reflected the narrow sectional attitudes of trade union leaders and officials: 'Each man knows his own trade, and the desires of his own union, but is both ignorant and indifferent as to the needs or desires of every other trade.'[17] There is, however, no evidence to suggest that union officials were out of step with the wishes and prejudices of their own rank and file members. Nor was this predilection for self-help and organizational autonomy the exclusive characteristic of the older craft unions. The general unions for semi- and unskilled workers which emerged after 1889 simply filled in some of the structural gaps inherited from the past 'and behaved each in its own industry or region as the other unions had long been behaving there'.[18]

There was, however, an even more fundamental objection to the method of legal enactment. It assumed that trade union leaders and members alike positively wished to involve themselves in formulating legislation and, if necessary, in pressing their claims in a court of law. Nothing, in fact, could have been further from the truth. As Pelling has observed: 'Involvement with the law meant for them, as for the individual worker, exposure to a hostile environment, where the stakes were very high and the dice might well be loaded. It is not very surprising that union leaders were inclinded to steer clear of the law whenever they could.'[19] In the late Victorian era it was usually the leaders of the weaker unions (with the notable exception of the cotton unions and to a lesser extent the miners) who were at all interested in obtaining legal support. Some of these leaders felt that their own interests would be better served by a system of compulsory arbitration than by one of collective bargaining. In those industries where the unions were too weak to compel the employers to enter into a stable collective bargaining relationship, there were obvious advantages to be gained from a system whereby improved terms and conditions could be imposed on the employers by law. Compulsory arbitration, however, never attracted more than a third of the votes within the TUC, where opinion was led by those unions who were strong enough to engage in collective bargaining. The growing hostility to trade unionism of the judiciary during the 1890s, culminating in the Taff Vale decision of 1901, in effect played into the hands of those who wanted to keep the law out of industrial relations. With the passage of the Trade Disputes Act of 1906, the non-interventionists won the day. From then on, voluntary collective bargaining was – and remains– the dominant method of rule-making.

Structure and government

The Webbs attributed 'nine-tenths' of the ineffectiveness of trade unionism to open competition for members between overlapping unions. The structure of British trade unions has in fact never ceased to engage the critical attention of even the most sympathetic observers. Yet, as the Webbs themselves pointed out, the structure of the movement was inextricably bound up with its purpose:

The whole history of trade unionism confirms the inference that a trade union, formed as it is for the distinct purpose of obtaining concrete and definite material improvements in its members' employment, cannot, in its simplest form, safely extend beyond the area within which those identical improvements are shared by all its members – cannot spread, that is to say, beyond the boundaries of a single occupation.[20]

This did not rule out the possibility of mergers between unions, which were common even in the 1890s. What it did ensure was that amalgamated unions comprising two or more occupational groups remained little more than loose federations of quasi-autonomous sectional interests.

The problems posed by the desire for occupational autonomy would have been less acute if it had been possible to define the precise boundaries of every trade and achieve a concensus within the movement as to where these boundaries lay. But boundaries were frequently unclear, providing a fertile seed-bed for inter-union squabbles which the movement as a whole was not as yet equipped to resolve. Not until 1939 did the TUC take upon itself, under the so-called Bridlington procedure, the role of arbiter and conciliator in inter-union disputes. In the engineering industry, for example, the ASE claimed the right to represent every kind of skilled man – a claim which was bitterly contested by smaller unions such as the Boilermakers' Society, the Pattern-Makers' Association and the Steam-Engine Makers' Society. In some areas the relations between different unions within the engineering industry were so bad that when one became involved in a dispute with an employer and strike action ensued, its principal rival would 'blackleg' by offering its own members for the vacant jobs. 'Scarcely a year passed', noted the Webbs, 'without the Trades Union Congress being made the scene of a heated accusation by one society or another, that some other union has "black-legged" a dispute in which it was engaged, and thereby deprived its members of all the results of their combination.'[21]

The craft unions, propelled as they were by the doctrine of vested interests, defined the boundaries of their organization according to occupational rather than industrial criteria. Their objective was to organize all members of the craft wherever they might be found, geographically and industrially, and exclude all non-members. Once this basic pattern of organization had been established, the unions of more recent origin – representing either operatives or unskilled workers – were obliged to follow it. The industrial diversity of the general unions accounts, in part, for their chequered career between 1889 and 1940. The cement which bound each craft union was not simply its economic bargaining power but also the sense of occupational status and social identity which it conferred on the individual members. Membership of a craft society confirmed the possession of appropriate skills. Membership of a general union, by contrast, was wholly instrumental in character. The general unions recruited thousands of unskilled workers in cyclical upswings when wages were rising and unemployment was low, only to lose them in droves during the ensuing recession. Most of them joined a union in the hope of higher wages, and as long as it met their aspirations they remained in membership. But the general unions found it difficult to mount an effective strike (if only because it was easy for employers to replace unskilled men with blackleg labour) and impossible to defend their members' wages in a period of rising unemployment. Lacking any real collective identity, the members quickly deserted the union when it failed to meet their expectations.

The development of trade unionism along occupational boundaries precluded any form of reorganization along industrial lines. The union which came nearest to the industrial model was the Miners' Federation of Great Britain, but in reality this organization was (at least until 1945) little more than a loose alliance of regional associations. In the railway industry, the ambition of the Amalgamated Society of Railway Servants to organize all grades was frustrated by the refusal of both the train drivers and firemen and the white collar staff to abandon their own respective unions. Elsewhere industrial unionism was never a practical possibility, nor did the movement as a whole develop any willingness to consider it seriously. At the Trades Union Congress of 1924, for example, a delegate from the MFGB proposed that the number of trade unions should be 'reduced to an absolute minimum', that the aim should be 'organization by industry, with every worker a member of the appropriate organization', and that a united front should be formed for the improvement of all workers' standards of living. The reaction of the delegates, however, clearly indicated that the tradition of autonomy was as powerful as ever. After investigating these proposals for three years, the TUC concluded that 'the varying structure and working of unions, the differing circumstances in the various trades and industries and the impossibility of defining boundaries (made) the general application of any particular scheme impracticable'. Further attempts in 1943 and 1962 to reopen the debate on structure within the TUC failed to elicit a constructive response from the great majority of affiliated unions.

The tradition that each union constitutes a sovereign body also explains the weakness of the TUC itself. When the TUC was established in 1868 it represented 'an annual demonstration of trade union strength, an expression of solidarity and an opportunity for leaders of the movement to discuss their problems'.[22] The discussion of problems, however, rarely produced a concrete strategy for action. The Webbs felt that by the 1890s the TUC had 'degenerated':

> The four or five hundred members coming from all trades and all parts of the kingdom are largely unknown to each other and new to their work. Each delegate brings to the meeting his own pet ideas and legislative projects. . . . They appear higgledy-piggledy in the agenda of the Congress sitting as a whole, the order in which they are discussed being decided by lot. The bewildered delegates, fresh from the bench or the mine, find themselves confronted with a hundred and fifty heterogeneous proposals, some containing highly technical amendments of the statutes relating to particular trades, others being mere pious aspirations for social amelioration, and others again involving far-reaching changes in the economic or political constitution of the country. All these come before Congress with equal authority; are explained in five-minute speeches; and as regards four out of every five, get passed without inquiry or discrimination.[23]

The Webbs were also critical of the cult of amateurism which prevailed among members of the Parliamentary Committee of the TUC – especially their refusal to enlist the help of professional advisers from outside the movement. Yet this amateurism was the direct result of the tradition of organizational sovereignty. The leaders and delegates of affiliated unions feared that if the TUC was allowed to develop into a large, professional bureaucracy, it would eventually pose a direct challenge to their own autonomy. Not until 1921 did they consent to the replacement of the ineffective Parliamentary Committee by a thirty-two man General Council, supported by a full-time general secretary and assistant secretary. This belated move did not, however, resolve the fundamental problem of how to transform the TUC into an efficient executive body with an appropriate degree of authority over its affiliated members, for the simple reason that there was no political will among the latter to see such a transformation occur. In these circumstances, the personality of the general secretary became a major factor in determining the degree of influence which the TUC could bring to bear over its affiliates and thus its credibility in negotiations with successive governments.

Within the TUC, the familiar struggle between the dictates of administrative efficiency and the pressure for democratic control was settled, on the whole, in favour of the latter. Within individual trade unions, however, the outcome was less clear-cut. In most craft unions the old suspicion of a permanent bureaucracy was very much to the fore. Constitutionally, the rank and file members were given the power to elect their full-time officials and, in a general meeting, determine the policy of the union. Central executive bodies were subject to various checks and balances designed to prevent them from arrogating power to themselves and losing touch with the ordinary members. The Webbs, however, noted a growing divergence between theory and practice. In small, local craft societies the concept of control by the members might still be attainable. In the larger national unions, however, it was soon seen to be totally unrealistic. The Boilermakers' Society, for example, without any formal consitutional changes, had by the 1890s become a bureaucracy run by an 'informal cabinet' of full-time officials. The Engineers were forced to recognize that it was impossible to achieve a unified strategy for the whole trade as long as every branch and district committee was free to go its own way and that the number of full-time officials at the centre would thus have to be increased.[24] The tendency for effective power to reside more and more with full-time officials was strongly reinforced by the increasing complexity of the union's business and the need for a common front against the associated employers.

The newer unions composed predominantly of unskilled workers tended to adopt a more centralized, less overtly democratic approach to the problem of internal government. The general secretaries and full-time officials of these unions were less hidebound by the tradition of the sturdy, independent craftsman and accorded priority to the effective marshalling of their limited bargaining power. This implied that the rank and file membership would have to accept the discipline of the union and follow the instructions of their full-time officials to a much greater degree than their counterparts in the craft unions. The different approaches reflected divergent organizational traditions. Most craft unions had grown 'bottom upwards' from the small local trade clubs of the eighteenth century; their members were only too well aware that their bargaining power was rooted in the possession of certain valuable skills. By contrast, the general unions which sprang up after 1889 owed much of their growth to the work of full-time organizers and much of their success, such as it was, to the negotiating skill of these same officials. Since their members typically lacked any real sense of *occupational* solidarity, the general unions had to endow themselves with an *institutional* stability. This in turn implied the establishment of a strong hierarchy of professional officers who could impose their collective will on the organization. The quality of leadership was always of critical importance to the survival of the union.

Yet all unions to a greater or lesser degree encountered the fundamental problem of controlling the behaviour of their members. Whatever differences there might be in the formal constitutional characteristics of individual unions, there was no way in which every dispute or grievance could be channelled up through the union's hierarchy. A general assembly of branch or district delegates would normally be able to reach agreement on the policy which the union should follow on certain general matters, such as demarcation, working practices and methods of payment. But this left a mass of potentially troublesome issues virtually untouched:

> . . . changes in methods and machines were constantly dispensing with old skills, and disordering status. From time to time such anxieties, grievances and vague resentments seemed to cumulate and reinforce one another; the men in some district would be seething with discontent; and yet the cause was not apparent, no issue had arisen of the kind with which union headquarters was used to deal. So when strife followed, it broke out suddenly; men suffering from a real but undefined sense of grievance formulated some unreasonable complaint; a trivial incident precipitated an unofficial strike. The men felt they had to take action into their own hands, because the union was no help to them. The officials at headquarters and the national executives were taken by surprise, and found fault with the men for breaking the agreement made in their name. The public blamed the leaders for being out of touch with the rank and file.[25]

The plain truth was, of course, that most unions had not yet established themselves as a prominent feature of labour relations *in the workplace.* Collective agreements and procedures negotiated by full-time officials at district or national level were in general only marginally relevant to most of the day-to-day problems which arose at workplace level. The gap was partially filled – but only gradually and imperfectly – by the emergence of the shop steward, in whom the roles of union activist and workplace representative were fused.

Conflict and co-operation

Progressive opinion in the pre-1914 era held that collective bargaining offered the most orderly method of adjusting terms and conditions of employment. The spread of collective organization among employees and employers alike was seen as a strong institutional bulwark against strikes and disorder. Yet it was also recognized that the application of *sanctions* by one side or the other was an integral part of the bargaining process:

> . . . it is impossible to deny that the perpetual liability to end in a strike is a grave drawback to the method of collective bargaining. So long as the parties to a bargain are free to agree or not to agree it is inevitable that, human nature being as it is, there should now and again come a deadlock, leading to that trial of strength and endurance which lies behind all bargaining.[26]

It was for this reason that the Webbs preferred the method of legal enactment to collective bargaining. But if a system of legal enactment had in fact been adopted, it seems likely that this would simply have transferred the main location of bargaining activity from industry itself to Downing Street and Westminster. This is, of course, precisely what happened when the economic problems of key industries such as coal mining and transport became too complex for the employers and unions themselves to resolve.

The pattern of strikes in the period from about 1889 to 1926 can be seen as a vindication of the argument that collective bargaining was a force for order and restraint in industrial relations. Those industries which experienced the highest levels of conflict (coal mining, railways and the docks) were those in which the employers were conspicuously reluctant to accept the claim of the unions to regulate terms and conditions of employment on a joint basis. By contrast, in industries where collective bargaining arrangements were well-established and the two sides had reached an institutional *modus vivendi* (such as cotton, iron and steel, printing and the boot and shoe trade), major disputes were rare. Yet it would be misleading to regard these decades as simply a transitional phase in the gradual movement of the British system of industrial relations towards institutional maturity. There were, in particular, two significant developments in these years which raised some awkward questions about the way in which the system was moving.

First, the structural development of collective bargaining at district and industry level and the absence of direct union involvement in workplace relations, though convenient for both sides, reflected a combination of circumstances which was not necessarily permanent. Most employers resented union interference with their right to manage their businesses and the level of unemployment in most years was such that 'troublemakers' could easily be replaced. From 1911 through to the end of the first world war, however, the average level of unemployment was far lower than it had ever been, thus removing the employer's labour market advantage. In 1911–13 low unemployment combined with a rising cost of living to produce both an unprecendented rise in trade union membership and a major increase in strike activity involving many different industries. As Pelling has observed, 'Men could more readily defy their employers when the supply of potential blacklegs was at its lowest'.[27] During the first world war the labour market tightened even further, the cost of living soared upwards, and there was a significant upsurge in union activity at *workplace* level. Ignoring the wartime prohibition on strikes and the disapproval of their own union leaders, coal miners, shipyard workers and engineers all took direct action at various times during the war. Some strikes occurred in pursuit of higher wages, some in protest against the 'dilution' of traditional skills and a few in opposition to the dismissal of fellow-workers. The lesson, however, was clear. Given favourable market conditions, well-organized workgroups would produce their own leaders and spokesmen who in turn would seek to encroach upon traditional managerial prerogatives and extend the frontier of joint regulation in the workplace. The assumptions of the formal system of district and industry-wide bargaining were being openly challenged.

It was against this background that the Whitley Commission was given the task by the government of investigating what had gone wrong with the established methods of rule-making in industry. The commission's first report (1917) clearly indicated the limitations of traditional collective bargaining:

> A permanent improvement in the relations between employers and employed must be founded upon something other than a cash basis. What is wanted is that workpeople should have a greater opportunity of participating in the discussions about and adjustment of those parts of industry by which they are most affected.

The report advocated the establishment of a structure of joint councils at industry, local and workplace level in order to secure for workers 'a greater share in and responsibility for the determination and observance of the conditions under which their work is carried on' and 'the greatest possible security of earnings and employment' in the interests of industrial peace and efficiency.

In some industries 'Whitley Councils' were set up at national level but the concept of formal joint consultation was rarely applied in the workplace. 'Whitleyism' left the main cockpits of industrial warfare untouched. In any case, the onset of heavy and prolonged unemployment after 1920 weakened the bargaining power of workgroups and buttressed the employers' determination to preserve their traditional right to manage their businesses as they thought fit. During the inter-war period, the main focus of union activity was on defending nationally negotiated terms and conditions against reductions. Not until the post-1945 period, when unemployment was once again reduced to virtually zero, did the demand for joint regulation in the workplace come once again to the fore. As in 1914–18, however, the initiative was taken by workgroups and shop stewards; union officials, employers and politicians alike were slow, even reluctant, to recognize the significance of this renewed 'challenge from below'. The normative influence of the traditional system of collective bargaining remained strong.

The second development involved the legal fiction that a strike was simply a 'trade dispute' involving one or more employers and one or more trade unions. In theory the voluntary, non-legal character of collective bargaining – underpinned by the doctrine of supply and demand – implied that there should be no *legal* obstacles which might prevent one party from meeting the other around the negotiating table on anything less than equal terms. The Trade Disputes Act of 1906 achieved this objective by protecting trade unions against action for damages arising from their involvement in a 'trade dispute'. Yet in so far as the Act assumed that the negotiation of terms and conditions of employment was of interest solely to the parties directly involved, it was a legal fiction even before it reached the statute book. The experience of the coal strike of 1893, when Gladstone instructed his foreign secretary Rosebery to offer his services as conciliator, implied that whenever the economy was faced with serious disruption, the government would intervene. In 1907 the mere threat of a national railway stoppage was enough to induce Lloyd George to intervene and force a settlement on the employers under threat of special legislation. The same response was forthcoming in a further railway dispute in 1911, a major coal strike in 1912, a strike in the London docks in the same year, and a stoppage in the South Wales coalfield in 1915. The inference was clear – trade unions in strategic industries and services need only threaten a stoppage and the government would force the employers to make an improved offer. In these circumstances a private trade dispute rapidly assumed immense public significance.

The system worked well enough as long as the government of the day was responsive to trade union pressure. When, however, the government refused to act, the consequences were far-reaching. The problems of the coal mining industry after 1918 furnished the raw material for the biggest single conflict in the history of British trade unionism. Even before 1914 it was obvious that the coal industry was slipping into decline due to a combination of rising costs, fragmented organization and inadequate capital investment. The mine owners' diagnosis was simple. British coal was becoming uncompetitive in overseas markets because its price was too high; prices must therefore be held down by reducing wage costs. The miners' answer was equally unambiguous. The industry would never be competitive as long as it remained in private hands; nationalization would enable uneconomic pits to be closed down and give the miners a decent living wage. The first world war only aggravated the industry's problems and the argument came to a head in 1919 when the MFGB decided on strike action in pursuit of their demand for higher wages and nationalization. Lloyd George persuaded them not to strike pending the report of a royal commission. A majority of the Sankey Commission, as it was known, basically accepted the miners' argument but no action was taken by the government. Indeed, as the industry's underlying position worsened during the post-1920 depression, the government dismantled the framework of wartime control and handed the industry back to the private owners. The immediate result was a successful lock-out, followed by drastic wage cuts.

In view of the government's refusal to involve itself directly in the coal industry's survival, the MFGB recognized that if further wage reductions were to be prevented the owners would have to be defeated in an all-out strike. Since the miners alone had insufficient bargaining power to achieve this objective, they needed the active support of other unions – especially those in the transport sector. In 1924 the TUC General Council was given the right to organize moral or material support for any union involved in a dispute which was likely to affect other workers. The return to the gold standard in April 1925 precipitated the crisis by inflating the price of British exports, including coal. Anticipating a further lock-out by the owners, in July the TUC organized an embargo on the movement of coal. The government then gave way and conceded a subsidy to the coal industry for nine months, pending the report of yet another royal commission. The Samuel Commission produced a set of compromise proposals which neither side could agree upon. The government's position was that the subsidy could not be extended and that it was up to the two sides to negotiate a settlement. The coal owners, however, could not envisage any settlement which did not entail a sizeable cut in wages, and this was never acceptable to the miners. Several members of the government agreed with the owners that the issue would only be resolved by a head-on collision which they were confident the miners would lose.

The TUC found itself obliged, somewhat reluctantly, to mobilize its resources in support of the miners, with the result that a General Strike was called on 3 May 1926. It lasted nine days and was then called off by the General Council; the miners, however, continued their dispute with the coal owners until the following November when they resumed work on the owners' terms. The problem for the TUC was essentially that of justifying the strike and its spokesmen were plainly on the defensive. Government propaganda stressed the threat to the constitution and to the authority of a democratically elected Parliament, thereby echoing Joynson-Hicks's famous statement of July 1925 that 'sooner or later this thing has got to be fought out by the people of this land. Is England to be governed by Parliament and the cabinet, or by a handful of trade union leaders?' The TUC strenuously denied that the strike in any way challenged the constitution – it was a perfectly legal attempt 'to protect the miners against a degradation of their standard of life' which was 'a menace to the whole world of labour'.[28] Yet a major confrontation between the state and one or more trade unions was always a distinct possibility once prime ministers cast themselves in the role of 'grand conciliator' and their governments adopted the method of legal enactment. For when governments refused either to enact laws which the unions wanted or to change existing legislation in response to union pressure, the resulting conflict inevitably raised wider political issues. Yet, by the same token, no government could stand idly by while a major industry was disrupted by a 'trade dispute'. Still less was it possible for post-1945 governments not to involve themselves directly in collective bargaining as increasingly important employers in their own right. The fundamental contradictions which lay at the root of the notion of 'free collective bargaining' became more and more conspicuous as time went by.

Political involvement

The traditional reason for trade union involvement in party politics was to persuade governments, Liberal and Conservative alike, to enact legislation which would either improve the terms and conditions of a specific group of workers or strengthen the general position of all trade unions *vis-à-vis* all employers for the purposes of collective bargaining. The fact that the Trade Union Act of 1871 and the Conspiracy and Protection of Property Act of 1875 were obtained from governments of different political colours seemed to vindicate this bi-partisan approach. Why, then, did the TUC eventually decide to throw its weight behind the idea of *independent* trade union representation in Parliament?

The main factor seems to have been the adverse trend in judicial decisions on trade union matters which was a marked feature of the late 1890s. The Court of Appeal's decision in *Lyons* v. *Wilkins* (1896), for example, seemed to nullify an important section of the 1875 Act by declaring that peaceful picketing was a common law nuisance. In *Quinn* v. *Leathem* (1901), the House of Lords found that an attempt by a union in dispute with an employer to bring pressure to bear on the latter by inducing customers to stop dealing with him was 'a combination to injure' and thus not protected against actions for damages. Finally in the famous Taff Vale case (1901), the Lords decided that, contrary to the apparent intentions of the 1871 Act, a trade union was a 'legal entity' and as such could be sued for damages in respect of acts committed by its officials. The Railway Servants were obliged to pay £23,000 in damages and costs to the Taff Vale Railway Company. In Phelps Brown's words:

> The effect on the unions was overwhelming. Henceforward if any member or officer committed any actionable wrong, the funds of the union might have to pay for it. The right to strike was not formally rescinded, for it was still thinkable that a strike should take place in which there was no breach of contract and no obstructive picketing, and in which the only object was the advancement of the legitimate interests of the strikers themselves. But these conditions could never be counted on: any dispute breaking out locally was liable to involve a union in heavy damages.[29]

The implications of what seemed to be a concerted judicial attack on the ability of trade unions to conduct collective bargaining were particularly alarming for the leaders of the newer, non-craft unions. It was they who had most to gain from favourable employment legislation and most to lose from restrictions on the right to picket.

They were also somewhat disillusioned with the Liberal Party in so far as it was practically impossible, outside the coal mining districts, to secure the adoption of working men as Liberal parliamentary candidates.[30]

To demand a reversal of hostile judicial decisions was one thing; to set up an independent organization for the purpose of electing genuine representatives of organized labour to Parliament was quite another. Some unions, notably the miners, were satisfied with the *status quo*; others were suspicious of the socialists, Marxists and 'intellectuals' associated with bodies such as the Independent Labour Party, the Social Democratic Federation and the Fabian Society. Consequently, when the Labour Representation Committee was formed in 1900, little more than a quarter of Britain's two million trade unionists were represented at the initial meeting. The objective of the LRC was to form 'a distinct Labour Group in Parliament, who shall have their own whips and agree upon their policy, which must embrace a readiness to co-operate with any party which for the time being may be engaged in promoting legislation in the direct interest of Labour, and be equally ready to associate themselves with any party in opposing measures having an opposite tendency'. To help the LRC achieve its objectives, the unions agreed to pay a levy from their members' subscriptions. In 1906 it succeeded in electing twenty-nine MPs and changed its name to the Labour Party.

A critical turning point in the new party's fortunes came in 1908 when the Miners' Federation decided to break its ties with the Liberals and affiliate to Labour. The electoral significance of this development was underlined in 1918 when of the fifty-seven Labour MPs elected in that year no fewer than twenty-five were members of the MFGB. The new constitution adopted by the Labour Party in that year, however, marked another turning point. Some trade union leaders wanted to keep the party in its original form – that of a small pressure group in Parliament composed exclusively of union representatives. Others, however, believed that it should become a mass party and seek to form a government in its own right. This, of course, meant that while the party might be led nationally and administered locally by middle-class intellectuals, the bulk of its financial resources would continue to be provided by the trade unions. It also posed the fundamental question of how the three major constituent groups within the party, namely the trade unions, the National Executive Committee and the Parliamentary Labour Party, were to devise an agreed programme of legislative proposals which would be pursued when the party attained power.

During the inter-war years this question remained unanswered. The experience of two Labour governments (1924 and 1929–31) suggested that Labour ministers would act in what they believed to be the national interest and would consciously stand above class or sectional interests. Consequently trade union leaders found that their relationship with a Labour government was not fundamentally dissimilar from their relationship with any other government. Trade union leaders who became government ministers were particularly anxious to prove their 'objectivity' and lack of class bias. The party leader, Ramsay MacDonald, was frequently critical of industrial action by the 'industrial wing' of the Labour movement and was not unduly sympathetic towards union pressure for specific pieces of legislation. The TUC soon realised, therefore, that its relations with Labour in government would not be easy. As Fred Bramley, the TUC general secretary, observed in 1925: 'The Labour party cannot have it both ways. If when in office we are to be detached from the Labour movement, we cannot be treated as an integral part of that movement when Labour is out of office.'[31]

This fundamental problem remained unsolved when Labour came to power in 1945, the only difference being that on this occasion there was a fair measure of agreement between the party and the TUC on what policies should be followed and the government had a massive majority with which to implement its programme. One of its most important policies, however, which had *not* been planned in advance, let alone agreed, was the appeal for wage restraint and higher productivity. The government, in effect, asked the trade unions to suspend their basic function – the determination of money wage levels through collective bargaining – in the national interest. The fact that the TUC did its best to comply with wage restraint for two years was not, however, indicative of any structural change in the relationship between the unions and the Labour government. The temporary success of the policy owed far more to the domination of the General Council by a small group of trade union leaders (notably Arthur Deakin of the TGWU) who not only commanded a massive block vote within the TUC but also enjoyed close personal relations with a leading figure in the cabinet, Ernest Bevin. For two years the General Council in effect became an arm of the government. It reverted to its traditional stance, however, when rank and file union members began to repudiate wage restraint and the death of Bevin deprived the government of its key link with the unions. After the collapse of wage restraint in 1950–1, the TUC was determined never to make such a one-sided arrangement with any government again.

Summary

The development of trade unionism in Britain since the late Victorian era has been shaped by two conflicting pressures. On the one hand, there is a profound belief on the part of leaders and members alike in the absolute sovereignty of each trade union and a corresponding determination to get the best possible terms and conditions of employment almost regardless of the wider implications. From this fundamental belief stems both the continuing attachment of most unions to the concept of free collective bargaining and their reluctance to see traditional occupational boundaries eroded. The belief that the possession of a job confers certain property rights on the job-holder has been inherited from the old craft unions and is now deeply entrenched among groups of workers who cannot be regarded as skilled in the traditional sense. Such rights, they feel, must be defended against encroachment by employers, governments and other trade unions. On the other hand, there are certain pressures which tend to encourage a sense of common interest *between* trade unions and to remind the members of each union that they are all part of the same movement. Attacks by the judiciary on the unions' ability to conduct an effective strike, the enactment of laws which in some way threaten the freedom of all unions or, as in 1926, the involvement of one union in a dispute which plainly has implications for other unions, have all at various times in the past encouraged the movement as a whole, acting through the TUC, to take some kind of concerted action. In general, however, it has always been much easier for individual unions to sink their differences and work together when they feel threatened by some external factor and are required to defend the *status quo.* Rarely have they been able to take a collective initiative for change.

It must also be recognized that the trade unions are themselves only part of the wider system of industrial relations. Their objectives, methods and structures have developed partly in response to their own internal needs and beliefs but also in response to pressures from the other two major participants in the system – the employers and the government. The tendency for the unions to devote most of their activity to the extension of common rules at district and national level must be explained at least partly in terms of the employers' resistance to the idea of joint decision-making on matters of substance in the workplace. Similarly the unions' deep-seated belief in self-help was greatly reinforced by the refusal of the state to do much beyond provide a conciliation service for the resolution of 'trade disputes'. It is at least arguable that if governments had followed the path indicated by the Webbs and shown more willingness to use legal enactment as a method of improving terms and conditions of employment, the trade unions would have been compelled to organize themselves accordingly. They might, for example, have established a strong central policy-making body capable of negotiating with governments and simultaneously imposing a greater degree of corporate unity on the movement as a whole. This might in turn have elicited a similar response from the employers' side, leading eventually to a much more centralized, homogeneous structure of institutions. Governments, however, failed to discard the legal fictions which surrounded the conduct of industrial relations, even after their own much-enhanced role as employers and managers of the economy had destroyed the assumptions on which those fictions were originally based. As a result, when governments, trade unions and employers were eventually forced to adjust to a greater degree of interdependence, the political, institutional and psychological strains were particularly acute.

2 Trade unions and the law

In its evidence to the Donovan Commission (1965–8), the TUC argued that the abstentionist character of British labour law was directly attributable to 'the competence of trade unions to safeguard the interests of their members'. Such indeed has been the prevailing view in trade union circles since the late nineteenth century. It could, however, convey a very misleading impression of the influence of the law on trade union behaviour. First, it tends to overlook the fact that prior to 1914 the weaker unions were by no means convinced that voluntary collective bargaining would serve their members more effectively than legal enactment and compulsory arbitration. Second, it also ignores the relatively recent upsurge of interest within the trade union movement in the enactment of laws which will either improve terms and conditions of employment or strengthen the bargaining position of the unions as a whole *vis-à-vis* employers. It would in fact be more accurate to say that the attitude of trade unions towards the law has rarely been homogeneous. While all trade union leaders have strongly resented the periodic attempts of the judiciary to erode their statutory immunities, some have realized that a more positive framework of legal rights could serve their interests better than the traditional doctrine of abstention. Since the mid 1960s successive governments have in fact departed from abstentionism as an overriding principle in an attempt to reduce the level of strike activity and curb the inflationary tendencies of collective bargaining. The chequered results of this new interventionism, however, have failed to resolve the long debate about the role of the law in industrial relations.

The long debate

'Law', as Professor Kahn-Freund has pointed out, 'is a technique for the regulation of social power'.[1] It follows that the view we take of the scope and purpose of legal regulation in industrial relations, as much as in any other sphere of human activity, depends on how we see the *distribution* of social power. If society is viewed as an agglomeration of pressure groups, any one of which can impose its will upon the others by the ruthless exploitation of its bargaining power, then the law may well be seen as the ultimate equalizing agent. By imposing obligations and restrictions on each pressure group, as well as recognizing its rights, the law will seek to ensure that all groups are kept in a state of general equilibrium which in turn will be synonymous with the national interest. If, by contrast, society is seen as an expedient (and inherently unstable) accommodation between groups or classes with fundamentally *unequal* power, then the role of the law will be viewed quite differently. In Hyman's words:

> Relations between employers and workers are governed by a contract of employment which is, in theory, freely agreed between the two parties. But the notion of a free contract between equals has little relevance to the real world. In practice the ownership of capital represents concentrated economic power, a legal entitlement to dominate; hence the employer can virtually dictate the broad outlines of the employment contract.[2]

But is it not the fundamental purpose of trade unionism to redress, through collective action, the natural inequality of the employee as an individual *vis-à-vis* his employer? Has it not achieved at least a measure of success in fulfilling this purpose? And has the law not been of *some* help along the way?

It is at this point that Marxists and political liberals begin to follow divergent paths. For while a liberal may well accept the argument that the distribution of power in society is unequal, he is likely to see some scope for corrective action by the state and to regard labour law as an important vehicle for such action. The law, he would argue, can have a significant effect on the ability of trade unions to act as a real countervailing force in industry by, for example, making it more or less easy for trade unions, first, to obtain recognition from employers, and, second, to enforce sanctions against employers with whom they are in dispute. A Marxist, however, is likely to reject this argument. He would argue that over the past century the state has become the committed ally of monopoly capitalism and that the non-interventionist tradition in British labour law reflects this alliance. For if industrial power is concentrated in few hands and the countervailing force of organized labour is, by comparison, weak then legal abstentionism must work in favour of the established power holders. Recent departures from the abstentionist principle have given the trade unions relatively little by way of legal support and have been motivated by a desire to integrate organized labour more fully into the established structure of power. The fundamental purpose of such integration is to weaken the power of trade unions and their members to frustrate the increasingly desperate attempts of late monopoly capitalism to resolve its own internal contradictions. Thus in Marxist eyes the law remains what it has always been – the handmaiden of capital.[3]

All this, however, is a long way from the debate which preceded the establishment of an abstentionist framework of labour law between 1871 and 1906. Ever since the repeal of the Combination Acts in 1824, workers have been legally free to form and join trade unions. The extent to which this freedom has actually been exercised, however, has depended heavily on the actions of employers, judges and trade unions themselves.[4] Until the very end of the nineteenth century the majority of the workforce was effectively excluded from trade unionism by the occupational and to a lesser extent industrial barriers erected by the established unions. Even where unions existed, there was no necessity for employers to negotiate with them about anything unless, of course, their bargaining power was such as to compel employers to recognize them. But the extent to which employer resistance could break the power of organized labour was also influenced by the attitude of the courts of law. In the hands of hostile judges, the common law proved to be an extremely malleable weapon against nascent trade unionism.

In the period between 1825 and 1871, there was a legal freedom to organize but no corresponding freedom to pursue the objectives of trade unionism. The mere threat to strike was held to be a 'molestation', 'intimidation' or 'obstruction' of an employer engaged in his lawful business; effective picketing was virtually impossible; the restriction of competition in the labour market was held to be a 'restraint of trade' and thus a criminal act. The 'restraint of trade' doctrine also deprived the unions of any status in civil law, to the point where in the famous decision of *Hornby* v. *Close* (1867), the Boilermakers' Society was denied legal assistance in seeking to prosecute an official who had embezzled its funds. This conflict between theory and practice emerged in the majority and minority reports of the first Royal Commission on Trade Unions (1867). The majority view sought to distinguish between justifiable and unjustifiable trade union activity. The formation of unions was justified by the imbalance of power in industry, but the active pursuit of 'coercive' objectives was seen as contrary to the general interest. The minority report, by contrast, argued that in practice it was impossible to draw a clear distinction between coercive and non-coercive methods. If trade union members were to derive tangible benefits from their collective power, they must be free to coerce employers just as employers were free to coerce them. Taken to its logical conclusion, the minority argument implied that, provided they did not commit crimes of violence, unions should be free to protect and advance their legitimate economic interests by any appropriate means.[5] The appeal of this argument was doubtless enhanced by the evidence of the trade union leaders themselves to the commission, which emphasized the orderly nature of collective bargaining and the respectability of their own (craft) unions.

The fact that the minority report was accepted by the government of the day and became enshrined in subsequent trade union legislation did not resolve the debate. Within the trade union movement itself there were those who argued for positive legal *support* for union activities. Outside the movement there were always voices to be heard arguing the case for greater legal *regulation* of collective power in the labour market, based on a clear distinction between 'legitimate' and 'illegitimate' union activities. These two themes were related in the sense that many trade unionists who might otherwise have been prepared to countenance legal support for collective bargaining declined to do so on the grounds that this might easily bring legal regulation in its train. The real clash of opinion, therefore, was between those who wanted more law in industrial relations and those who did not. When, from the 1950s onwards, the combined effects of full employment, rising expectations and accelerating inflation appeared to challenge the logic of non-intervention, the old debate on the role of the law once again assumed an immediate significance for public policy.

The framework of abstentionism

The fundamental purpose of the legislation enacted in 1871, 1875 and 1906 was to remove from the unions any liability for their actions under the common law as interpreted by a hostile judiciary. The Trade Union Act of 1871 gave the unions protection from the 'restraint of trade' doctrine. It did not, however, confer a corporate legal personality on them, so that they could not make legally binding agreements and could not sue or be sued for damages. This implied that while the internal rules of a trade union could not be enforced by law, neither could its funds be touched by employers who claimed that they had been damaged by its actions. The Conspiracy and Protection of Property Act of 1875 laid down that as long as a trade union was acting 'in contemplation or furtherance of a trade dispute', it would enjoy immunity from any action for criminal conspiracy unless it was guilty of a criminal act. The Act also made picketing somewhat easier by expressly permitting workers to attend at or near a place in order *merely* to obtain or communicate information from or to other workers not on strike. These gains soon proved to be paper thin, but at the time they were of immense satisfaction to the moderate, respectable craftsmen who presided over the TUC.

By the 1890s, however, the climate of middle-class opinion in general, and of judicial opinion in particular, had grown perceptibly cooler towards trade unionism. One factor, no doubt, was the appearance of the 'new' general unions and the large-scale strikes in which they were involved. Another was the growing concern over the craft unions' resistance to new working methods in manufacturing industry. The government appointed another royal commission, which once again considered the case for a more interventionist legal framework. Various suggestions were advanced which would have conferred a much more active role in dispute settlement on the government, the most radical being compulsory arbitration. The members of the commission, however, found that majority opinion on both sides of industry was against the imposition of legally binding awards:

> A succession of witnesses had shown them how, industry by industry, up and down the country, parties to the wage bargain had been working out methods that suited their own circumstances and generally finding, if only by trial and error, a way to voluntary agreements honourably observed. The majority thought they should let well alone. . . . The tasks and methods of industrial relations were repugnant alike to judicial procedure and imposed settlements . . . . And there was the less need to consider regulation when what was unregulated was working on the whole so well.[6]

The employers' and trade unions' expressed preference for making rules and resolving disputes over their application and interpretation by voluntary methods allowed the government to reject the idea of *uninvited* intervention. The Conciliation Act of 1896, by establishing a state mediation and conciliation service, confirmed the government in its role of 'benevolent neutral'.

The judiciary, however, responded to the rising level of industrial conflict in the late 1890s by seeking to establish clear, legal limits to trade union activity. In *Lyons* v. *Wilkins,* for example, the Court of Appeal held that peaceful picketing was both a 'nuisance' at common law and a 'watching and besetting' under the 1875 Act.[7] In *Quinn* v. *Leathem,* the House of Lords made it clear that the methods employed by trade unionists in pursuit of a trade dispute could entail *civil* liability for conspiracy. Vigorous industrial action against an employer could therefore be seen as a 'combination to injure', exposing union officials to claims for damages. In the Taff Vale case, the Lords struck their most damaging blow at the unions' ability to mount effective strikes by deciding that such damages could be enforced against union funds. This decision required the Lords to assume that, contrary to the express provisions of the 1871 Act, a registered trade union was a legal entity which could be sued for torts (civil wrongs).

The government's response was to set up another royal commission in 1903 which, three years later, came down in favour of a comprehensive code of labour law. Opinion within the TUC, however, had moved decisively in the opposite direction. All that most trade union leaders and the twenty-nine newly elected Labour MPs wanted from Parliament was a return to the degree of legal immunity which they thought had existed after the passage of the 1875 Act. The Trade Disputes Act of 1906 met their wishes. It gave the unions complete immunity from legal action in tort and redefined picketing in a way which appeared to favour the unions. Above all, it sought to remove liability for civil conspiracy and inducing breaches of employment contracts from trade unionists engaged in prosecuting a trade dispute. A trade dispute was defined in terms which appeared to cover every conceivable kind of industrial action, including inter-union disputes. The legislators' intention was to give the unions comprehensive immunity from judge-made liabilities, and for the next half century it looked as though they had succeeded.

The triumph of the abstentionist doctrine did not, however, remove the need for further legislation in industrial relations. Some statutes, notably the Trade Union Act of 1913 and the Trade Disputes Act of 1965, were promulgated in response to renewed attempts by the judiciary to set limits to union activity. The 1913 Act followed the Osborne case in which the Law Lords invalidated the use of union funds in support of the Labour Party. The 1965 Act sought to reverse the Lords' decision in *Rookes* v. *Barnard,* in which it was held that a *threat* to break employment contracts in order to enforce a closed shop constituted intimidation and as such was not protected by the 1906 Act. Other laws reflected the realization that some 'trade disputes' might threaten the well-being of the community. Thus the Emergency Powers Act of 1920 gave the government broad authority to preserve essential supplies to the community in the event of major industrial disruption. The Trade Disputes and Trade Unions Act of 1927 sought to deter another general strike by, among other things, stipulating criminal liabilities for strikes designed to 'coerce' the government. This Act, however, was hardly ever invoked before its repeal in 1946. Most of the 'labour' laws enacted between 1906 and 1971, however, were essentially in accord with the spirit of voluntarism. Factories Acts laid down minimum safety standards in workplaces, while various Compensation Acts provided for minimum compensation from employers in the event of injury sustained at work. The Fair Wages Resolutions of the House of Commons stipulated that private contractors engaged on public work should observe certain employment standards. Finally the Trade Boards Act of 1909 laid down a legal minimum wage in certain industries where it was recognized that voluntary collective bargaining would be difficult to establish. Nevertheless the assumption behind the wages council system was that each council would encourage the growth of voluntary machinery in the industry it covered.

In 1906 the debate between the advocates of legal enactment and the supporters of collective bargaining was finally resolved in favour of the latter. From then on the TUC gradually lost interest in pressing Parliament for the kind of protective legislation (such as a national minimum wage) which had been very important to some of its members in the late Victorian era. In the absence of pressure from either the unions themselves or from Labour MPs, successive governments took the view that the parties to collective bargaining were best left to do the job in their own way. Consequently the scope of statutory protection was and remained extremely narrow. The law did nothing to encourage or regulate collective bargaining. Employers were free to refuse recognition, to dismiss or otherwise victimize trade unionists and to break collective agreements. Trade unions were free to apply what sanctions they could against recalcitrant employers and force them to the negotiating table. Even the House of Lords accepted the logical implications of voluntarism. Thus in the Crofter case (1942), Lord Wright observed that the law 'has for better or worse adopted the test of self-interest or selfishness as being capable of justifying the deliberate doing of lawful acts which inflict harm, so long as the means employed are not wrongful . . .'.[8] It was therefore inappropriate for judges to draw common law distinctions or make moral judgements about what unions should or should not be allowed to do. If employers were free to pursue their legitimate interests by any lawful means, the same rights must be extended to trade unions. In short, the role of the state in industrial relations was governed by a firm and increasingly deep-seated belief in 'collective *laissez-faire*'.

The challenge to abstentionism

The assumptions which underpinned the doctrine of abstentionism and the broad social and political consensus which it attracted remained largely inviolate during the immediate post-war period. Even the Labour government's attempt to hold down the level of wage settlements in 1948–50 did not really challenge abstentionism in so far as it relied entirely on persuasion and was never presented as anything other than a short-term response to a severe economic crisis. No minister sought to deny that free collective bargaining was anything less than the normal way of deciding terms and conditions of employment. The difficulty which succeeding governments faced was that the fundamental weaknesses of the British economy made it increasingly subject to balance-of-payments deficits and inflationary pressures. Moreover the rapid increase in the size of the public sector after 1945 meant that the government was now a very large employer in its own right. While it was obliged by custom and practice to engage in collective bargaining, either directly or indirectly, with unions in the public sector, it was also compelled to take a view about what level of pay settlements was consistent with the state of the economy. It was then caught up in the logic of intervention. For once it had decided on a 'norm' for pay increases in the public sector, it could hardly ignore the level of settlements in private industry. In the inflationary environment of the 1950s an annual 'wage round' emerged and with it an annual 'going rate' for settlements. Public sector employees would not willingly settle for less than workers elsewhere were getting. Consequently the Conservative government of the day was reluctantly drawn into a series of conflicts with well-organized groups of their own employees (the railwaymen in 1955, health service employees in 1957, London busmen in 1958) in an attempt to enforce pay norms.

In the private sector the government initially relied on the traditional methods of publicity, exhortation and example. It was hoped that if the government itself was seen to be standing firm against inflationary pay claims in the public sector, private employers would follow suit. This hope was destroyed in part by the government's own failure to pursue a consistent strategy on pay. In the aftermath of sterling crises, when deflationary policies were being pursued (as in 1956–8 and 1961–2) the government's attitude was much more uncompromising than in cyclical upswings when expansion was the order of the day. A more fundamental reason for the failure of exhortation, however, lay within the bargaining system itself. Part of the problem was institutional in the sense that neither the trade unions themselves nor the employers' associations with whom they negotiated, were organized in a way which would have enabled them to implement government guidelines – even had they been willing to do so. Moreover, the agreements made at industry level were in some key sectors becoming less and less relevant to what was actually happening in the workplace. In engineering, motor cars and several other manufacturing industries, the post-war years witnessed the growth of bargaining over pay within the workplace itself. Consequently, even if their respective organizations decided to observe government norms at national level, shop stewards and managers at plant and company level were still free to negotiate better terms. But these structural characteristics in turn only reflected the attitudes and preferences of the parties themselves. Reared on the tradition of 'collective *laissez-faire*', both sides took the view that it was their business to negotiate agreements which met their needs. In the context of free collective bargaining, the appeal to some vague, undefined 'national interest' struck an unfamiliar note.

Recognizing the ineffectiveness of exhortation in its purest form, governments adopted a more interventionist stance. They set up a series of 'impartial' agencies at national level whose tasks were both educative and (increasingly) investigatory. The first of these bodies – the National Incomes Commission (1962–4) – was supposed to examine specific wage claims and settlements referred to it by the government. It failed, however, to achieve its objectives, partly because the TUC refused to co-operate with any body which sought to restrain wages while ignoring prices and profits. The NIC was replaced by the National Board for Prices and Incomes (1965–71) which, as its name implies, had more wide-ranging terms of reference. Its main task was to investigate and seek to change 'old habits, inherited attitudes and institutional arrangements' which were thought to restrain productivity growth and encourage inflation. Having investigated particular pay and price-fixing arrangements, the board would make recommendations for change to the employers and trade unions concerned. It was assumed, of course, that both sides would act upon the board's advice. It was also assumed that the thousands of employers whose collective bargaining arrangements were *not* investigated by the board would follow the spirit of the policy by initiating institutional changes which would tie the movement of pay within their establishments much closer to the growth of productivity. The success of the board's activities depended entirely on the co-operation of employers and unions. It had no power to enforce its recommendations on the parties and was in no sense an arbitrator. It was essentially a catalyst to change and, like all such bodies, it needed time to establish its credibility in the eyes of trade unions and employers and thereby win their confidence.

Unfortunately the marked deterioration in Britain's economic performance during the mid 1960s, culminating in the devaluation of the pound in November 1967, not only deprived the board of the time it needed but compelled it to become more involved in short-term wage restraint and neglect its long-term reformist role. The urgent need to deflate the economy after the major sterling crisis of July 1966 forced the Labour government to impose a six-month statutory freeze on pay and prices, with criminal sanctions against those who flouted it. Writing in the shadow of the freeze, Flanders observed that: 'Public opinion . . . is not at all appalled by these drastic infringements on the freedom of collective bargainers. It rather welcomes the determination of the government to make its temporary policies work. . . . The experience of the freeze . . . is undermining the belief in voluntarism as an absolute principle'.[9] But what did these 'drastic infringements' actually amount to? After the freeze was over the government faced the same problem as before – how to ensure that collective bargainers conformed to the official guidelines on pay. All that the various Prices and Incomes Acts of 1966–9 enabled the government to do was *delay* the implementation of those pay settlements and price increases which it knew about and of which it disapproved. Thousands of collective agreements which broke the policy inevitably slipped through the 'monitoring' procedure operated by the Department of Employment. The threat of legal sanctions was simply meant to buttress voluntary observance of the policy, and in the absence of sufficient volunteers the policy ultimately collapsed.

This did not, however, signify the abandonment of the *concept* of an incomes policy. As the problems of inflation and low productivity grew more acute during the 1970s, so successive governments resorted to increasingly detailed regulatory 'codes', backed by the force of law, in an attempt to restrain pay and prices. The defunct NBPI was replaced by the short-lived Pay Board (1973–4) and the more durable Price Commission (1973–9). Strikes in support of pay claims which were in breach of the prevailing norms were said, on more than one occasion, to be a direct challenge to parliamentary democracy and the ability of the government to govern. The public was frequently left with the impression that the country's entire future hinged on whether or not a particular union or group of workers would accept a given offer. Yet by the end of the 1970s the institutions of wage determination had undergone no radical change. More importantly, the hostility on both sides of industry to the concept of *permanent* regulation of wage bargaining by the state was as strong as ever.

As successive governments took an increasing interest in the substantive outcome of collective bargaining, they also grew more apprehensive about its behavioural characteristics. A critical assumption on which the doctrine of abstentionism rested was that voluntary procedure agreements were the most effective way of avoiding direct conflict. Employers and unions alike would feel committed to observing only those rules which they themselves had made. Yet the growth of unofficial and unconstitutional strikes in certain key industries during the 1950s and 1960s seemed to suggest that militant shop stewards were deliberately exploiting the voluntary nature of procedures and disrupting production in pursuit of 'irresponsible' demands. While it was frequently acknowledged that the trade unions themselves were not the initiators of such strikes, they were nevertheless blamed for failing to control their members and permitting their authority to be flouted with impunity. Concern was also expressed over the 'undemocratic' nature of the closed shop and the apparent domination of most unions by small cliques of militants and communists. The burden of much comment in the press and the media generally was, in a nutshell, that full employment had given the unions more power over society than ever before and that they were abusing it. Indeed, as the economy staggered from crisis to crisis in the mid 1960s and the public debate on what was wrong with Britain intensified, so government ministers were openly critical of certain aspects of trade union behaviour and increasingly hostile to unofficial strikes.

As on three previous occasions (1867, 1894 and 1903) the appointment of a royal commission reopened the whole debate about the role of the law in industrial relations. By 1965, however, the tradition of 'collective *laissez-faire*' was an obvious anachronism in a society in which the state had assumed overall responsibility for managing the economy and maximizing public welfare. The government had already declared an interest in ensuring that the supply of manpower to industry was improved in both qualitative and quantitative terms in the form of the Industrial Training Act (1964) and the Redundancy Payments Act (1965). While the Donovan Commission (as it came to be known) was in session, the government imposed its six-month freeze on pay and prices and continued thereafter to use the law as an aid to voluntary restraint. The question before the commission, therefore, was not whether the law *should* play a more active role but *how* this might be best done. The answer, however, depended in turn on the view which was taken of what the law could and could not be expected to achieve in terms of influencing *behaviour* in the workplace.

There was the popular view –expressed most lucidly by Andrew Shonfield in his 'Note of Reservation' to the Donovan Report – that the tradition of legal abstention had allowed and even encouraged the trade unions to become 'over-mighty subjects':

> With the growing dependence of people on the reliable performance of services required for tolerable living in crowded urban communities, the employment of collective power of groups of producers to disrupt the lives of people who have no means of helping themselves raises new problems. . . . It will become less possible in the circumstances which are unfolding to distinguish, in the sharp traditional style of the English Common Law, between public authority and power and the 'private' power of organizations with collective functions, which control the supply of essential goods and services not obtainable from any alternative source.[10]

The trade unions, he argued, had responsibilities to the rest of the community and the law should spell these out in unambiguous terms. The rules which unions required both their members and employers to observe could, for example, help to sustain restrictive practices and should therefore be subject to public scrutiny. An Industrial Relations Commission should be established in order, among other things, to compel the more conservative employers and unions in each industry to negotiate the kind of productivity agreements which their more progressive competitors or colleagues had already achieved. In short, the law would act as a device for spreading efficient working practices throughout an industry more quickly than would otherwise be the case. Similarly, he argued in favour of a presumption in law that all collective agreements were legally binding contracts. This would encourage dynamic employers to innovate more rapidly because it would introduce a much-needed element of predictability into workplace relations. Legal enforceability would also bring tangible benefits for the unions since management 'would be induced to enlarge the scope of the collective bargaining, if the reward for doing so were to allow it to plan for more rapid change in a climate of security'.[11]

The Donovan Report itself, however, proceeded from less ambitious assumptions about what the law could achieve. Its analysis of the shortcomings of the industrial relations system centred on the declining effectiveness of industry-wide agreements and the corresponding growth of informal, autonomous and fragmented bargaining in the workplace. The growth of unofficial strikes was seen primarily in terms of the lack of formal procedures at plant and company level:

> As long as no effective method for the settlement of grievances exists, no one can expect a threat of legal sanctions to restrain men from using the advantage they feel able to derive from sudden action in order to obtain a remedy for grievances which cannot be dealt with in an orderly fashion. Self-help has always been the response to the absence of 'law and order'. In industrial relations, 'law and order' can be created only by effective collective bargaining arrangements.[12]

Donovan rejected the case for legal restrictions on the right to strike on two counts: first, that they would be ignored by the strikers themselves (as they had been during two world wars when all strikes were illegal); and second, that they would not in themselves encourage the reform of procedures. There was little point in giving the force of law to collective agreements as long as they retained their traditional form. Unless an agreement was drawn up in clear, precise language, it could not be enforced in a court of law. Donovan added, however, that once the parties had reformed their procedures by voluntary action, it would then be possible 'to distinguish the cases in which unconstitutional strikes have been the result of inadequate procedures from those in which strike-proneness is due to irresponsibility or to agitation by eccentrics or subversives'.[13] The employer would then be able to exercise his legal rights by dismissing those workers who broke procedure agreements.

Donovan's attitude to the law was in fact rather ambiguous – a reflection, no doubt, of divergences of opinion between the members of the commission. On the one hand, its strategy for encouraging the reform of bargaining structures and practices was fundamentally voluntarist in character. The Commission on Industrial Relations (CIR), which was to concern itself with the problems of longer-term institutional change at plant and company level, was given no legal powers with which to enforce its recommendations. Its success would depend entirely on its ability to persuade managements and trade unionists to improve their procedures and practices. On the other hand, some of its recommendations reflected a more interventionist and restrictive approach. Overturning a century of tradition, it suggested that trade unions should register and be given corporate, legal status. It also proposed that the immunity from action for inducing breaches of employment contracts conferred by the 1906 Act should in future be restricted to registered unions and those acting on their behalf. Had this proposal been enacted it would have exposed unofficial strikers to claims for damages. Moreover, Donovan accepted that closed shops might result in injustice to individuals and recommended that trade union rule books should be scrutinized by the registrar in order to ensure that individual members had a right of appeal to the union's Executive Committee.

An equally significant strand in the commission's thinking was its recognition of the emerging discrepancy between the theory of voluntarism and the practical results. Advocates of legal abstention had always assumed that what was unregulated by law would be covered by voluntary agreements. By the mid 1960s, however, it was obvious to any impartial observer that this was by no means the case. In his evidence to the commission, Allan Flanders pointed out that the traditional absence of legal support for collective bargaining was responsible for the inadequate growth of joint regulation in British industry. There was a particularly large gap in the private sector, where some 85 per cent of non-manual workers were covered neither by collective agreements nor by statutory regulation. He also emphasized that, by comparison with collective agreements in the USA, collective agreements in Britain typically covered a narrow range of substantive issues, which was in turn indicative of an inadequate level of internal joint regulation. The commission accepted this argument and gave the CIR the task of promoting trade union recognition and the extension of collective bargaining by the traditional method of case-by-case inquiry, persuasion and publicity. It was also envisaged that by bringing recognition disputes within a clear institutional framework, the possibility of further multi-unionism would be greatly reduced. The question of penalties for a refusal to comply with the CIR's recommendations would, said Donovan, 'need to be reviewed in the light of experience'.[14] Finally, the commission proposed that all employees should be given a legal right not to be unfairly dismissed. The intention here was to encourage employers to improve their dismissal arrangements and spur employees and unions to negotiate satisfactory joint procedures. Once again, however, the commission's argument implied some dissatisfaction with the impact of free collective bargaining in this field.

From the vantage point of the late 1970s it is possible to take a more objective view of the Donovan Report than was possible at the time. When the report was published in 1968 the dominant reaction was one of profound disappointment. Politicians were looking for a short, sharp 'legal' antidote to unofficial strikes. Donovan offered none. Instead it emphasized the crucial significance of *management* attitudes and behaviour and the need for long-term institutional reform at plant and company level. A major theme in the report was the changing structure of authority *within* the trade unions and the implications of this change for collective bargaining. Trade union leaders and officials, said Donovan, could not be 'industry's policemen' – they had to respond to the expressed wishes of their members. The real solution to the problems of unofficial strikes, inflationary wage claims and low productivity lay in a total rethink of industrial relations policy on the part of senior management, followed by specific initiatives for change. Nevertheless the commission's specific proposals for changing the law added up to a decisive rejection of the abstentionist tradition. The commission accepted that not only was there considerable scope for extending the statutory floor of individual rights to which all employees should be entitled but that in certain circumstances the law could act as a spur to collective action. The difficulty facing the commission – as Lord Donovan himself admitted in an unhappy addendum to the report – was to satisfy the popular demand for quick solutions.[15]

The Labour government's response was contained in a White Paper ('In place of strife') which was more decisively interventionist in tone than the Donovan Report. It enunciated four principles as the basis of a national industrial relations policy – the reform of collective bargaining, the extension of trade union rights, new aids to those involved in collective bargaining and, finally, new safeguards for the community and for individual workers against the exercise of coercive power. Much of the White Paper's underlying analysis and some of its specific proposals were derived directly from the Donovan Report. The point at which they parted company was on the use of criminal sanctions against strikers. The White Paper proposed to give the secretary of state for employment a discretionary power to impose a twenty-eight day 'conciliation pause' in cases where strikes had occurred in breach of procedure. A breach of such a 'pause' would entail a financial penalty. It also proposed that the secretary of state should be able to order a secret ballot where a major, official strike was threatened. The Donovan Commission had in fact considered both ideas and rejected them, primarily on the grounds that they were unlikely to achieve their intended objectives. Had they become law, it is safe to assume that they would rarely have been invoked.

Nevertheless the so-called 'penalty clauses' possessed an immense symbolic value to both the government and the TUC. For the government they represented a clear message to the electorate that ministers were determined to do something about Britain's strike problem. For the TUC they represented a blatant attack not only on the right to strike but also on the entire voluntary tradition of British industrial relations. Faced with a revolt among its trade union-sponsored backbenchers, the government agreed to drop the 'penalty clauses' in return for a 'solemn and binding' undertaking by the TUC (June 1969) to use its best endeavours in the settlement of unofficial disputes.[16] This agreement marked a major step forward by the TUC and strengthened the authority of the General Council over the affiliated members. Yet its success inevitably depended very much on the personal skills of the general secretary, Vic Feather. In the succeeding months, every unofficial strike which the general secretary was unable to settle was projected by the press as a breach of the 'solemn and binding' agreement. Voluntary effort, it seemed, was a wholly inadequate substitute for a clear framework of legal penalties and deterrents.

The Industrial Relations Act, 1971

Although this Act was the work of a Conservative government, its philosophy and provisions owed far more to the notions and prejudices of lawyers than to pressure from employers. It not only removed the statutory bedrock of abstentionism (by repealing the Acts of 1871, 1875 and 1906) but proceeded from quite different assumptions about the relationship between industrial behaviour and the law. The authors of the Act clearly shared Andrew Shonfield's view that the traditional abstention of the law had allowed the unions to acquire too much power. This concentration of power could, in their view, be broken down, first by surrounding the strike weapon with a new range of civil liabilities which, it was confidently assumed, most employers would eagerly exploit to restore order to their strike-torn workplaces. The second limb of the strategy was to confer new rights on the individual worker and groups of workers which would in total strengthen their position *against* the union to which they belonged. Faced with this two-pronged assault on their power, one led by employers and the other by their own members, it was anticipated that the trade unions would become a much more cautious and co-operative influence in British industry. Two critical assumptions, however, were made – first, that employers and union members alike would actually make use of the rights which the Act gave them, and second, that eventually the unions themselves would come to accept the new legal framework and work within it. In the event, neither of these assumptions was justified.

The cornerstone of the Act was that the unions as organizations had to be 'brought within the law'. This was to be achieved by encouraging them to register with the Registrar of Trade Unions who in turn was given the task of scrutinizing their general objectives under the Act. Only registered unions could call themselves 'trade unions' under the Act; an unregistered union simply became an 'organization of workers' with no legal rights and open-ended liabilities. A registered union was given a corporate, legal personality (thereby removing the keystone of the 1871 Act) and a very limited immunity in respect of industrial action. All collective agreements negotiated after the date on which the Act came into force would be regarded as binding in law unless the parties inserted a specific clause to the contrary. It was indeed fundamental to the Act that all trade unions, registered or not, were legally responsible for the actions of their officers and 'agents' (namely shop stewards) and, in accordance with the Taff Vale judgement, that their funds were liable to damages. If a union committed an 'unfair industrial practice', of which there were eleven specified in the Act (which include inducing breaches of employment contracts as well as commercial contracts), then the injured party could take the union to the newly established National Industrial Relations Court and claim damages. The intention here was to force union officials to control their shop stewards and prevent them from breaking agreed procedures.

The practical difficulties which followed from this simplistic conception of the structure of authority within trade unions, however, were graphically underlined by a series of strikes in the docks during the summer of 1972. In *Heaton's Transport* v. *TGWU*, the NIRC and the House of Lords both held that the union (unregistered) was liable for the apparently unofficial activities of its shop stewards in the docks and that liability could only be avoided by a withdrawal of the stewards' 'credentials'. While no doubt legally correct, this judgement was in practical terms a nonsense.[17] The entire history of labour relations in the docks underlines again and again the readiness of the dockers to follow 'unofficial' leaders and the corresponding brittleness of their loyalty to the union. If the TGWU *had* disciplined its stewards in the prescribed manner it would simply have destroyed what little hold it retained over the dockers themselves – an outcome which would have been exactly contrary to the Act's intentions.

The rule that unions were responsible in law for the actions of their agents was intended as a deterrent to unofficial strikes, the assumption being that many such strikes occurred because union officials failed to control their stewards and rank and file members. The 'emergency' provisions in the Act, which were intended to combat large-scale official stoppages, reflected a quite different line of thought. Under sections 138–45 of the Act, the secretary of state was empowered to order a secret ballot before the commencement of a large-scale, official stoppage and to impose a 'cooling-off' period once it had begun. The assumption behind these provisions was that workers were frequently ordered or otherwise induced to participate in major stoppages against their wishes by militant union leaders and officials. Far from having too little power over their members, trade union leaders apparently had too much. It followed, therefore, that many such strikes could be avoided if the 'silent majority' was given an opportunity to express its true feelings and repudiate the authority of its own leaders. The emergency provisions were put to the test on only one occasion and failed miserably. In April 1972 the railway unions began an official work-to-rule in pursuit of their annual pay claim. The government applied to the NIRC and obtained a fourteen-day 'cooling-off' period so that further negotiations could take place. The unions suspended their work-to-rule and resumed negotiations. At the end of the fourteen-day period, however, no agreement had been reached and the work-to-rule began again. The government then got an order from the NIRC requiring the unions to ballot their members on whether or not they wished to accept British Rail's last offer. The overwhelming majority of railmen voted against acceptance. The government then retired from the dispute and left the parties to negotiate on an improved offer. The 'emergency' provisions were not invoked again.

The attack on the internal authority of the unions proceeded from similar assumptions of latent dissatisfaction within the mass of rank and file members. It was a fundamental principle of the Act (section 5) that every worker had a right to join *and not to join* a registered trade union of his or her choice. This principle obviously struck at the heart of the closed shop, the enforcement of which was declared an 'unfair industrial practice'. The authors of the Act were obliged to recognize, however, that the closed shop brought some advantages to employers and unions alike. Consequently the post-entry closed shop was reinstated under the title of 'agency shop'. Where an official agency shop existed, workers who refused to join the appropriate union were required to pay the equivalent membership fee to a charity or, failing that, were liable to be dismissed by the employer. But the authors of the Act could not really bring themselves to accept that the freedom of the individual should be subordinate to the interests of collective organization, even in the cause of order and discipline in the workplace. They feared that even an agency shop might be dominated by a clique of militants unless the members were provided with legal safeguards. Thus an agreed agency shop could be challenged by 20 per cent of the workers involved and the CIR was then obliged to conduct a ballot. If two-thirds of those voting decided to terminate the agency shop, then it was duly terminated. In any case an agency shop could only be operated by a *registered* trade union and as the vast majority of unions refused to register, the number of agency shop agreements negotiated under the Act was minuscule. Indeed, the attack on the closed shop proved to be a total failure. The vast majority of managers and trade unionists continued to operate their traditional arrangements and very few non-members chose to make use of their legal rights. The inference was that the coercion and injustice which the authors of the Act associated with the closed shop was largely a figment of their own imaginations.

The attempt to bring union rules within the law failed for the same reason. It was assumed that the individual union member *needed* new, stringent safeguards against the tyrannical behaviour of shop stewards and branch officials. Registered unions were required to specify the powers and duties of their officials – especially the power to authorize industrial action and the circumstances in which that power might be used. Yet the thinking behind this provision attached far too much importance to formal rules *per se* and largely overlooked the fact that no matter how explicit the rules of any organization might be, their practical significance would always be subject to a web of informal customs and practices. Given the low level of member participation in union business in the branches, there has always been a tendency for the policy of most trade unions to be determined by a small number of activists. Indeed, the same is true of practically every other kind of voluntary organization. The belief that this 'problem' could be resolved by the imposition of an elaborate system of formal checks and balances of the internal power structure of every trade union defied over a century of practical experience.

The failure of the Act to weaken the internal authority of the trade unions suggests that most members did not regard the exercise of this authority as an intolerable infringement of their personal freedom. The very fact that workers join trade unions at all implies that they are prepared to accept certain limitations on their freedom in return for the benefits of collective organization. It is hardly surprising, therefore, that in 1971–4 many trade union members reacted strongly against a legal framework which appeared to challenge the basis of trade union organization in the workplace. As Weekes *et al.* concluded, the repudiation of these sections of the Act by management and trade unionists alike 'must raise doubts about the ability of the law to protect individual rights in the field of employment, unless these rights are seen to command wide support or serve the interests of the parties to collective bargaining'.[18]

It would be wrong, however, to conclude that the Act was nothing more than a partisan assault on the trade unions. In the post-Donovan era no legislator could ignore the role of other factors in generating disorderly industrial relations. Various sections of the Act were, therefore, predominantly reformist in intention. Like the Donovan Commission, the authors of the Act wanted to bring more formality into workplace bargaining and simultaneously encourage managements to negotiate better procedures. The Donovan proposals for safeguards against unfair dismissal, for example, were broadly followed in the Act. There is little evidence, however, that they provided an effective spur to procedural reform in this field.[19] An attempt was also made to tackle the problems of multi-unionism and employer resistance to collective bargaining. A clear procedure was laid down with the specific intention of promoting trade union recognition, eliminating strikes over recognition issues and avoiding inter-union conflict over bargaining rights. The new formula for order was the Sole Bargaining Agency (SBA), under which a registered trade union could be given exclusive and legally enforceable bargaining rights in respect of a defined bargaining unit. This arrangement was so attractive to some white collar organizations who had struggled long and hard against both employer hostility and competition from staff associations that a few decided to defy TUC policy and register under the Act. The difficulty was that the reformist intentions of the Act were largely undermined by the authors' obsession with trade union power. Having set up a Sole Bargaining Agency, for example, the authors then proceeded to give as few as one-fifth of the employees covered by the agency the power to repudiate it. Moreover, the fact that most trade unions did not register while many staff associations and 'house' unions *did*, and obtained SBAs from their employers, actually aggravated the problem of multi-unionism and fragmented bargaining.

Various post-mortems on the Act were being held long before its repeal in 1974. Apologists for the Act have claimed that it failed to achieve its objectives because the unions refused to co-operate with it. Once they had decided not to register, most of the Act's provisions were bound to be under-used or ineffective since they assumed that in time the unions as a whole *would* decide, however reluctantly, to co-operate. In a trivial sense this claim is, of course, valid. But we need to ask *why* the unions opposed the Act so vigorously and, equally important, why most employers were either hostile or indifferent towards it. Their attitude may of course be partly explained in terms of a deep-seated suspicion, born of the century-long dominance of abstentionism, of lawyers and legalism in industrial relations. But the real explanation probably lies in the nature of the Act itself. From a trade union point of view, the Act could be seen as a blatant attack on traditional freedoms and immunities, which in a sense it was. It could also be seen as an attempt to reduce the influence of trade unionism in industry and to sweep away the hard-won gains of a century. This view, however, would be unfair. The authors of the Act accepted that trade unionism *could* be a force for order in industry but they erred in seeking to impose on employers and unions alike a series of legal rules which in total attempted to distinguish patterns of behaviour which were fair and reasonable from those which were not. In theory some of their intentions could have been fulfilled if employers as a whole had elected to make use of their rights. In practice, however, very few did so. In the words of Weekes *et al.*:

> Employers generally refused to see their industrial relations as a problem and the 'disorder' described by others was often defended by managements because it gave them flexibility. Certainly management seemed anxious to avoid the loss of control to outsiders which they felt the use of the new legal institutions implied. In so far as any of them saw the need for change, strategies other than the use or threat of law were generally preferred.[20]

The implied assumption that the majority of British workplaces were dominated by strike-happy shop stewards and that demoralized managers spent most of their time appeasing unreasonable demands was totally at variance with reality.

In this sense it could be said that the failure of the Act, at least in the minds of most observers, answered with finality at least some of the arguments in the debate which had begun over a century before. At the core of the Act was the belief, expressed in 1867, 1894, 1903 and finally in 1965–8, that a comprehensive legal framework would have a profound effect on industrial behaviour. The task of the NIRC was to apply the Act and thereby put on record the judgement of the community about what was 'fair and reasonable' in industrial relations. The fundamental difficulty which confronted the NIRC, however, was the divergence between what the lawyers who drafted the Act considered 'fair and reasonable' and what was normal, acceptable behaviour to the vast majority of employers and trade unionists. The size of the gap is clearly illustrated by various pronouncements made by the president of the NIRC, Sir John Donaldson, on the role of his court in settling disputes. For although he accepted that the court had an important *conciliatory* role to play, he argued that disputes should be decided on the basis of the legal rights of the parties rather than their industrial strength. Yet the development of collective bargaining in Britain over the previous century had emphasized again and again the importance of marshalling coercive power and applying it within an emerging framework of voluntary procedures. Donaldson's definition of 'good industrial relations', namely 'a relationship based on the observance of the law, respect for the rights of others and due regard for the general interests of the rest of the community', was similarly out of step with tradition. The long supremacy of legal abstentionism and 'collective *laissez-faire*' meant that there was no institutional mechanism through which a wider public interest could be introduced into the deliberations of collective bargainers. The agreements which they made were essentially their own business and what was in their interests must, by definition, be in the interests of the community as a whole.

The dichotomy between the lawyers' and the practitioners' view of what constituted good industrial relations was forcibly brought home by Donaldson on more than one occasion in the docks' dispute during the summer of 1972. In the Heaton case, for example, the employer who initiated the action intimated that he wished to withdraw his complaint after the first fine of £5000 had been imposed on the TGWU by the NIRC. Donaldson, however, refused to permit this, arguing that proceedings could not be terminated until they had run their natural course.[21] It did not matter that the docks were in the meantime threatened by a total shutdown. A national dock strike, said the President, was a 'short-term danger' which had to be faced in order to uphold the rule of law. This was not a doctrine which commended itself to trade unionists, employers or, ultimately, to government ministers.

The post-1974 legal framework

The repeal of the Industrial Relations Act in 1974 did not bring a return to the tradition of abstentionism. The criticisms levelled at this tradition by the Donovan Commission had not been invalidated by the experience of 1971–4. The *bias* of legal intervention, however, was decisively altered by the legislation which replaced the 1971 Act. While certain sections of this Act sought, however unsuccessfully, to encourage the growth of collective bargaining and strengthen the basic floor of individual employment rights, the main emphasis was on curbing the use of collective power. By contrast, the legal framework which emerged in 1974 and 1975 and which, at the time of writing, is about to be amended, reinstated the voluntary principle as the keystone of the industrial relations system and established certain rules with a view to ensuring that this same principle worked more effectively than in the past. Following Donovan, it assumed that collective bargaining was the best method of conducting industrial relations. It further assumed that without a measure of legal support it would be difficult, if not impossible for trade unions to extend collective bargaining to large groups of employees whose terms and conditions were still determined unilaterally by employers. It also recognized that, given the inadequate coverage and substantive poverty of collective bargaining in Britain, many employees had too little protection against their employers and that the law could play an important regulatory role in this field. Nevertheless, in spirit as well as in letter it was much closer than the 1971 Act to the Donovan Commission's relatively modest conception of what the law can and cannot achieve in industrial relations.

The principal objective of the Trade Union and Labour Relations Act of 1974 (TULRA) was to repeal the 1971 Act and, with the help of a further Amendment Act in 1976, restore the traditional immunities from criminal and civil action. The legislation of 1906 and 1965 was re-enacted and the principle of union liability for the actions of its agents set aside. A new and important qualification, however, was introduced. Only a trade union which could prove its *independence* from employer influence or domination was entitled to enjoy the various immunities and rights conferred by the law. These included the right to receive from an employer information which was held to be essential for bargaining purposes, the right to be consulted about redundancies, the right to paid and unpaid time off work for union representatives and members, and the right to be consulted about occupational pensions schemes. In addition, members of independent trade unions were protected against dismissal for their activities in or membership of such unions. Consequently, although TULRA reintroduced the principle of public scrutiny of a trade union's rule book and activities (this time by the certification officer), the purpose and effect of this scrutiny was quite different from the corresponding provision in the 1971 Act. Under that Act a union had to show that its rule book conformed with a variety of legalistic, common law notions; under the post-1974 framework a union was simply obliged to prove that it could function as an independent, autonomous organization.

The second important innovation introduced by TULRA was the establishment of the Advisory, Conciliation and Arbitration Service (ACAS). This body took over the day-to-day conciliation functions of the Department of Employment and assumed responsibility for the longer-term reform of collective bargaining in place of the defunct Commission on Industrial Relations. The DE (formerly the Ministry of Labour) conciliation service had over the previous decade lost the confidence of many trade unionists, who believed that in the era of incomes policy no government department could take a genuinely neutral view in disputes involving pay. The CIR, having started its life in 1969 with considerable union goodwill, forfeited this support through its enforced association with the Industrial Relations Act. The thinking behind the establishment of ACAS was that a genuinely independent national agency could make a valuable contribution both to the settlement of disputes and the reform and extension of collective bargaining. Its role was, however, conceived in thoroughly voluntarist terms. In the words of its first chairman, Mr Jim Mortimer:

> The emphasis is strongly on investigation designed to help employers and unions in situations where they have themselves requested assistance. This emphasis is deliberate. The Service must work to win the confidence of employers and unions and it must not give the impression of wanting to 'lecture' them. Public agencies are most effective in industrial relations when people are disposed to listen to what they have to say. . . .[22]

In the second half of the 1970s, ACAS successfully established itself as an important conciliatory force in industrial relations. The major criticism which its activities attracted arose, ironically, from its statutory obligation to extend collective bargaining. Some employers questioned its impartiality in recognition disputes and claimed, somewhat unfairly, that it would always be prejudiced against an employer who resisted a union recognition claim. This aspect of the service's work, however, became less and less important with the passage of time.

The main purpose of TULRA was to 'normalize' labour law and restore the voluntary principle. It was closely followed by the Employment Protection Act of 1975 (EPA) which sought to achieve two major objectives – first, the strengthening of individual employment rights and second, the encouragement of collective bargaining. Most of the new individual rights were designed to increase employment security and impose corresponding limitations on *managerial* power. They included a right to a guaranteed payment for workless days; a right to paid suspension from work on medical grounds; a right to paid maternity leave and to return to work on terms and conditions not less favourable on the expiration of such leave; and a right to time off work for trade union and public duties. The Act also improved the safeguards for employees when their employment was terminated by, for example, increasing the minimum periods of notice, imposing new requirements on employers to consult in advance with employees threatened with redundancy and strengthening the remedies for unfair dismissal. In total, therefore, the 'individual' provisions of the Act marked the largest single step which had yet been taken in Britain towards a full legal recognition of the concept of job property rights.

The 'collective' provisions of the 1975 Act were designed not only to promote the procedural extension of collective bargaining but also to provide some support for an extension in the substantive scope of collective agreements. The rules covering trade union recognition, however, were intended simply to encourage a dialogue between the two parties and recognized in turn that this could not take place without mutual goodwill and voluntary effort. The role of ACAS was to bring the pressure of public policy to bear on employers who refused to discuss a reasonable *prima facie* claim from an independent trade union for recognition. The validity of the claim itself was then investigated by ACAS by means of a 'fact-finding' inquiry. If the facts of the situation supported the union's claim (and this was a matter for ACAS itself to determine) then efforts were made to persuade the employer to concede recognition. Only when these efforts had obviously failed did the possibility of legal sanctions arise, and these could hardly be described as draconic. The ultimate sanction consisted merely of a legally binding award by the Central Arbitration Committee (CAC) improving the terms and conditions of those employees in the proposed bargaining unit *as if* collective bargaining had actually taken place. There was nothing in the Act which directly *compelled* an employer to recognize a union for bargaining purposes – there was simply a presumption that employers would behave reasonably and accept a claim which had been validated by a responsible public agency.

The provisions in the Act which dealt with the substantive outcome of collective bargaining were similarly designed to encourage voluntary action. These consisted of a general obligation on employers to disclose to recognized, independent trade unions *information* essential to the conduct of genuine collective bargaining. Several European countries during the 1970s introduced some form of compulsory disclosure, while in Britain the Industrial Relations

Act placed a duty on employers to disclose information to registered trade unions, where it would accord with 'good industrial relations practice' to do so, and/or without which the unions would be materially impeded in collective bargaining. The 1975 Act merely reaffirmed this duty, subject to certain safeguards for the employer's business. A Code of Practice on disclosure issued by ACAS in 1977 gave more detailed guidance to employers and trade unions on what kind of information *might* be essential for bargaining purposes but no hard and fast rules were laid down. Claims by trade unions that an employer was unreasonably refusing to disclose information were heard by the CAC but the sanctions which the latter could apply were nominal and, up to the end of 1979, very few complaints had been referred to it. The real focus of activity was at plant and company level, where some managements responded to union pressure by formulating their own policies on disclosure. It was recognized on both sides, however, that the problems of adjusting bargaining procedures and techniques to a greater volume of information – especially financial information – were unlikely to be resolved without a degree of mutual trust and a sustained effort to improve understanding. This was not, therefore, an area in which precise, detailed rules *could* be imposed on collective bargainers.

When the legislation of 1974 and 1975 was enacted, the TUC anticipated that the support it gave to the extension of collective bargaining would be of particular benefit to those unions who sought to organize white collar workers in the private sector, sometimes in the teeth of employer hostility. The need to extend collective bargaining in the white collar sectors of employment was regarded as vital to the long-term strength of the trade union movement in view of the past and projected growth of this type of employment and the downward trend in manual work. The practical results of legal support, however, were much less dramatic than either its advocates or its critics originally anticipated.

First, the need for unions to prove their independence in order to claim legal rights and immunities did not prevent the continued growth of staff associations and 'house' unions. To pass the test of independence, a union had to show that it was 'neither under the domination or control of . . . nor liable to interference leading towards control, by an employer or employer group arising out of the provision of financial or material support or by any other means' (TULRA, section 30). There were, however, no precise statutory guidelines under which the independence or effectiveness of a trade union could be evaluated. In these circumstances much depended on the subjective judgement of the certification officer, who tended to take a relatively liberal view of the representative capacity of those organizations which the TUC had long regarded as suspect. Consequently, over the period 1975–9 far more staff associations received certificates of independence than were refused them. Since many of these were claiming and receiving bargaining rights in respect of white collar workers in expanding areas of employment, they threatened to erect a major obstacle in the way of continued growth by TUC affiliated unions.

Second, the very limited role of sanctions in the statutory recognition procedure meant that the extent to which ACAS succeeded in fulfilling its statutory obligations depended almost entirely on its ability to persuade hitherto reluctant employers to accept a union recognition claim. In practice the number of formal reports issued by ACAS was very small in relation to the total number of references and was confined largely to those disputes where a trade union came up against deep-rooted employer hostility. By October 1978 some 1207 recognition claims had been referred to ACAS under section 11 of the EPA, of which 654 had either been withdrawn or settled by conciliation. In only 145 cases had ACAS gone to the length of publishing a report. Conciliation, therefore, played a vital part in the operation of the statutory procedure. Under the 1975 Act, ACAS had no power to force an employer to concede a claim, and indeed it would be contrary to the spirit of voluntarism, as well as to the realities of industrial relations, if collective bargaining could be imposed on an employer who was fundamentally unwilling to negotiate in good faith. The legal power conferred on ACAS was confined to the functions of investigation and report. It was obliged by law to ascertain the wishes of employees themselves yet, as the House of Lords made clear in the Grunwick case, an employer was under no legal obligation to co-operate with an ACAS inquiry.[23] Moreover, the length of the statutory recognition procedure allowed a hostile employer to 'play for time' in the expectation that the union recruiting campaign in his establishment would eventually lose momentum, and that the level of membership would fall, thus undermining the basis of the claim for recognition. These factors together help to explain why a large proportion of the published reports in which ACAS recommended that the union involved should be recognized were not implemented.

Those sections of the 1975 Act which were designed to strengthen individual rights broadly achieved their objective, but the impact on industrial relations was less than dramatic. The safeguards against unfair dismissal, for example, had a very limited impact on voluntary procedures, possibly because the safeguards themselves did little more than confer on the individual a right to compensation for unfair dismissal in certain circumstances. Employers could be fined for dismissing an employee unfairly but they were not obliged by law to reinstate that employee. Moreover, the way in which the unfair dismissal provisions were interpreted from 1976 onwards considerably lessened the chances that a given dismissal would be unfair. In 1973 the NIRC laid down that industrial tribunals should regard themselves as 'specialist industrial juries' and adopt a 'broad approach of common sense and common fairness' in deciding claims for unfair dismissal.[24] In effect this was an open invitation to tribunals, when applying the general test of fairness in dismissal cases, to say what *they* would have done had they been in the employer's shoes. Consequently, the general direction of tribunal decisions over the next three years imposed more exacting requirements on employers as their role of 'specialist juries' developed into that of 'disseminators of good practice'. In 1976, however, the High Court intervened and instructed tribunals that their task was simply to decide whether or not the employer had acted reasonably in the circumstances, a rule which has been incorporated into the Employment Act 1980.[25] In a range of decisions covering such issues as selection for redundancy, the right of management to reorganize its business and the relevance of warnings, the Employment Appeals Tribunal (established in 1976) effectively strengthened the position of the employer.[26] Although the main body of case law still emphasizes the importance of following procedures when dismissing employees, the operation of this section of the law can no longer be regarded as a drastic limitation on managerial rights, if indeed it ever could be so regarded.

Before closing this brief discussion of the current legal framework, we must mention four other pieces of legislation which have been enacted in order to strengthen the rights or otherwise improve the terms and conditions of individual employees. The Health and Safety at Work Act (1974) marks the latest and easily the most ambitious advance along a regulatory path stretching back to the first Factories Acts. Despite a relatively favourable reception within industry, it is difficult to evaluate the effectiveness of this Act if only because many employers have found the cost of implementing it to the full almost prohibitively expensive. The Equal Pay Act (1970), despite a six-year implementation period, has not apparently succeeded in achieving its overriding objective of ensuring that female employees receive an equal rate of pay with men for doing work which is either the same or broadly similar in nature. The Sex Discrimination Act (1975) and the Race Relations Act (1976) are still too recent in origin to permit a real assessment of their effects. From the volume of case law to date, however, it would appear that very few employees are aware either of their rights under this legislation or of the procedure they must follow in order to compel an employer to observe the law. Once again the sanctions which can be applied to an employer who is found by an industrial tribunal to be in breach of the law are mild. The assumption is that the vast majority of employers will comply with them voluntarily and that sanctions will not be needed.

Although it may be premature to offer a final evaluation of the impact of the post-1974 legislation on labour relations in the workplace, the evidence to date suggests that it has on the whole been modest. Apologists would, of course, argue that any legislation which is essentially supportive of voluntary action must by definition be undramatic in its impact. They would argue that no law can, for example, preserve the level of employment in a period of severe economic recession when the available number of jobs is falling rapidly (as in 1975–7). All it can do is delay or soften slightly the impact of market forces on the enterprise. They would also point out that collective bargaining cannot be imposed on unwilling employers and that sanctions are no substitute for organized persuasion. Nevertheless, some trade union leaders have expressed disappointment with the practical effects of what, after all, amounts to a major package of employment legislation. The reasons for this limited impact have been summarized thus:

> Many employers had developed policies and practices which were in advance of the minimum standards specified in the legislation. Many others, for whom this was not the case, were able to continue much as before, presumably due to the lack of people at their workplaces with the knowledge or inclination to draw attention to the law or invoke its requirements.[27]

It should be noted this legislation simply provides yet another manifestation of a major underlying theme in the historical relationship between trade unions and the law. Once an Act is on the statute book, it is the task of the judges to say precisely what the law means in a given set of circumstances. Usually the main effect of judicial interpretation is that the law means rather less than the trade unions assumed it did. This was certainly true of the framework legislation of 1871, 1875 and 1906 and our experience with the post-1974 statutes has in many respects been the same.

Are the unions above the law?

At the time of writing, the use of coercive power by trade unions and workgroups is still a major political issue. Indeed, the disruptive strikes which occurred in several major industries and services during the winter of 1978–9 has sharpened the long-standing controversy over the role of the law in industrial relations. The Conservative Party returned to office in May 1979 with a commitment to correct the imbalance between the rights and responsibilities of trade unions which the legislation of 1974 and 1975 was alleged to have created. But what is the nature of this imbalance, and can it be corrected by amending the law? Critics of the Labour government's legislation contend that under its auspices the unions acquired new and potentially dangerous powers in three areas – an immunity from the legal consequences of strike action, the extended use of picketing, and the growth of the closed shop. However, the Conservative government's Employment Act (passed in August 1980) seeks to limit union power in each of these areas, and the likely impact of the Act's amendments must now be discussed.

Under the 1906 Act (re-enacted in 1974), a trade union is given immunity from actions for damages on the grounds that, by calling a strike, it has induced its members to break their contracts of employment *provided* the union is acting 'in contemplation or furtherance of a trade dispute'. The 1906 definition of a trade dispute was always broad enough to cover practically every type of collective labour dispute, including inter-union conflicts. All that the 1974 Act did was to make the definition even more explicit and thus remove any conceivable uncertainty. In 1976, however, by an amendment to TULRA, the Labour government extended this immunity to cover the inducement of breaches of *commercial* contracts, a point which had been shrouded in uncertainty since the early 1960s. This enabled a union in dispute with an employer to apply sanctions against a third party (such as a customer or supplier of the firm involved) without liability for damages. Some judges were clearly disturbed by this extended immunity and in a series of cases the Court of Appeal sought to narrow it. It was held that the motive behind a particular action against a third party and its closeness to the trade dispute itself should be tested objectively. If a union applied sanctions against a third party, it must be done genuinely and directly *in furtherance* of a trade dispute and not undertaken either 'in connexion with' or 'as a consequence of' a trade dispute or for some other motive.[28] The House of Lords, however, has overruled this approach. In the Express Newspapers case, for example, Lord Diplock pointed out that Parliament had clearly intended that trade union officials should have 'a wide discretion to exercise their own judgement as to the steps to be taken in an endeavour to help the workers' side in any trade dispute to achieve its objectives'. If this was the case, then it was lawful for a union to inflict a 'a disastrous loss' on a third party 'who might be a stranger to the dispute with no interest in its outcome'. The Lords added that if this immunity was too wide – and Lord Salmon's critical reference to the behaviour of pickets in a dispute at the Charing Cross hospital clearly implied that, in their view, it was – then it was for Parliament to change the law. Whether it will do so is at present uncertain, but the Employment Act contains no provisions to this effect.

If the government decided to reduce the unions' immunity and impose an objective test on the 'golden formula', there would be more scope for employers to apply for *interlocutory injunctions* restraining unions from taking industrial action. An injunction clearly constitutes a powerful weapon against strikes in so far as, once a stoppage has been brought to a halt and union members have resumed work, union officials and stewards are likely to encounter great difficulty in persuading them to resume action once the legal proceedings have been concluded. If, of course, a union can show that it is acting 'in contemplation or furtherance of a trade dispute', then an injunction should not be granted. Indeed, a 1976 amendment to TULRA specifically instructs the courts that, when they are considering a request for an interlocutory (that is, temporary) injunction, they must 'have regard' to the likelihood that the party against whom the injunction is sought will be able to show that he is acting in contemplation or furtherance of a trade dispute. But if Parliament should decide to restrict the unions' immunity against third party claims, this will undoubtedly create uncertainty about the kind of action that can and cannot be taken in order to increase the effectiveness of a strike. In these circumstances aggrieved third parties will feel encouraged to apply for injunctions, which the courts will no doubt be disposed to grant.

A narrower view of what constitutes a lawful trade dispute would obviously have implications for the right to picket. The right of workers to picket the premises of their employer, with whom they are pursuing a lawful trade dispute, is protected by TULRA in exactly the same terms as it was protected by the 1906 Act: such picketing is lawful provided it is confined to 'peacefully obtaining or communicating information or peacefully persuading any person to work or abstain from working'. In reality, of course, the purpose of picketing is to deter non-strikers from entering the employer's premises. In many situations the dividing line between peaceful persuasion and physical intimidation is impossible to draw. Indeed, there must always be an element of intimidation wherever picketing is effective. Moreover, the law does not recognize the existence of vehicular traffic. Vehicles can only be stopped if pickets are there in sufficient force to intimidate the drivers. The total unreality of the law has in effect placed the power to decide whether or not picketing is lawful in the hands of the police. If they wish to disperse or prosecute pickets for obstructing the highway, intimidation or a breach of public order, a long line of judicial decisions gives them the authority to do so. A further problem arises in the case of 'secondary' picketing. Strictly speaking the term 'secondary' picketing should only be applied to action which is at *one* remove from the primary dispute. In recent years, however, the term has been applied to *any* industrial action other than that which is taking place at the employer's premises. The effectiveness of this weapon has been demonstrated in several major disputes over the past decade and the advocates of restriction clearly see this as a major loophole in the law.

The new Employment Act mounts a frontal assault on secondary picketing by promulgating a new definition of lawful picketing which in effect confines it to the employee's own place of work. Only a trade union 'official' may participate in picketing a workplace where he is not employed. Outside these new boundaries, a picket who induces a worker to break his contract of employment by picketing somewhere other than his own place of work can be sued in tort. The effectiveness of this new approach remains to be seen. Should Parliament also take a narrower view of the immunities which can be claimed 'in contemplation or furtherance of a trade dispute', secondary picketing is likely to be the target of more and more court injunctions. Whatever changes are made in the law, however, it seems more than likely that in the forseeable future the only effective way of preventing a large body of well-organized workers from picketing an establishment as vigorously as they can will be the same as in the past. This means that there must be a sufficiently large body of police present who can by simple physical force preserve the right of non-strikers to go on working.

The third area of concern is the closed shop. Under the Industrial Relations Act the closed shop was not prohibited *per se*; the law simply made the *enforcement* of a closed shop (by the dismissal of non-unionists) an unfair industrial practice. We noted that this section of the Act was virtually ignored by managers and trade unionists alike and that very few closed shops were challenged. The authors of TULRA would no doubt have preferred to avoid any reference to the closed shop, thereby restoring the pre-1971 situation. Unfortunately they were required to define a closed shop and permit action to enforce it in order to maintain the unfair dismissal provisions of the 1971 Act. An employee who refused to join a union which operated or was a party to a closed shop (or 'union membership agreement') could under TULRA be fairly dismissed unless he could show that he had a 'genuine religious objection' to trade unionism. While some unions have been showing less tolerance towards non-unionist objections to closed shops in recent years, the operation of this section of TULRA did not generate much litigation. One reason may lie in the fact that since 1976 an employee who is barred or expelled from union membership in circumstances where his job depends on such membership has had a right of appeal to an independent review committee operated by the TUC. A more likely explanation, however, is that many closed shops have in practice been operated in a more liberal spirit than the letter of the law implies. Many agreements exclude not only those who have religious objections to membership but also those who class themselves as 'conscientious' objectors. The closed shop does not in fact depend primarily on legal support for its strength but on the cohesion of union members in a given workplace and on the willingness of the employer to comply with its provisions.

Why, then, have more and more closed shops been formally negotiated with employers since 1974? To some extent the increase in the number of employees covered by formal union membership agreements is more apparent than real because they simply represent the formalization of well-established, informal arrangements. Formalization has in turn been encouraged by the 'Ferrybridge Six' case (1976), in which an industrial tribunal held that if an employer wished to claim immunity from a complaint of unfair dismissal arising from the enforcement of a closed shop, he must ensure that the requirement of union membership is imposed consistently on *all* workers covered by the closed shop. Consequently it is now very much in the employer's interest to commit a union membership agreement to writing and define precisely those groups to whom the agreement applies.[29] The spread of closed shops may also, however, reflect a more widespread recognition among employers and trade unionists alike of the advantages which 100 per cent membership can bring. This is particularly relevant in the white collar field, where inter-union competition for members is frequently encountered and where a union membership agreement can, if granted at the initial recognition stage, exclude all competitors. Consequently the level of membership at which a closed shop is likely to be both requested and conceded has fallen well below the traditional 75–80 per cent benchmark.

The recent spread of the closed shop has given a new impetus to the opponents of this institution. One point which is frequently made is that the principle of compulsion which lies at the heart of the closed shop is incompatible with the claim that trade unions are voluntary bodies. As the Donovan Commission pointed out:

> If (the employee) is to obtain or retain employment where there is a closed shop, he has no choice but to join the trade union and pay a subscription. . . . Once a member of the union, the individual has to comply with any relevant decisions it may make; if he does not he may be disciplined, and if things go too far he may eventually be expelled and lose his job in consequence. So far as he is concerned, therefore, the trade union is no longer a 'voluntary' organisation. . . .[30]

Consequently the closed shop may lead to great injustice being done to individuals who fall out of favour with shop stewards or lay officials in the workplace.

The authors of the 1980 Employment Act undoubtedly share this belief and the following amendments are proposed in order to strengthen the position of the individual objector. First, the grounds on which an employee can lawfully remain outside a closed shop, and thereby retain his employment, have been widened to include reasons of 'conscience' or some 'deeply held personal conviction'. Second, employees who at the time of a closed shop being introduced are not members of the appropriate union and subsequently do not join are permitted to remain non-members. If an employee who falls into either of the above categories finds himself dismissed on the grounds of non-membership, the dismissal will be unfair. In practice neither of these amendments is likely to have much effect on the majority of closed shop agreements. A recent survey of 136 union membership agreements has reported that two-thirds of them place no obligation on existing non-members to join the union. Since the vast majority also provide exemption to the 'genuine religious objector', an extension of such clauses to cover 'conscientious objectors' in general should present few difficulties.[31]

A more radical innovation is the provision in the Act requiring new closed shop agreements to be approved in a secret ballot by 80 per cent of the employees to whom the agreement will apply. In workplaces where union membership is already high, there is no reason why this should cause much difficulty. If union representatives have agreed with management on the need for a closed shop and have drafted a procedural document giving effect to this arrangement, then presumably both sides will use their best endeavours to persuade the workforce to accept it. Faced with organized persuasion on this scale, the vast majority of employees are likely to vote for the closed shop. Difficulties may arise, however, if a closed shop is being proposed for a workplace or bargaining unit in which union membership is considerably below the 80 per cent level. In these circumstances the main effect of the Act may be to postpone a union application for a closed shop until the membership level has been increased to something near 80 per cent. In view of the recent trend in favour of introducing closed shops at membership levels well below 80 per cent, the new rules will either slow down the spread of closed shops or else encourage union activists in the workplace to make greater efforts to increase their membership. In any event, the existing pattern of union membership agreements will not be affected.

Finally, it must be remembered that the decision whether or not to introduce a closed shop is entirely a matter for the parties themselves. There has never been a legal obligation on any employer to have a closed shop, nor is there any legal procedure which a union can invoke in order to secure a closed shop. The law merely provides a measure of support for closed shops by permitting employers to dismiss non-members in certain circumstances. The Employment Act simply redefines those circumstances in a way which marginally strengthens the position of the individual objector. There is no reason to suppose that employers and union representatives will have difficulty in adjusting the terms of their membership agreements to take account of the new rules. In these circumstances it seems likely that most closed shops will continue to operate in broadly the same way as before.

The remaining provisions of the Act are similarly modest in intent. The recognition procedure embodied in section 11 of the 1975 Act (see pages 65–6) is to be repealed, but in view of the very limited impact of this procedure since 1975 the effects of repeal are likely to be insignificant. The abandonment of this procedure is little more than a timely recognition of the fact that it has failed to achieve its objectives. The Act also gives individual employees a statutory right not to be unreasonably excluded or expelled from a trade union and empowers industrial tribunals to determine complaints arising under this provision. This may be seen as an additional safeguard for employees who work in closed shops and is designed to discourage arbitrary behaviour on the part of union activists and shop stewards. Since there is no evidence of widespread discrimination against individuals, this provision is unlikely to be used very often. Nevertheless it may be a useful deterrent in the small minority of cases where an individual *has* been treated unfairly. Finally, the Act seeks to encourage the use by trade unions of secret ballots, especially where industrial action is about to be undertaken or ended and also in union elections. This encouragement takes the form of a subsidy from the government to offset the administrative costs of running secret ballots. The assumption here is, of course, very familiar, namely that a secret ballot allows the silent and, by implication, moderate majority of union members to make their views known to their leaders. The validity of this assumption in relation to the calling of industrial action has already been discussed (see pages 55–6) and the role of ballots in union elections is discussed in Chapter 4. It may simply be noted at this point that it is easy to exaggerate the likely effects of ballots on the pattern of workplace behaviour.

In summary, the assertion that between 1974 and 1979 trade unions gained sweeping new *legal* powers seems at variance with reality. If the bargaining power of organized labour *has* increased since 1974, the reasons must be sought outside the sphere of legislation. Most of the enactments of 1974–6 were, in fact, concerned with individual rather than collective rights, so that, while it is possible to argue that some of them have imposed unreasonable burdens on employers, it can hardly be maintained that in themselves they have enhanced the power of *trade unions*. The legal status of the unions is still based on the traditional *immunities* which were restored and marginally strengthened in 1974 and 1976 after the temporary interruption of 1971–4. In this narrow, technical sense, therefore, it can be said that the unions are 'above the law'. For over a century it has been recognized that the process of fixing terms and conditions of employment and preserving industrial peace is primarily a matter for voluntary effort. It has also been recognized that the consequences of collective action are likely to bring those who take such action into direct conflict with the precepts of the common law – hence the continuing significance of legal immunities. If these immunities were restricted, the effectiveness of the strike weapon could in certain circumstances be reduced, and determined employers would be given a significant bargaining counter which they do not have at present. But as long as free collective bargaining remains the dominant form of rule-making in industrial relations, the unions arguably must be free to pursue their legitimate bargaining objectives and improve their members' terms and conditions without having to cross a mine-field of legal liabilities. The inducement to behave 'reasonably' is best regarded as a function of the day-to-day bargaining relationship between unions and managements and the general climate in which bargaining takes place.

The challenge to the tradition of legal abstentionism has come not so much from the growth of union power as from the changing role of the state in British society. Over the past forty years the government has become both the biggest single employer in the country and the overall manager of the economy. In these circumstances it is hardly surprising that successive governments have moved, albeit with varying degrees of conviction, towards a fundamental redefinition of their role in industrial relations. No longer does government simply 'hold the ring' while the other two parties proceed to resolve their differences. The development of a more interventionist legal framework, the increasingly active role of government agencies in the labour market and the attempt to curb the inflationary consequences of collective bargaining all add up to an implicit declaration that the state now has objectives and needs of its own which employers and trade unions alike must take into account. It is obvious that there must be *some* congruence between the interests of the state as an employer and those of employers as a whole but to regard this partial affinity in Marxist terms would be a gross distortion of reality.

The problem for governments is that the bargaining power of trade unions and workgroups is increasingly and inevitably directed against *them* rather than against private employers. Politicians would be less than human if they did not occasionally succumb to the temptation to devise a system of legal sanctions which could in theory be used to break the stranglehold which well-organized workgroups have on vital services and supplies. Practical experience, however, suggests that the application of penal sanctions to large groups of workers or their organizations is unlikely to be effective and may even be counter-productive. Experience also suggests that, in McCarthy's words, there is 'no necessary connexion between a more responsible and interventionist policy by government and the volume of legal sanctions'.[32] It would, therefore, be more sensible to see the future role of the law in terms of the contribution which it *could* make towards encouraging a climate of opinion in industry which is more receptive to constructive initiatives for change.

3 Growth and structure

One important yardstick by which the social status and influence of trade unionism can be measured is the rate at which its aggregate membership is growing. Applying this yardstick to the decade 1969–79, one can only conclude that – contrary to the message of the opinion polls – the appeal of trade unionism has grown stronger. The growth in aggregate membership is particularly striking when set against the overall stagnation of the period 1952–67. At the beginning of the 1960s the failure of the trade union movement to increase its very modest penetration of the expanding white collar occupations was frequently underlined by outside observers. Shanks, for example, attributed this failure to the conservative, 'cloth-cap' image of trade unionism. 'To be a trade unionist', he wrote, 'is to align oneself with those at the bottom of the social ladder at a time when the predominant urge is to climb it.'[1] Thus the fact that since the late 1960s the trade unions have been much more successful in recruiting white collar workers requires explanation. We also need to ask whether this growth reflects a particular combination of circumstances which may well disappear in the 1980s or whether British society is now moving inexorably towards a state of almost total unionization.

The dimensions of union growth

The main features of trade union growth since the 1960s have been well documented by Price and Bain.[2] The first point to note is that since 1968 union membership has grown not only in terms of absolute numbers but also in density. Density is, of course, a much more informative yardstick of union success since it relates aggregate membership to the size of the labour force and measures the extent to which unions are penetrating their 'market'. The significance of the post-1968 period is underlined in Table 1.

Table 1 *Total trade union membership and density in the UK, selected years, 1892–1976*

Year	*Labour force* ('000s)	*Annual change in labour force* (%)	*Total union membership* ('000s)	*Annual change in union membership* (%)	*Density of union membership* (%)
1892	14,126		1,576		11.2
1913	17,920		4,135		23.1
1920	18,469		8,348		45.2
1933	19,422		4,392		22.6
1945	20,400		7,875		38.6
1948	20,732		9,362		45.2
1952	21,252		9,588		45.1
1962	23,432		10,014		42.7
1967	23,809		10,188		42.8
1968	23,667	−0.6	10,191	0.0	43.1
1969	23,603	−0.3	10,470	+2.7	44.4
1970	23,446	−0.7	11,178	+6.8	47.7
1971	23,231	−0.9	11,126	−0.5	47.9
1972	23,303	+0.3	11,351	+2.0	48.7
1973	23,592	+1.2	11,447	+0.8	48.5
1974	23,689	+0.4	11,755	+2.7	49.6
1975	23,522	−0.7	12,184	+3.6	51.7
1976	23,538	+0.1	12,376	+1.0	52.5

The data on unionization by sector and industry suggests that in all but a handful of cases (notably agriculture, construction and distribution) there was a general increase in union density between 1948 and 1974.

The significance of this development is seen in true perspective when set against the well-known changes in the industrial and sectoral *distribution* of employment which have occurred in Britain over the post-war period as a whole. In simple terms, the industries with the highest densities of union membership (coal mining and the railways) have declined sharply, while those in which union density has traditionally been low (banking, insurance and finance, professional and scientific services, distribution and various leisure services) have expanded (see Table 2).

Table 2 *Union membership and density in selected industries in the UK, 1948–74*

Industry	*Labour force* ('000s)	*Union membership* ('000s)	*Density* (%)	*Labour force* ('000s)	*Union membership* ('000s)	*Density* (%)
Coal mining	802.7	675.3	84.1	314.0	302.1	96.2
Railways	694.9	612.1	88.1	224.0	217.0	96.9
Footwear	139.5	92.8	66.6	87.1	68.8	79.0
Cotton and other textiles	928.5	457.0	49.2	596.7	243.8	40.9
Agriculture and forestry	785.9	215.7	27.4	415.5	92.3	22.2
Construction	1353.7	613.2	45.3	1428.8	388.1	27.2
Port and inland water transport	155.7	123.2	79.1	81.5	77.2	94.7
Post Office and telecommunications	353.2	283.4	80.2	509.7	448.1	87.9
Distribution	2167.9	325.3	15.0	2810.1	321.8	11.4
Insurance, banking, finance	425.9	137.1	32.2	680.5	305.1	44.8
Health	525.9	204.6	38.9	1175.2	715.8	60.9
Education and local government	1280.5	792.2	61.9	2752.4	2356.0	85.6
Hotels and catering	708.1	n.a.	—	824.2	42.5	5.2
National government	724.1	480.6	66.4	623.7	564.5	90.5

In declining high-density industries the unions have on the whole further strengthened their position. In one declining sector – agriculture – and in construction they lost ground heavily during the period under review. In one expanding sector – distribution – they also lost ground. Elsewhere, however, they improved their position, with particularly impressive advances in the rapidly growing health, education and local government sectors.

Most of the growth in employment opportunities has occurred in those industries and services where non-manual jobs far exceed manual jobs. In 1951 the proportion of the labour force in white collar employment was 30.8 per cent; by 1971 this proportion had risen to 42.7 per cent and continued to grow during the 1970s. Up to the mid 1960s the growth of white collar unionism did not quite keep pace with the growth of white collar employment, so that the density of unionism in these occupations declined very slightly (to 29.6 per cent) between 1948 and 1964.[3] Between 1964 and 1974, by contrast, white collar union membership increased faster than the white collar labour force, with a particularly sharp upsurge in 1969 and 1970 (see Table 3). The penetration of white collar unionism was particularly impressive in manufacturing industry, where density rose from 12.1 per cent in 1964 to 32.0 per cent in 1974.

The growing proportion of women in the labour force also has important implications for trade unionism in so far as women were once alleged to be more difficult to organize than men. In fact, while the tendency has been for white collar unionism to expand faster among men than women, the reverse has happened in manual employment (see Tables 4 and 5). The remaining differential between male and female union density may well be attributed to the large number of women who are only part-time employees and as such have less incentive to join a union.

It seems clear, therefore, that up to the late 1960s the stagnation of aggregate union membership and union density reflected 'a marked inability or reluctance' on the part of the unions themselves 'to develop their representative position beyond those occupations and industries in which they had historically been relatively strong'.[4] Why, then, was there such a dramatic break in membership trends in

Table 3 *Trends in manual and white collar union membership, 1964–74*

	Union membership ('000s)			*% increase*	
	1964	*1970*	*1974*	*1964–70*	*1970–4*
White collar	2684	3592	4263	+33.8	+18.7
Manual	7534	7587	7491	+0.7	–1.3
	Union density (%)			*% increase*	
White collar	29.6	35.2	39.4	+5.6	+4.2
Manual	52.9	56.0	57.9	+3.1	+1.9

Table 4 *Union membership by sex, 1964–74*

	Male ('000s)			*Female* ('000s)		
	1964	*1974*	*% increase*	*1964*	*1974*	*% increase*
White collar	1681	2593	+54.2	1003	1629	+62.4
Manual	6329	5927	−6.2	1206	1561	+29.4
Total	8010	8565	+6.9	2209	3190	+44.4

Table 5 *Union density by sex, 1964–74 (%)*

	Male			*Female*		
	1964	*1974*	*Increase*	*1964*	*1974*	*Increase*
White collar	33.4	44.5	11.1	24.9	32.6	7.7
Manual	60.0	64.7	4.7	32.6	42.1	9.5
Total	51.4	56.9	5.5	28.6	36.7	8.1

1969 and 1970 – a break which broadly continued, albeit at a more modest pace, during the 1970s? If, in Shank's terms, it was 'the smell of the music hall and the pawnshop' which discouraged many white collar workers from joining a trade union in the 1950s, what factors came into play after 1968 which in total appear to have removed this constraint on growth? Why, in addition, have unions found it easier to recruit workers and win collective bargaining rights in some industries than in others?

Factors affecting union growth

Changes in the aggregate level of union membership used to be explained almost entirely in terms of the economic cycle. It was observed that major upswings in union recruiting activity coincided with periods of economic expansion and that, by the same token, union membership tended to fall when the level of economic activity was declining. This hypothesis has a certain plausibility. When order books are full, unemployment is falling and the general level of prosperity is increasing, businessmen will be more willing both to avoid strikes and to pass on wage increases in the form of higher prices. They may also be less inclined to dismiss or discriminate against trade union members. Consequently workers will have more incentive to join a trade union because they know that its efforts to improve their wages and conditions are more likely to succeed. Unfortunately the 'prosperity' theory – at least in its crude form – does not stand up to close analysis. The evidence from several countries suggests that by no means all periods of rising prosperity have been associated with union growth and, conversely, that not all downswings can be correlated with declining membership.[5] The theory also overlooks the defensive functions of trade unionism. Why, one might ask, should workers join unions in 'boom' periods when market forces are already working in their favour and yet desert them in downswings when their need for countervailing power is so much greater?

Recent empirical work suggests that changes in the level of union membership are strongly influenced by the relationship between three economic variables – the rate of change in prices, the rate of change in wages and the level of unemployment.[6] Since increases in wage rates tend to lag behind price rises, a sudden acceleration in the latter may well induce employed workers to take appropriate action to protect their real incomes. Trade union members, for example, may seek through their representatives to renegotiate existing wage agreements or adopt much more ambitious targets for the next annual pay round. Non-unionists may be induced to join a trade union in the hope that it will defend or enhance their living standards. To the extent that unions succeed in negotiating increases in money wages and salaries which keep pace with or exceed the rate of inflation, the lesson is not likely to be lost on non-unionists. As Price and Bain have argued:

> Price rises generally have a positive effect on union growth because of the 'threat effect' – the tendency of workers to unionise in an attempt to defend their standards of living against the threat posed by rising prices – and wage rises will have similar impact because of the 'credit effect' – the tendency of workers to credit wage rises to unions and to support them in the hope of doing well or even better in the future.[7]

Historically, the major upswings in trade union membership have extended over several years (such as 1901–20 and 1934–47) in which the rate of price inflation has been relatively high and unemployment either relatively low or falling.

The boom in union membership which began in the late 1960s and continued throughout the 1970s requires a more detailed explanation. If the rate of price inflation is the most important influence over union growth, how do we account for the fact that the rate of membership growth was higher in 1969 and 1970 than in succeeding years when the rate of inflation was on average considerably greater than in the late 1960s? One explanation is provided by the Bain–Elsheikh model, which suggests that the relationship between prices and union growth is non-linear, that is, that prices do not have a *constant* effect on union growth. Once price inflation exceeds 4 per cent its effect on union growth continues but at a more modest level.[8] In behavioural terms, therefore, it seems that the *initial* impact of accelerating inflation on living standards is the most effective recruiting officer for trade unionism. Another variable emphasized by Bain and Elsheikh is unemployment. The rate of union growth after 1970, and more especially after 1974, would have been higher had it not been for the restraining effect of rising unemployment. In 1970 registered unemployment stood at 2.5 per cent and over the next two years it rose to a peak of 3.7 per cent before falling back to 2.5 per cent in 1973. Between 1974 and 1976, however, the unemployment rate more than doubled, which presumably damped down the effect of high and rising inflation on union growth. Nevertheless the 'threat effect' of inflation was strong enough to keep union membership on a rising trend.

Changes in pay relativities and differentials may also have assisted union growth. The membership explosion which occurred in 1969 and 1970, for example, was partly triggered by the collapse of the Labour government's incomes policy. In 1967–8 this policy was vigorously enforced against some workgroups while others escaped relatively lightly. As the policy began to crumble in 1969, so the sense of injustice which it had generated found expression in a sharp increase in both the level of pay claims and the level of strike activity. Not only was there a dramatic increase in the number of working days lost but the proportion of strikes arising over pay issues also rose sharply. To the extent that major, well-publicized stoppages resulted in pay increases which exceeded the general rate of inflation, they underlined the relevance of militant collective action and enhanced the appeal of trade unionism to hitherto unorganized workgroups.

It is likely that concern over relativities has continued to be a positive influence on the level of union membership during the 1970s, though perhaps for different reasons. In the late 1960s, the sense of injustice was caused by an apparently discriminatory incomes policy. In the 1970s, by contrast, it is more likely that dissatisfaction has arisen as a result of incomes policies which have imposed flat-rate increases on all groups, thereby compressing differentials and relativities. This compression has aroused particularly strong resentment among white collar groups. Between 1970 and 1975 the average pre-tax earnings differential between white collar and manual men fell by 11 per cent, and a similar compression occurred in the differential between white collar and manual women. The earnings differential between skilled and unskilled manual workers also declined sharply over the same period, although where skilled workers were represented by their own craft unions this erosion was far less pronounced. Since pay differentials are inextricably linked with occupational status, many white collar workers are likely to have been attracted by the emphasis which white collar unions typically place on grievances of this kind.

The influence of unemployment on the growth of union membership, however, seems more problematic. The Bain–Elsheikh model suggests that relatively high unemployment will discourage union membership by reducing union bargaining power. It is doubtful, however, whether the relationship between the level of demand for labour and the bargaining power of the trade unions is in reality quite so simple. As Blackaby has pointed out:

> Those trade unions which, in any round of wage negotiations tend to set the target figure which subsequent negotiators aim to reach are not usually in industries which feel themselves under much threat from unemployment; or if they do feel such a threat, they may well not be persuaded that a rapid increase in money earnings would increase unemployment. Unemployment tends to fall not on those leading the wage bargaining process but on those who are on the margin of the labour force.[9]

Consequently one would expect unemployment to have a differential impact on bargaining power. Circumstances can also be envisaged, however, in which the *threat* of unemployment has a positive influence on union membership, particularly among white collar employees. The merger boom of the late 1960s, for example, eventually generated a plethora of rationalization programmes, plant closures and redundancies. For a significant number of white collar workers, security of employment was no longer assured. More recently the development of micro-process technology has, in effect, placed a question mark over the future of thousands of traditional clerical jobs. This sense of uncertainty may have induced many white collar staff to join a union for basic self-protection. If they feel threatened by technological and organizational change then at the very least they will see that collective representation could be needed if they are to obtain the best possible severance terms.

Non-economic factors may also have played a role. Workers in general and white collar employees in particular are usually reluctant to join a trade union unless it is either recognized by their employer for bargaining purposes or else has very good prospects of getting recognition. They tend to see trade unionism as a vehicle for achieving certain concrete objectives and their decision to join or not to join a union is likely to be determined by their assessment of how far it can in practice achieve those objectives. Consequently, many of them see little point in joining if their employer is overtly hostile to trade unionism and in such circumstances some may even be afraid to do so. There is little doubt that in the past the active hostility of employers has, at least in certain industries, proved to be a powerful obstacle to the expansion of union membership. From 1968 onwards, however, governments adopted a more interventionist stance in favour of extending collective bargaining and it is generally assumed that this change in the political climate may well have caused some employers to concede recognition who would otherwise have resisted it. In the light of our experience with the statutory recognition procedure established in 1975, it would obviously be unwise to put too much emphasis on political and legal factors, but it is conceivable that they may have exerted some influence on otherwise reluctant employers.

The economic and non-economic factors mentioned above have contributed in varying degrees to the upswing in union membership which began in 1969 and continued during the 1970s. We must also note, however, the presence of *structural* factors which are of longer-term significance in the process of union growth. Recent work by Bain and Elsheikh, for example, has thrown more light on the reasons why the level of unionization varies from one industry to another. The most important single factor seems to be the average size of establishment in an industry:

> . . . the larger the establishment the more interested its employees are likely to be in joining trade unions. For the larger the number of employees the more likely they are to be treated not as individuals but as members of groups, to have their terms and conditions of employment determined not by the personal considerations and sentiments of their managers but by bureaucratic rules which apply impersonally to all members of the group to which they belong, and hence to come to the conclusion that the most effective way of modifying these rules in their favour is by collective rather than individual bargaining.[10]

Another significant factor is the nature of the product market in which the establishment operates. *A priori* reasoning suggests that in an industry where labour costs are a large proportion of total costs and where competition is such that the loss of income from a strike is not easily made good, employers may be unwilling to offer a protracted resistance to unionization. By contrast, monopolistic or oligopolistic industry may be more difficult for a union to penetrate initially because employers may be less vulnerable to coercion. Once trade unions have established themselves in such industries, however, they find it easier to maintain their membership than they do in the more competitive industries where firms may be vulnerable to cost increases and may 'run away' in search of low-cost unorganized areas (or countries). The extent to which employers can avoid unionism in this way obviously depends, however, on whether their product market is local or national in nature.

In the public sector the relationship between unionization and market structure is likely to be quite different from that in the private sector. In Britain public corporations are legally obliged to recognize appropriate trade unions and engage in collective bargaining. Consequently the assumption which holds in the private sector, namely that employers will resist collective bargaining until compelled to do otherwise, does not apply in publicly owned industries and services.

The general conclusion seems to be that, as determinants of inter-industry variations in unionization, the characteristics of the labour force have become less important over the past thirty years and the structural context in which people work, more important. The tendency of women, for example, to have a negative effect on unionization has declined in step with the growing proportion of the female labour force which has become organized. Similarly, an industry which employs large numbers of part-time workers can be effectively organized if its structural and market characteristics are such that many or most of the full-time workers in the industry also join trade unions. The presence of white collar workers or craftsmen no longer affects the degree of unionization to the extent that it once did. Indeed, as Bain and Elsheikh conclude:

> . . . as unions are increasingly accepted as part of the structure of British society and union membership becomes increasingly widespread, it becomes less dependent upon the self-selection of individuals with similar personal characteristics and attitudes and more dependent upon the characteristics of the firms and industries in which individuals work.[11]

This does not necessarily mean, of course, that the last two decades of the century will witness the same rate of union growth as the 1970s. It does, however, suggest that forecasts of renewed stagnation or even decline which are based exclusively on the changing composition of the labour force must be treated with considerable reserve.[12]

The pattern of organization

It was argued in Chapter 1 that a major underlying theme in the historical development of British trade unionism was the conflict between, on the one hand, the pressure for sectional representation and organizational autonomy and, on the other, the need for broader unity and concerted action. The post-1968 upswing in union membership has done nothing to resolve this conflict; indeed in some respects it has probably aggravated it. Hyman has pointed out that in the late Victorian era the new general unions were 'essentially *residual* in their recruitment patterns, filling the numerous and often complicated gaps left by the earlier structure of trade unionism'.[13] The white collar unions of the post-war years found themselves in exactly the same position, except that the gap they were seeking to fill was steadily expanding year by year. For most manual unions the choice has been between expansion through merger and, in the absence of suitable candidates for acquisition, stagnation and decline. Consequently, though the number of unions has continued to fall, there has been little change in the underlying structural characteristics of British trade unionism.

The classical method of analysing trade union structure relies on the familiar distinction between craft, industrial and general unions. Craft unions are popularly associated with groups of workers who have one particular skill or a set of related skills. Industrial unions are those which organize all workers in a given industry, skilled and unskilled alike. General unions are those which recruit anyone and everyone,regardless of their skill or the industry in which they work. Although, however, this approach may once have been valid, it has long since ceased to accord with the structural realities of British trade unionism. Although there are still a number of pure craft unions in existence, their total membership is insignificant. There are no pure industrial unions at all, in the sense that while a small number of unions still claim industrial status, they have never succeeded in achieving the aspirations of those who founded them. Most of the larger unions are 'general' in the sense that they represent more than one occupation in more than one industry or service, but to say so hardly furthers this analysis.

A much more useful approach was developed several years ago by Turner, who made a critical distinction between 'closed' and 'open' unions.[14] A closed union is, in simple terms, one which imposes some restriction on entry. Such restriction may be either *vertical* or *horizontal* in nature. Most of the traditional craft unions were vertically closed but horizontally open – in other words they were prepared to accept all workers who possessed the appropriate skill qualifications across a range of industries but were not prepared to lower their barriers to entry within any industry. Technological change, however, has always posed a threat to such barriers. In the late nineteenth century, for example, the craft union in the boot and shoe industry was compelled to open its doors vertically and admit non-craft operatives. In the engineering industry, the response of the ASE to technological change was more conservative. On the one hand, it gradually opened its recruitment vertically within the engineering industry but, on the other, it began to recruit horizontally among skilled men in all the metal-working trades *and* it preserved its craft-based system of internal government. In the printing industry the craft unions' response to technological change was delayed until the 1950s when competition from the open unions in the industry forced a reappraisal of recruitment policies. By contrast, the two unions which are nearest to the industrial model – the NUR and the NUM – have pursued vertically open recruitment strategies while remaining horizontally closed. Even so their vertical openness has been limited by the existence of separate organizations for both white collar staff and craftsmen. These constraints are particularly obvious on the railways where all the white collar grades are organized by the TSSA and where many of the 'craftsmen' (in this case the engine drivers) are represented by ASLEF, which is closed both horizontally and vertically.

Whether a union is open or closed depends very much on the occupational characteristics of its members and the sources of its bargaining power. As Turner has pointed out, closed unions are restrictionist:

> not merely in the sense that they base themselves on a capacity to control the supply of labour to particular occupations and maintain an exclusive claim to employment within those occupations but also in the sense that they have little intrinsic interest in increasing their numerical strength. Indeed their interest lies rather in the opposite direction – of limiting the intake of labour

to the jobs that they control and thereby restricting also the membership of the union itself.[15]

Such unions are unlikely to follow expansionist policies and if they merge at all they are likely to do so with other closed unions in a defensive alliance along the lines of the Boilermakers, Shipwrights and Blacksmiths (ASBSBSW) in the shipbuilding industry and the National Graphical Association in the printing industry.

By contrast, the bargaining strength of those unions that are vertically and horizontally open lies not in the exclusive control of key skills but in strength of numbers. Such unions are unlikely to recognize any industrial or occupational limitations to their recruiting activity (unless, of course, they have agreed with other unions not to compete for members in a given industry or company) and often owe much of their growth to mergers. The TGWU, for example, originated from an amalgamation of several unions in the docks and road transport in 1921, from whence it established itself in the engineering industry by merging with the Workers' Union in 1929. The fact that there were opportunities for a general union to expand in the engineering industry in turn reflected the reluctance of the AEU (as the ASE became in 1920) to open its ranks vertically. Subsequent mergers, however, have given the TGWU strong representation in a wide range of industries and services. The merger with the National Union of Vehicle Builders in 1972, for example, made the TGWU the dominant union in the motor car industry. It has also established a white collar subsidiary – the Association of Clerical, Technical and Supervisory Staffs – which competes with other non-specialist white collar unions for members. One major factor in the success of the union's growth strategy has been its willingness to leave its various subsidiaries with a degree of autonomy. The GMWU, by contrast, has in recent years been unable to attract amalgamation partners, so that despite having similar opportunities for expansion the union has failed to extend its membership to anything like the same degree as the TGWU. An open membership policy does not, in short, guarantee that membership will actually expand. In practice much depends on the political acumen of the leadership and on the nature of the image which they succeed in projecting of themselves and their organization.

The significance of these factors is clearly illustrated by the response of individual unions to the expansion of both white collar and public service employment. In the private sector ASTMS has

Table 6 *Expansion of white collar union membership, 1966–77*

Union	*Membership* ('000s) *1966*	*1977*
ASTMS	72	441
APEX (formerly CAWU)	76	150
TASS (formerly DATA)	73	183
BIFU (formerly NUBE)	58	116
	279	890

been conspicuously more successful in recruiting new members than its major competitors (see Table 6).

Since the late 1960s ASTMS has pursued a vigorous strategy of horizontal and vertical expansion which has carried the union into a wide range of white collar occupations in both the public and the private sector. The success of this strategy may be attributed to the professional skill of the union's full-time officials, reinforced by an adroit use of the media and by the charismatic leadership of the general secretary, Clive Jenkins. The growth of APEX – a union which is equally open both horizontally and vertically – has by comparison been modest. One reason for this differential rate of growth must surely be the relatively unaggressive image of APEX. The other unions mentioned above, BIFU and TASS, have been more constrained by both horizontal and vertical barriers to expansion. As the National Union of Bank Employees, the former encountered strong opposition within the banking sector from well-established staff associations and its attempts to expand horizontally into other sectors of finance were frustrated by competition from both staff associations and ASTMS. TASS has succeeded in breaking out of its traditional base in engineering-drawing offices but its future prospects are still determined by the limits of the engineering and metal-working industries, and even here it continues to face competition from ASTMS.

The public sector itself has witnessed some significant changes in the pattern of both white collar and manual union membership. The expansion of local government employment between 1964 and 1974 gave a powerful stimulus to NALGO, which represents the hierarchy of white collar staff in local authorities. The growth in NALGO's membership has also been stimulated by the union's tendency to adopt less 'gentlemanly', more militant bargaining postures since the late 1960s. The corresponding expansion of employment in education has not, however, brought much benefit to the largest union for teachers, the NUT, whose membership fell slightly during the 1970s. One reason may well be the growth of competition from the smaller National Association of Schoolmasters, which doubled its membership between 1969 and 1976, when it reached 86,000. The bargaining stance of the NAS places far more emphasis on differentials and on the need to reward specialist skills, which seems to have evoked a positive response from many career teachers in secondary schools.

The pattern of manual union membership in the public service sector has been changed by the recent growth of NUPE and COHSE. The National Union of Public Employees organizes manual workers in local government and the health service and more than doubled its membership between 1967 and 1977. This rate of growth is particularly significant in the light of the union's long struggle to build up its membership base and win bargaining rights in the face of strong opposition from both the TGWU and the GMWU. Its recent success is due to a combination of vigorous leadership and spontaneous action. The present general secretary, Alan Fisher, has given the union a firm identity as *the* organization for manual workers in the public service sector and has vigorously conducted a long campaign against low pay. Equally if not more important has been the use of key groups of workers in demonstrations of the union's bargaining power. In the autumn of 1970 and again in the winter of 1978–9, the selective use of industrial action by NUPE greatly reinforced the union's bargaining stance and reminded its members that to be low paid is not necessarily to be powerless. On a smaller scale, the Confederation of Health Service Employees used the same formula of publicity-conscious leadership and direct action to expand its membership during the 1970s. In this case, however, future growth is likely to be limited by the union's horizontal confinement to the National Health Service and, of course, by the factor which is likely to affect the prospects of all public sector unions, namely the future level of tax-financed expenditure.

The way in which changes in the pattern of employment and union membership over the post-war period as a whole have affected the 'pecking order' within the TUC is illustrated in Table 7. The table underlines both the success of the TGWU in strengthening its position as the largest single union (chiefly at the expense of the

Table 7 *Union membership, 1945–77*

	1945		*1966*		*1977*
Union	*Membership* ('000s)	*Union*	*Membership* ('000s)	*Union*	*Membership* ('000s)
TGWU	984.8	TGWU	1428.0	TGWU	2022.7
AEU	704.3	AEU	1054.6	AUEW	1155.4
GMWU	605.0	GMWU	793.0	GMWU	945.3
NUM	533.4	NUM	412.9	NALGO	709.3
NUR	409.8	NALGO	360.7	NUPE	693.1
USDAW	274.6	USDAW	366.3	USDAW	441.5
ASW	176.0	ETU	293.2	ASTMS	441.0
UPW	145.3	NUPE	250.1	EETPU	420.0
ETU	133.0	NUR	227.8	NUT	288.8
T&GWU	118.7	ASW	188.1	NUM	258.7

AUEW and GMWU) and the growing significance of the largest white collar unions within the TUC. It is worth repeating, however, that the factors which account for the growth of trade unionism *per se* do not necessarily explain why some unions have expanded their membership at a much faster rate than others. Here we need to examine, in much more depth than is possible in a study of this kind, a range of variables such as the quality of union leadership, the nature of a union's internal organization, the perceived image of a given union and of its leader, the effectiveness of its merger strategy (if any) and the personal and occupational characteristics of its actual and potential membership.

Mergers and concentration

It is still commonly argued that Britain has too many trade unions and that multi-unionism at plant, company and industry level has been a major contributor to strikes, inflation and low productivity. As we noted in Chapter 1, certain union leaders have on various occasions in the past sought to convince their colleagues of the necessity for rationalization and the elimination of fragmented bargaining arrangements. They have, in short, recognized the point made by the Webbs nearly eighty years ago, namely that multi-unionism weakens the bargaining power of organized labour. Given the impracticability of a wholesale reconstruction of the movement on industrial lines (with one union per industry), significant rationalization can only be achieved through mergers. The tendency for trade unions to combine is almost as old as trade unionism itself, so that the advocates of amalgamation have the force of tradition behind them. The real issue is not whether mergers in general should be encouraged but rather the speed with which they should occur and the direction they should take. Thus the Donovan Commission observed that:

> The total number of unions is declining and there is some indication that membership is being concentrated in the larger organisations, but it is obvious that a very real contribution could be made to the problem of multi-unionism if some of the more important and wide-ranging organisations could be induced to combine with each other.[16]

Donovan was anxious to speed up the process in general and, more specifically, to encourage mergers between craft unions in the engineering and construction industries.

In general, Donovan's wishes have been carried out. Between 1968 and 1978, trade union membership increased by 28 per cent, while the number of trade unions declined by 22 per cent. Over the same period, the average membership per union rose from 17,000 to 28,000. Tables 8 and 9 summarize the key trends. Table 8 illustrates the rapid fall in the number of small trade unions; Table 9 shows the extent to which membership is heavily concentrated (as of 1978) in the twenty-six largest unions.

Since the Donovan era there have been several major amalgamations which have simplified the overall pattern of representation in certain industries. In the construction industry, for example, the formation of the Union of Construction, Allied Trades and Technicians (UCATT) in 1972 brought together under one umbrella the painters, decorators and woodworkers in the industry. In the motor car industry, the merger between the TGWU and the NUVB has concentrated the majority of unskilled and semi-skilled workers in one organization. In general engineering, the AUEW has taken under its wing – albeit in the form of a loose federation – the foundryworkers', draughtsmens' and civil engineering unions. Textiles, insurance and printing have also witnessed significant moves towards rationalization and concentration. At the time of writing, several proposals, involving some of the ten largest unions,

Table 8 *Number and size of trade unions, 1966–78*

Number of members	*Number of trade unions* 1966	*1968*	*1970*	*1972*	*1974*	*1976*	*1978*
Under 100	126	114	108	83	80	69	72
100–499	147	137	134	136	138	143	135
500–999	68	63	57	45	52	47	48
1,000–2,499	89	88	66	67	69	60	62
2,500–4,999	65	60	55	56	52	45	37
5,000–9,999	30	33	34	33	31	30	26
10,000–14,999	22	18	14	13	11	8	9
15,000–24,999	18	19	22	18	18	15	14
25,000–49,999	19	15	13	18	17	17	19
50,000–99,999	20	20	17	13	14	14	14
100,000–249,999	9	10	14	14	14	14	15
250,000 and more	9	9	9	11	11	11	11
Total number of unions	622	586	543	507	507	473	462

are being openly canvassed and may soon come to fruition. Before discussing future developments, however, it would be useful to discuss briefly the various factors which impel unions to consider merger proposals.

The pressures of competition for members have been an important influence on merger activity, especially in the white collar sector. The decision of DATA to become the Technical and Supervisory Section of the AUEW, for example, may well owe something to the recruiting activity in the engineering industry of unions such as ASTMS, APEX and UKAPE. The same influence may also have impelled the NUVB to join the TGWU, with whom there was considerable overlap in potential membership. Allied to the problem of competitive recruitment is the common desire among the established unions in a given industry to ward off a possible takeover threat by a large union with extensive interests outside the industry. It has been suggested, for example, that some of the mergers, both actual and prospective, involving unions in the textile industry have been motivated by a determination to restrain the future growth of the TGWU in this industry.[17] The incentive to amalgamate will be particularly strong if, as in textiles, employment and therefore

Table 9 *Distribution of union members among unions*

Number of members	*Number of unions*	*Total membership ('000s)*	*Total number of unions (%)*	*Total membership of unions (%)*
Under 100	72	4	15.6	0.0
100–499	135	34	29.2	0.3
500–999	48	34	10.4	0.3
1,000–2,499	62	103	13.4	0.8
2,500–4,999	37	134	8.0	1.0
5,000–9,999	26	169	5.6	1.3
10,000–14,999	9	112	1.9	0.9
15,000–24,999	14	267	3.0	2.1
25,000–49,999	19	711	4.1	5.5
50,000–99,999	14	947	3.0	7.3
100,000–249,999	15	2263	3.2	17.3
250,000 and more	11	8335	2.4	63.6
Totals	462	12,376	100	100

aggregate union membership is falling and established unions are facing a serious long-term loss of income.

This brings us to a range of factors which, through their effects on the firms in a given industry, can have a major impact on the organizational horizons of the unions. Technological change, for example, can help to blur some of the traditional demarcation boundaries which have fragmented the pattern of union membership. This factor has been and will continue to be of considerable significance in craft dominated industries such as shipbuilding and printing. A more powerful influence, however, arises from changes in the structure of industry itself. It is hardly coincidental that the most intensive periods of merger activity within the trade union movement have also witnessed exceptionally high levels of merger activity among firms themselves. There are several reasons why we should expect there to be a causal relationship between company and union mergers. Mergers often generate widespread uncertainty about employment prospects and are frequently associated with plant closures and redundancy. In such circumstances, a decision by the relevant unions to pool their resources may be seen as an attempt to strengthen their collective bargaining position. Mergers may also lead to a growth in the size of bargaining units and may thereby encourage small, local unions to merge with national unions in order to protect their bargaining rights. There is unlikely to be a similar pattern of recognition arrangements in two or more newly merged companies and the only logical solution may be for the unions involved to merge themselves.[18]

Since the average size of employment units will almost certainly continue to grow in the forseeable future, the tendency for union membership to become concentrated in a small minority of very large unions is likely to continue. This does not necessarily mean, however, that the amalgamation process will be either painless or rapid. Nor will it inevitably lead to a gradual coalescence of unions on industrial lines. In certain industries, notably textiles and printing, and in certain sectors of public service employment, there may eventually be one or two dominant unions which will have emerged through a series of *vertical* amalgamations. In other industries, however, the trend is likely to be in favour of *horizontal* concentration. In engineering and metal-working, for example, a merger between the EETPU and the AUEW would strengthen the interests of skilled men and form a powerful counterweight to the TGWU with its base in the semi- and unskilled grades. In the railway industry, there does not seem to be the remotest possibility that ASLEF will merge with the NUR or the TSSA. The problems of amalgamation are not merely caused by the need to mesh two different rule books and two different internal structures, which may in themselves be complex enough. As a delegate from UCATT told the 1977 TUC conference, many amalgamations have only regrouped the competitors and changed the location of the conflict. The rock on which many proposed mergers have foundered is that the unions involved have incompatible occupational interests and conflicting bargaining objectives. It is inconceivable, for example, that many – if indeed any – white collar unions would merge with a large manual union in the interests of industrial solidarity. For the same reason, the surviving craft unions are likely to see their future in terms of merging with other craft unions either in the same or in a closely related industry. The prospect of being swallowed up by one of the giant general unions, with the consequent erosion of differentials and status, is likely to continue to encourage mergers between craft unions and between white collar unions to the exclusion of unwelcome outside interests.

The role and functions of the TUC

Before the formation of the Labour Party, the main function of the TUC was to discuss and promote legislation affecting the interests of organized labour. After 1900 the parliamentary activities of the TUC became less important but it was not until 1921 that the old Parliamentary Committee was disbanded. By then the main problems facing the trade union movement were economic rather than legal in character. With the onset of the post-war depression, a strong tendency arose in most industries to reduce wages. The leaders of the non-craft unions realized that the employers' wage-cutting strategy could only be countered by co-ordinated action. The body capable of imposing some kind of co-ordination was, of course, the TUC. But this in turn raised the old problem of how to balance the need for closer unity with the deep-seated desire for organizational autonomy. The constitutional changes which took place after the first world war, therefore, did not challenge the tradition of union sovereignty. All they did was to vest a few limited powers in the hands of a new co-ordinating body called the General Council.

Since its inception, the General Council has represented the largest and most powerful unions within the TUC. By 1978 the council had 41 members representing 30 of the 115 unions affiliated to the TUC. The members themselves are elected to represent the 18 trade groups into which the TUC is currently sub-divided (see Table 10).

Election to the General Council is by the block vote of all the unions represented at the annual congress. This system has produced several complaints from both inside and outside the TUC that election to represent any trade group is virtually impossible without the support of one or more of the giant unions. This implies that candidates from the smaller unions must be politically acceptable to the leaders of the large unions. Consequently, although it is rare for members to lose their seats once elected, there is always the possibility that they might do so for reasons which have little to do with their ability as members of the General Council. Another perennial problem is that of devising a fair and equitable ratio of seats to the size of the membership constituency. Table 10 reveals that there are great discrepancies between different trade groups and suggests that the smaller groups such as shipbuilding, iron and steel, textiles and agriculture are over-represented in relation to, say, transport, printing, electricity and public employees. It would of course be remarkable if the composition of the General Council had

Table 10 *Distribution of trade unions in TUC General Council by trades*

Trade group	*Seats*	*Number of* *Unions*	*Delegates*	*Member-ship* ('000s)	*Affiliation fees** £'000s
1 Mining and quarrying	2	3	61	295.1	50.1
2 Railways	2	3	42	280.4	47.6
3 Transportation (excluding railways)	5‡	6	100	2141.9	364.1
4 Shipbuilding	1	1	12	129.9	22.1
5 Engineering, founding, vehicle building	4	10	78	1389.4	236.2
6 Technical, engineering and scientific	2	4	55	679.7	115.5
7 Electricity	1	1	32	420.0	71.4
8 Iron, steel and minor metal trades	1	9	33	146.7	24.9
9 Building, wood-working and furnishing	2	4	44	390.1	66.3
10 Printing and paper	1	6	82	420.9	71.5
11 Textiles	1	15	29	125.6	21.3
12 Clothing, leather and boot and shoe	1	6	42	267.6	45.5
13 Glass, ceramics, chemicals, food, drink, tobacco, brushmaking and distribution	2	9	72	596.7	101.4
14 Agriculture	1	1	16	85.0	14.4
15 Public employees	5‡	11	193	2197.1	369.6
16 Civil servants and post office	3‡	12	146	999.0	160.6
17 Professional, clerical and entertainment	2	10	62	404.2	68.7
18 General workers	3	3	73	945.3	160.7
	39†	112	1172	11,865.3	2012.5

*20p per member from 1 January 1978
‡An additional seat was given to these groups by the 1977 Congress
†Plus two seats for women workers making 41 seats in all on the General Council

changed exactly in step with the rapid changes in the composition of the organized labour force which have occurred over the past decade. Nevertheless it would seem that the current membership of the council is too heavily weighted in favour of declining industries dominated by manual workers.[19]

The role of the TUC general secretary is commonly described as one of responsibility without power. Under rule 10 of the TUC constitution he is merely elected by the congress and sits in an *ex officio* capacity (without a vote) on the General Council. Yet, ever since the 1920s the general secretary has at most times been widely regarded as the spokesman and living embodiment of the TUC. His personality and public image have a profound effect on the status of the TUC in the eyes of trade unionists, employers, government ministers and the community as a whole. It must be remembered, however, that his influence over the General Council depends on his own political and diplomatic skills rather than on his constitutional powers. All the post-war general secretaries have spent most of their working lives within the TUC bureaucracy, and indeed length of service seems to be the main qualification for the post. The idea of appointing someone directly from the upper ranks of a major affiliated union, still less of introducing new blood from outside the TUC, is fundamentally at variance with the traditions of the organization. The present incumbent, Len Murray, succeeded the late Vic Feather in 1973 after twenty-six years' service in the TUC. Feather himself succeeded George Woodcock in 1969 after thirty-two years' service. To the outsider, it seems improbable that anyone whose working life has been spent within one organization will be likely to take an unduly critical view of that organization when, in late middle age, he reaches the top of the hierarchy.

This does not mean that every general secretary has been content to leave the job exactly as he found it. Feather, for example, responded to the pressures of the time by developing the industrial 'trouble-shooting' role of the general secretary. His successor was much more involved in discussions with Labour ministers, at least up to May 1979, on a wide range of economic and social issues. Given the Labour government's commitment to winning and retaining the active co-operation of the TUC, the change of emphasis which Murray brought to the job was inevitable. The point is that the way in which a particular general secretary defines his role and performs it depends on the interaction between his own personality and the circumstances in which both he and the General Council members find themselves. Thus, despite the modest constitutional position of the general secretary, neither the parameters of the job itself nor the moral authority of the various incumbents have remained static.

The constitutional powers of the General Council itself are, by contrast, explicitly defined, although they too have gradually changed over the years and are always subject to the overriding moral influence of both the Council and the general secretary at any given time. These powers are defined in rules 11 and 12 of the constitution. Rule 11 obliges affiliated unions to keep the General Council informed of any major disputes in which they may become engaged, either with employers or among themselves. Only if there is a breakdown in collective bargaining is the General Council allowed to give advice to the unions involved. If this advice is accepted and a strike or lock-out ensues, the council is obliged to organize material or moral support. It was the operation of this rule which underpinned the role of the council in 1926. Since then, however, the TUC has been extremely reluctant to involve itself in organizing 'material or moral support' for a specific strike. In 1955 rule 11 was amended so as to allow the General Council to intervene in the early stages of a dispute involving an affiliated union if members of other affiliated unions were likely to be affected by it. In 1969 this rule was extended at the famous Croydon congress to cover unofficial and unconstitutional strikes which threatened to throw other union members out of work. There is little doubt that the General Council has made good use of this rule and that the 'peacemaking' functions of the TUC have consequently become more important. Perhaps the most dramatic illustration of this role in recent years was the General Council's attempt to find a solution to the miners' dispute of 1973–4. Following the government's decision to put British industry on a three-day week and the obvious breakdown of negotiations between the NUM and the government, the TUC intervened with an offer which committed the General Council to dissuade affiliated unions from quoting an exceptional miners' settlement, if such a settlement was allowed, in support of their own wage claims. The government rejected the offer, but had it been taken up it would have subjected the moral and constitutional authority of the TUC to a severe test.

The General Council also has powers under rule 12 to intervene in inter-union disputes. In 1920 a Disputes Committee was set up to resolve conflicts of interest in the field of recruitment and recognition between affiliated unions. The rule *requires* affiliated organizations to submit their disputes to the committee and to abide by the committee's findings on pain of expulsion from the TUC. The role of the committee was strengthened in 1939 with the adoption of the 'Bridlington Principles' which urge affiliated members to agree on spheres of influence, to refrain from 'poaching' another union's members, to agree on conditions of transfer, not to accept members of other unions who are in arrears with their contributions, under discipline or engaged in a trade dispute and to inquire about an applicant's past or present union membership. These principles were extended by the special Croydon congress in 1969 in two ways. First, *official* strikes over inter-union disputes are now prohibited until the TUC has had an opportunity to examine the issue and affiliated members involved in an inter-union dispute are obliged to notify the TUC immediately. Second, where an *unofficial* stoppage occurs over an inter-union dispute, the unions involved are required both to notify the TUC and take immediate steps to get their members back to work.

The gradually expanding role of the Disputes Committee illustrates the continuing commitment of affiliated unions to resolve their internal problems by voluntary machinery. Over the past sixty years the committee has evolved its own guidelines and criteria, based on case law and precedent, and enjoys a unique moral authority within the TUC. Through the traditional methods of inquiry and fact-finding, the committee can often find a rational solution to some highly emotional conflicts. Above all it acts as a valuable safety-valve through which the disputes that inevitably arise from competitive recruitment can be resolved. Union officials can in effect discharge their obligations to their own rank and file members by passing a dispute to the committee, which can in turn be blamed for an adverse decision. It is occasionally argued that the Disputes Committee tends to favour the larger unions and thereby discourages dissatisfied groups within these unions from 'voting with their feet' by joining smaller organizations. There is no evidence, however, that the decisions of the committee have discriminated against smaller unions.[20] The committee has also been criticized for failing to promote strutural change within the trade union movement. But this is not its function and indeed never could be. To be successful, a strategy for structural reform would need to be based on a much wider consensus than that which is represented on the Disputes Committee and the latter would undoubtedly weaken its own moral authority if it ever attempted to adopt a reformist role.

Such, then, are the constitutional powers of the TUC. Their

effectiveness depends overwhelmingly on the consent of the affiliated members and the ultimate penalty for non-compliance, namely disaffiliation and expulsion, has seldom been invoked. The ETU, for example, was expelled from the TUC in 1961, and then only briefly, for proven electoral malpractices. In 1971–4, some twenty unions were expelled for refusing to adhere to the official policy of non-co-operation with the Industrial Relations Act. But the use of this sanction is necessarily exceptional. If the TUC ever found itself in the position of having to expel two or three of the major unions which have seats on the General Council, its own credibility as a representative body would be damaged. The status of the TUC with governments and employers' organizations depends largely on its ability to represent the collective viewpoint of the great mass of British trade unions and this in turn depends on argument, persuasion and compromise.

The absence of constitutional 'teeth' has frequently been the subject of criticism by otherwise sympathetic outsiders. Allan Flanders, for example, noted in the mid 1960s that there was 'as yet no strong demand within the movement, such as existed after the first world war, for far-reaching reforms in the TUC's constitution; no proposals to transform it into a truly federal structure on the lines of the central union organisations in the Scandinavian countries and West Germany'.[21]

At the end of the 1970s the situation is unchanged. Although the events of the intervening period have combined to strengthen the moral authority of the TUC, there is no demand within the movement that the powers of the General Council should be strengthened and, by implication, the sovereignty of the affiliated members eroded. The continuing avoidance of constitutional change and the corresponding commitment to voluntarism is often singled out by critics as both the cause and consequence of the conservative, defensive role of the TUC. David Low's famous caricature of the TUC as a cart-horse evokes the image of a ponderous organization whose members harbour a profound suspicion of new ideas and maintain a corresponding devotion to those arrangements and institutions which have 'stood the test of time'.

Leading trade unionists have occasionally conceded that such criticisms are not without substance. They would accept, for example, that the TUC normally achieves its maximum effectiveness when defending the *status quo* against an external threat. The posture which the General Council seems to find most congenial is that of reacting to initiatives and pressures which emanate from outside the trade union movement. The few that come from within the TUC, such as the various proposals for structural reform which have arrived on conference agendas, always seem to fall foul of established interests. Indeed the council only seems to take a major initiative itself when a real crisis is looming and the government of the day appears unable or unwilling to act. Two examples spring readily to mind – first, the TUC's offer in January 1974 to make the miners a special case and, second, the proposal for the introduction of a flat-rate incomes policy launched in July 1975 and accepted by the Labour government. In more normal times, however, the will to take major initiatives is less evident.

The reasons are not difficult to find and would hardly come as a revelation to members of the General Council. First, the TUC represents a wide range of occupational interests and aspirations which are not necessarily consistent with each other. This diversity, and the scope for internal conflict which it brings, has if anything been sharpened by the arrival in strength of white collar unions over the past decade. On the occasions when, for example, the TUC has either actively supported or reluctantly acquiesced in incomes policies which have promulgated flat-rate or equity-based norms for pay increases, some white collar union leaders have expressed strong opposition. This is hardly surprising in view of the importance which white collar unions in general attach to maintaining or increasing pay differentials. But it hardly accords with the interests of those unions who represent large numbers of unskilled, low-paid workers, whether in the public or the private sector, and whose bargaining objectives may be better served by an effective, equity-based incomes policy. Such conflicts are never far below the surface, as the report of the General Council in 1970 recognized:

> The TUC has the perennial problem of reconciling the special interests of particular unions, or groups of members, with the general interests of the trade union movement, and of deciding when which set of interests should prevail. This has on occasion led the TUC to make general statements which, because they are capable of different interpretations, offend none and are minimally acceptable to all. A propensity not to offend and not to appear to be interfering with union autonomy has historically often led the TUC to eschew taking initiatives.

The traditional way in which motions submitted by individual unions are presented by the General Council for debate at the annual conference, that is, by 'compositing' several motions into one, not only saves time but also helps smooth over such differences of interest. Usually, therefore, there is a tendency to find the lowest common denominator and to emphasize those matters which unite the affiliated members. Motions in defence of the *status quo* (for example, the closed shop) or in favour of the restoration of something which has existed in the past (for example, free collective bargaining) always attract the highest levels of support.

The second reason behind the TUC's reluctance to take initiatives and generally behave in a more directive manner may be found in the relationship between the TUC and its affiliates. Every trade union leader knows that the authority which he enjoys as leader depends on the ability of himself and his full-time officials to represent the interests of their members and bargain effectively on their behalf. The same applies to the authority of both the general secretary and the General Council *vis-à-vis* the affiliated membership. As the council observed in their 1975 report to congress:

> It would be meaningless for the general council to be given powers to direct and instruct unions unless unions in their turn have the same power over their members. What a union can do would, and must, ultimately be determined by its members. The only real sanction the TUC has is suspension or expulsion: the use of other sanctions, such as the imposition of fines on unions, is neither desirable nor practicable, and in any case it would run directly counter to the way in which the TUC has been developing in recent years which is to win the support of unions for agreed policies by argument and persuasion.

In so far as the moral authority of the General Council has been strengthened over the past twenty years – and there is ample evidence to suggest that it has – the key factor has been the ability of the council to represent a common viewpoint in discussion and negotiations with governments and to win concessions from them on major issues of policy.

This leads us to another major criticism which has been levelled at the TUC in recent years – namely that it has acquired too much political influence, to the extent that it now holds a power of veto over a wide range of government policies. The criticism was first heard in the aftermath of the Labour government's withdrawal of the proposals to introduce penal sanctions against strikers contained in the White Paper 'In place of strife' (1969). It was repeated when the TUC's policy of non-co-operation ensured that most of the Industrial

Relations Act of 1971 remained a dead letter. But it was greatly sharpened by the experience of 1974–6, when the Labour government and the TUC sought to implement an agreed set of economic and social policies. The logic behind the 'social contract' was that, in an inflationary age, union members might be induced to moderate their claims for higher money wages if their 'social wage' was improved. Consequently, in its first year of office, the government introduced food subsidies, froze council house rents, retained the system of price and dividend control it inherited from its predecessor and generally sought to safeguard the 'social wage'. In return, affiliated unions were supposed to keep their pay claims in line with, but not ahead of, the cost of living. In a year of rapidly accelerating inflation, however, the wages side of the contract was virtually unenforceable and by the spring of 1975 the TUC recognized that a clearer, firmer guideline was needed. By then Britain's rate of inflation was moving far ahead of the average for Western Europe and sterling was subject to heavy speculative pressure. The TUC-inspired £6 pay limit which was adopted by the government for the wage round of 1975–6 and observed by the vast majority of negotiators helped to reduce the rate of inflation marginally, but renewed pressure on sterling in 1976 brought a large IMF loan and a fundamental reappraisal of the government's economic strategy.

In 1976 the government finally had to accept that the reduction in living standards implied by the sharp increases in the price of oil in 1973–4 could no longer be postponed. In accepting the IMF loan, the government was forced to make a reduction of £1 billion in public spending and phase out many of the improvements in the social wage which had been introduced in 1974. Incomes policy was further tightened up in 1976–7, public spending was reduced by a further £1.5 billion and the government's industrial strategy was quietly buried. Meanwhile average living standards fell and unemployment rose to more than double the level of 1974. Alarmed at the extent to which the government's economic policy was increasingly determined by orthodox Treasurey doctrines, the TUC began to develop its own alternative economic strategy. This involved a more vigorous use of import controls, the imposition of restrictions on capital movements and a major increase in job-creating public expenditure. The government, however, disregarded these alternatives. Indeed, after 1976 both the government and the TUC dropped any pretence that the 'social contract' as originally conceived was a viable proposition. At the annual conference of 1977 even Jack Jones, general secretary of the TGWU and the union leader whose views were reputed to carry most influence with the government, was moved to complain about the excessive influence of senior civil servants. This prompted a delegate from the Society of Civil and Public Servants to warn the General Council not to exaggerate its influence with the government: 'The General Council visits the corridors of power. The Treasury boys live there.' At the same conference the prime minister criticized free collective bargaining and asked for another year of co-operation from the TUC in holding down pay settlements to 10 per cent. The affiliated members responded by passing a resolution in favour of an immediate return to free collective bargaining. The government, however, continued to pursue an incomes policy and the following year senior ministers even intimated that collective bargaining should be permanently regulated. It could hardly be said, therefore, that the influence of the TUC over the Labour government in its post-1976 phase was in any sense excessive.

With a Conservative government in office, the TUC is likely to find itself occupying an even more modest role in national policy-making – at least initially. Opposition to Conservative policies will undoubtedly unite the affiliated members and the General Council will be called upon to defend the established rights of the movement. It would be unfortunate, however, if the next four years were allowed to slip by without further extension of the co-ordinating and advisory role of the TUC. There is considerable scope for improvement in, for example, the basic information services which the TUC bureaucracy provides for the affiliated members. A greater degree of professionalism in this field will not, however, be possible without a realistic increase in the income which the TUC receives from its affiliates. In 1976 the total income of the TUC from affiliation fees was only £1.7 million, or rather less than 2 per cent of the total annual income of the affiliated unions. This reluctance to provide the TUC with adequate funds is less the result of tight-fistedness on the part of the unions as a consequence of the traditional suspicion of large, central bureaucracy which lies at the heart of British trade unionism. The determination to keep the TUC under tight financial control exactly mirrors the traditional preference for autonomy and self-help among the affiliated unions. The problem of providing a better service to the affiliates therefore begs the fundamental question of how the relationship between the TUC and its member unions is to develop over the next few years. At the time of writing there seems to be little willingness to face such questions.

The industrial consequences of union structure

The structure of British trade unionism has frequently been criticized for its baffling complexity and apparent lack of rationality. Indeed, the abolition of multi-unionism has been a *cause celebre* with generations of reformers. Employers have criticized multi-unionism on the grounds that it causes demarcation disputes and encourages competitive militancy by trade unions. It is doubtful, however, if there is much substance in this argument. The significance of demarcation issues as a cause of strike action has greatly diminished since the 1920s, and in recent years they have made a negligible contribution to the overall level of strike activity. Competitive militancy is only likely to arise where two unions are seeking to recruit and represent the same group of employees. The fact that there are several unions in a given plant or company need not entail competitive bargaining if they have clearly-defined and mutually agreed spheres of interest. The number of unions *per se* in an establishment or industry is, therefore, not necessarily a key variable in the state of inter-union relations. Conflict or competition can be as disruptive among the few as among the many. In any case it is easy to exaggerate the extent of multi-unionism. One survey of the engineering industry in the late 1960s, for example, found that of the total number of establishments covered (432), one-third had no more than two unions, one-half no more than three unions and almost two-thirds no more than four unions present. Moreover, in many of these establishments, some of the unions had so few members that they made no attempt to represent them. For practical purposes the dominant union was the bargaining agent for *all* manual employees.[22]

From a different ideological perspective, other critics, following the Webbs, have argued that fragmented representation simply weakens the bargaining power of the unions themselves and thus plays into the employers' hands. However valid this point may have been in the pre-1914 era, when the institutionalization of labour relations in the workplace had barely begun, there seems little substance behind it in current circumstances. Again, provided that there are stable boundaries between the representational interests of different unions, there is no reason why they should not bargain effectively on behalf of their members. Industrial unionism in itself would not remove the possibility of conflict between occupational groups within the bargaining unit. If, for example, there was only one union for all grades of staff on British Rail, there would still almost certainly be conflict *within* the union over the differentials of skilled men (for example, train drivers). In this sense one could say that if ASLEF did not exist, it would have to be invented. It is equally clear that many white collar workers may well have preferred to remain outside the scope of trade unionism if the institutional choice facing them had been limited to the white collar sections of large manual trade unions. The rapid growth of white collar unionism over the past decade hardly suggests that the majority of white collar recruits believe that their bargaining power will be weakened by joining an organization which caters exclusively for their own occupational interests.

Multi-unionism is such a well established feature of British industrial relations that it would be surprising indeed if the parties themselves had made no attempts to circumvent the practical problems of co-ordination which arise. At *industry* level, the response has in some cases been the establishment of a Joint Industrial Council on which representatives of all the recognized trade unions come together and negotiate with the representatives of the appropriate employers' federation. In other cases the trade unions have formed a federation of their own for the purpose of either developing a common approach to services and policy-making or bringing themselves together for negotiating purposes. With the declining importance of industry-wide bargaining, however, there has been a tendency to move away from the second type of federation. The largest bargaining federation which remains is the Confederation of Shipbuilding and Engineering Unions, representing the twenty-three principal unions which negotiate with the Engineering Employers' Federation. But although the CSEU still plays a strategic role in collective bargaining at industry level, the growing importance of plant and company bargaining in engineering has eroded its significance. On the rare occasions that a major dispute has occurred at national level, both the EEF and the CSEU have found it increasingly difficult to maintain a united front the longer the dispute has lasted. In other industries, notably building and printing, the once-important union federations have virtually disappeared.

As the structure of collective bargaining has changed in many industries over the past twenty years, especially in the manufacturing sector, so the focus of achieving inter-union co-operation has shifted to the workplace. The principal agents in achieving co-operation at this level are, of course, the shop stewards of the various unions involved. The extent to which stewards do in practice co-operate in a multi-union workplace depends partly on the internal organization of the unions involved, partly on the attitude of the employer and partly on the personal relationships of the stewards involved. The interaction of these variables produces significant differences in the pattern of union co-operation both within and between industries. In some workplaces the representatives of certain unions find it difficult to co-operate for bargaining purposes; in others there is full co-operation between them. The problem of accounting for these differences is discussed in more depth in Chapter 5. The general point which must be made in conclusion is that where union representatives have a genuine desire to work together, any institutional barriers which stand in the way can usually be overcome. But the will to co-operate must always be subject to the congruence between the underlying objectives of different unions and, even more, to the way in which officials and shop stewards interpret these objectives.

4 Leaders and members

An analysis of the structure of British trade unionism inevitably raises fundamental questions about the internal organization of the unions themselves. One cannot criticize the existing pattern of relationships *between* unions without at the same time analysing the relationship between leaders and members *within* individual unions. Since most of the larger unions are to a greater or lesser degree coalitions of diverse occupational and industrial interests, it may seem surprising that their leaders have been so successful in holding them together and inducing them to follow specific corporate objectives. Some critics would argue that effective leadership is only possible because most unions of any size have long ceased to be democratic in any meaningful sense. They are, in effect, a collection of oligarchies in which power is concentrated in the hands of a few office-holders and popular control is virtually non-existent. This belief is frequently expressed in the form of opinion poll surveys which report that a majority of the general public and also of trade unionists themselves are of the view that trade unions tend to be controlled by small cliques of 'militants' and 'extremists'. But if this belief is justified, how do we account for both the apparent willingness of the mass of rank and file members to be effectively denied a say in how their unions shall be governed and their acquiescence in policies which are allegedly at odds with their own wishes?

Two plausible explanations spring to mind. First, it may be that the vast majority of union members consciously trade some of their freedom as individuals for the tangible benefits which collective action brings. Such a trade-off goes to the heart of collective organization. In Hyman's words:

> A union can wield effective job control only if, and to the extent that, it can mobilise disciplined collective action on the part of its members. Such collective discipline is in turn dependent on members' willingness to subordinate, where necessary, their own immediate wishes or interests to

common rules and collective decisions . . . it is only through the power *over* its members which is vested in the trade union that it is able to exert power *for* them.[1]

If this explanation is valid, we would expect to encounter among many ordinary members a strong commitment to the principles of association and collective action juxtaposed with an equally profound indifference towards the practical problems of running the organization itself.

A second and not necessarily inconsistent explanation is that within every union there are means whereby members who are not office-holders can, if they choose, influence the decision-making process. Trade unions do after all claim to be democratic organizations and must be seen to be responsive to the wishes of those whom they represent. The fundamental problem which the decision-making arrangements, both formal and informal, of every trade union are designed to resolve is that of 'how to combine administrative efficiency with popular control'.[2] Every trade union has sought to overcome this problem in its own way, so that the balance between power exercised *for* the members and power exercised *over* them varies considerably from one union to another. Nevertheless a number of common themes are visible and need to be discussed.

Democracy versus oligarchy

Clegg has advanced a simple theory of trade union government which rests on four principles. First, the rank and file members meet in their branches and elect representatives to an annual (or in some cases biennial) conference. Second, the conference decides what the general policy of the union shall be. Third, an elected executive council or committee is responsible for administering the union's affairs on a day-to-day basis within the policy guidelines laid down by the conference. Finally, a chief executive officer, usually called the general secretary, performs such administrative tasks as are delegated to him by the executive body and supervises the union's full-time officials.[3] Not every union conforms to this theory even in outline but it is near enough reality to serve as a useful starting point for discussion.

The theory draws attention to the role in union government of the three democratic concepts of election, representation and mandate. For most rank and file members the principal method of direct participation in the affairs of their union is by voting at branch level.

Here they may elect the general secretary and/or president, the members of the national executive body and delegates to the annual conference. In most unions, however, the full-time union officials are appointed rather than elected and general secretaries, once elected, tend to hold office until they retire. Only in the AUEW are all the union officials subject to periodic re-election. The systematic appointment of officials can, of course, be defended on the grounds of efficiency and continuity. A more trenchant criticism of the electoral process is that in most unions it has consistently failed to attract the participation of more than a tiny minority of the electorate. But low levels of participation in branch elections are probably inevitable in view of the declining significance of the branch itself. Thus, in a survey conducted in the early 1950s, Roberts found that the branch was in general the preserve of the activist minority within each union and that the ordinary member had ceased to attend branch meetings.[4] An investigation of branch life in the TGWU by Goldstein concluded that, judged in terms of its contribution to 'well-informed participation in the common tasks of the democratic operation of the union', the branch as an institution had failed.[5] In these circumstances it is hardly surprising that turnout at branch elections has been consistently low (usually less than 15 per cent) and that the voting preferences of union activists have been disproportionately represented. Where, by contrast, elections are held at the workplace itself (as in the NUM) the normal level of participation is much higher. The introduction of postal ballots in the ETU (1956) and the AUEW (1972) has certainly improved the level of participation, but in both unions the proportion voting is still less than 40 per cent.

If the electoral system fails to give voice to the opinions and aspirations of the vast majority of members who do not turn up at branch meetings, it is at first glance difficult to see how the concepts of representation and mandate can be put into effect. It has frequently been argued, for example, that most union conferences do not in fact discharge their constitutional responsibility of determining policy. They meet infrequently and tend to discuss policy issues only in very general terms. They may pass resolutions in favour of broad political and social objectives but these are hardly likely to affect the day-to-day running of the union, nor is it practicable for conferences to lay down detailed guidelines for collective bargaining. In unions such as the TGWU and GMWU which negotiate in a wide variety of industries and services, an issue which is of direct concern to one group of members may be of little interest to the others. If the disinterested majority are allowed to determine the union's policy on issues of which only minority groups have any practical knowledge, then the quality of the decisions made is likely to suffer. Multi-unionism is also likely to negate any effective control over collective bargaining by the conference of any one union. As Clegg has pointed out, in most major industries no single union has the power to determine the bargaining objectives and strategies of the union side as a whole. Conference resolutions on pay and conditions, for example, are always subject to modification by the representatives of other unions. The process of developing a common bargaining position 'gives a great deal of power to the full-time officers or executive members who almost invariably lead union delegates at meetings of this kind and frequently comprise the whole delegation'.[6]

In these circumstances how meaningful are the mandates which conference delegates give to their executive bodies? The executive councils of many unions are made up of full-time officers who are usually branch or regional secretaries. These are the 'professionals' who normally have years of practical experience behind them as administrators and negotiators. Describing the emergence of the professional cadre in the Victorian unions, the Webbs made their famous observation that 'the growing mass of business and the difficulty and complication of the questions dealt with involved the growth of an official class, marked off by capacity, training and habit of life from the rank and file'.[7] The problem of ensuring that full-time officials do not lose contact with the rank and file has been approached in different ways. In the AUEW, for example, divisional officers and executive council members are subject to triennial elections. Yet, given the advantages which incumbents tend to hold over newcomers, it is rare for office-holders to be denied re-election. By contrast, unions such as NALGO and the NUR provide for executive bodies composed entirely of lay representatives. In the NUR all members of the executive are elected for three years and are then obliged to return to their former jobs. Such solutions, however, are exceptional and in most unions full-time officials, whether at district, regional or national level, have considerable security of tenure.

The same problem arises in respect of the chief executive officer or general secretary. In strict constitutional terms his role is usually that of merely implementing the decisions of the executive body. In practice, however, he can effectively dominate the decision-making machinery of his union. Indeed, in the immediate post-war period the success of the Labour government's incomes policy depended to a considerable extent on the authority of a few general secretaries. Obviously the chief officer's influence at any time is a function of his own political and negotiating skills as well as the expectations of those whose servant he is supposed to be. These expectations are in turn likely to be influenced by the various problems and pressures, external and internal, which the union is facing. As the environment changes, so the personal authority of the general secretary may also fluctuate. Nevertheless the overall impression is one of stability. Once a chief officer is elected, he tends to hold office until he himself chooses to go, and during his tenure he can normally exert considerable influence over the general direction of the union.

In summary, the various *de facto* limitations on popular control which are evident in the internal arrangements of practically all trade unions appear to support those who maintain that all labour organizations are subject to an 'iron law of oligarchy'. According to Michels's classic analysis, there is an irresistible tendency for power to concentrate itself in the upper reaches of every trade union regardless of how 'democratic' its formal constitution may be.[8] The practical need for administrative efficiency must always, in short, override the theoretical commitment to popular control.

The concept of inevitable oligarchy, however, has long been out of favour as an explanation of union government. Some have argued that democracy does not require *active control* by the rank and file members in order to be effective. There is a continuum of involvement ranging from direct participation in union affairs by, say, holding office and voting in elections to passive legitimation of the *status quo* by simply paying an annual subscription. Any voluntary organization tends to be run by the activist minority and the absence of mass participation does not necessarily infer the absence of democracy. After all, the members *can* vote if they choose to do so and if they do not then one can only presume that they are broadly satisfied with the *status quo*. If, however, they feel that the power structure of the union is too heavily weighted against them and that any form of constitutional protest would be pointless, they can always vote with their feet and if necessary form a breakaway union.

This argument is, however, profoundly unconvincing. The spread of the closed shop has effectively deprived many union members of the power to vote with their feet, while the history of breakaway unions is in general one of unrelieved failure. Even if a dissident minority of members did succeed in breaking away from their union, this would not in itself challenge the authority of the union's leadership. Indeed the 'parent' union would in these circumstances almost certainly seek the support of the appropriate employers in denying any form of recognition to the breakaway body. This is precisely what happened to the breakaway Glass and General Workers' Union at Pilkington in 1970. The formation of this union owed much to the dissatisfaction of many members of the GMWU with the performance of their union during the prolonged stoppage at the Pilkington glass works. Yet without recognition from the company and in the teeth of hostility from the GMWU, the breakaway organization could make no progress and soon disappeared.[9] The reluctance of employers to recognize breakaway unions in circumstances where well-established bargaining arrangements already exist is hardly surprising. The denial of recognition, however, must inevitably deprive breakaway organizations of their *raison d'être*.

A more plausible explanation of the general indifference of union members towards their organizations is that for most of them the union as an institution is not a salient feature of day-to-day life in the workplace. Motivated by instrumental collectivism, they see the union simply as a means of achieving tangible improvements in pay and conditions and as long as it meets their expections they are not unduly disturbed if the union is led by individuals whose political outlook is at variance with their own. A recent study of the Union of Post Office Workers by Michael Moran, for example, suggests that the dichotomy between the 'militant' attitudes of the active minority who run the union and the 'moderate' opinions of the non-activist majority does not necessarily infer the absence of internal democracy. The majority of the members in Moran's sample appeared quite happy to leave union business in the hands of the activists and tolerated their pursuit of 'radical cultural' goals provided that the union continued to function as an effective negotiating machine.[10] A variation on this theme is that in those sectors of manufacturing industry where bargaining on matters of substance at workplace level has become very significant over the past twenty years, many union members are likely to regard their shop steward as the living embodiment of the union. In their eyes the steward *is* the union and by comparison with his activities the mundane business of the union branch, the resolutions of the annual conference and the pronouncements of the general secretary may be of marginal significance. For them the election of a shop steward may be the only election which is likely to have any effect on their pay and working conditions.

The uneven development of workplace bargaining, however, implies that the above explanation cannot be relevant in all circumstances. There are many industries and services in which a standard framework of pay and conditions is negotiated nationally, leaving little scope for supplementary bargaining at local level. Even in industries where company and plant bargaining is widespread, full-time officials frequently take the lead in negotiating annual increases in pay and other major agreements. Consequently for many union members the activities of the organization outside their own workplace is of considerable significance. Moreover, it is always conceivable that members may on occasion become dissatisfied with their union's negotiating performance and may wish to register dissatisfaction. Assuming, therefore, that it is not practicable for them to vote with their feet, they may suddenly decide to take a more active interest in union affairs. What avenues are open to them by which they can induce the leadership of their union to be more responsive to their wishes? Such avenues generally fall into two categories – those which are built into the formal structure of the organization and those which emerge informally from the pattern of inter-group conflict within the union.

Formal checks and balances: the AUEW

One way of reducing the risk that a union will fall into the hands of oligarchs is to erect constitutional barriers against the concentration of power. It was noted in Chapter 1 that the governmental systems of the Victorian craft unions reflected a deep-seated determination on the part of the ordinary members to prevent the growth of a top-heavy, unresponsive bureaucracy. This principle is still evident in the constitution of the AUEW (Engineering section) which is the direct historical descendant of the ASE. It has often been pointed out that the AUEW constitution is founded on the same principle of the separation of the powers as the constitution of the United States, and exhibits the same strengths and weaknesses.

The federal nature of the AUEW constitution is reflected in the power of the 267 district committees which operate within the union. The members of each of these committees are elected annually by the branches and are responsible primarily to the branches. Consequently they are not little oligarchies in their own right but are subject to the same democratic scrutiny as every other section of the union hierarchy. The committees have certain disciplinary powers over the membership but, more importantly, they have retained their traditional role in collective bargaining. They have a general, supervisory authority over the agreements which are negotiated with employers in their district. They also have the power to approve the initiation and termination of strike action in their district without reference to any higher authority. Finally, no shop steward can be officially recognized by the union until his election by the membership has been formally franked by the district committee. This degree of decentralization can of course be defended quite simply on the grounds that the diversity of the engineering and metal-working industries makes some measure of local autonomy inevitable. But it also implies that the national policy of the union on any issue of substance can be virtually ignored by a district committee.

The district committees elect two delegates to serve on the twenty-six divisional committees under which the districts are grouped. The functions of these committees, however, are relatively modest, being confined to the discussion of resolutions sent by branches and districts *en route* to the annual conference and the election of two delegates to the conference itself. At divisional level the membership as a whole (voting in the branches) elects a full-time organizer who is responsible for negotiating with employers within the division and ensuring that the industry's disputes procedure is followed.

The annual conference itself is officially termed the National Committee and comprises fifty-two lay members representing the twenty-six divisions. According to the constitution, the National Committee 'shall discuss the past and future policy of the union, with a view to giving the Executive Council instructions for the ensuing year, and may initiate any policy which they think would be beneficial to the union'. In short, the National Committee is the legislative branch of the union and is formally superior to, as well as constitutionally separate from, the Executive Council. Senior officers of the union may attend the National Committee and participate in the discussions but cannot vote. The seven-member Executive Council is supposed to implement the policy laid down by the National Committee. But in order to ensure that this body does not become the preserve of any one faction, every member of the executive must submit to the verdict of the total membership every three years, which on this occasion votes in seven electoral divisions. To complete the separation of the powers, the union also has a judiciary in the form of an appeal court. This court comprises eleven rank and file members, elected triennially from eleven electoral divisions, whose task is to adjudicate on complaints.

If an elaborate system of constitutional checks and balances, reinforced by the general principle of accountability through the ballot box, was synonymous with membership control, then the AUEW would be a model of democracy. In practice, however, the main result has been the development of a unique system of two-party conflict. Over the last twenty years union elections have been closely contested by 'two highly organised and ideologically opposed electoral organisations which, having many of the trappings of parties, are worthy of the title'.[11] The parties concerned represent, respectively, the 'establishment' and the 'opposition'. Until the late 1960s the establishment party controlled the main constitutional organs of the union at national level and held the principal offices. Ideologically it has usually been identified with orthodox Labour Party policy. Between 1967 and 1974, however, the more left-wing opposition party (or 'progressives', as they called themselves) gained ground by intense campaigning in a small number of high-polling branches. Their most notable achievement was the capture of the presidency of the union in 1967 by Hugh Scanlon, a former communist who won with communist support. The introduction of postal ballots in 1972, however, increased the level of participation in elections and brought additional support to the establishment party. How successful the opposition will be in organizing the enlarged electorate remains to be seen.

The paradox of the party system within the AUEW is that the craftsmen who designed its constitution more than a century ago almost certainly never envisaged that the union would become an ideological battleground. As Clegg has pointed out, when the ASE was founded, 'All members had the same interests in preserving the power of the union by insisting on the observance of the rules and customs which ensured uniform treatment and protection for every member. There was no room here for organised opposition, and no need for it.'[12] So why has a party system developed? One reason must surely be the growing involvement of union leaders in national politics and policy-making. The overt support of Hugh Scanlon's predecessor, Lord Carron, for the Labour government's incomes policy and his hostile attitude towards unofficial strikers (an attitude echoed by government ministers in the 1960s) undoubtedly presented the opposition party with an opportunity to make electoral capital among active members in the branches, some of whom must have been on the receiving end of Carron's strictures. Another paradox is that, while the existence of an opposition party is in no way sanctioned by the union's constitution, the formal system of checks and balances and the traditional attachment to the electoral principle effectively guarantees its continued vitality. Moreover, since the establishment party needs an organized opposition in order to justify its own existence, it seems unlikely that it will seek to remove the opposition party by changing the union's rule book.

While close electoral contests *may* be indicative of a healthy internal democracy, the party system within the AUEW is not necessarily synonymous with popular control. In this union the struggle is between two well-organized factions each of which constitutes only a small minority of the total membership. The constitution of the union, historically designed to prevent the emergence of centralized bureaucratic leadership, now ensures that the internal power struggle cannot be extinguished from the top. The consequences of factionalism for the union's effectiveness have in general been adverse. Its constitution appears to have discouraged amalgamations and it has therefore failed to expand its membership base as successfully as its larger rival, the TGWU. Those unions which *have* amalgamated with it are still constitutionally autonomous, leaving the AUEW as little more than a loose federation. Its efforts in the field of research and education have been consistently poor. Above all, however, it seems to have failed in the primary task of collective bargaining. The past decade has witnessed a serious erosion of engineering craftsmen's differentials and a steady decline in the number of skilled men in the industry. Occasionally, the dissatisfaction of skilled groups within the union becomes articulated in open protest, as in 1977 when toolmakers at British Leyland threatened to form a union of their own. The apparent inability of the union to weld its constituent groups into an effective, unified force is reflected in its record of industrial action. It has seldom risked a sustained official stoppage at national level in the engineering industry and when it has done (as in 1979) the results have been modest. Selective strikes at plant level (as in 1972) have been even less successful. The growth of workplace bargaining in the industry has, of course, contributed to the strategic weakness of the union at national level, but the union leadership also seems incapable of arousing and maintaining the commitment of the mass of rank and file members. To the extent that this is true, it is an ironic comment on the most formally democratic union in Britain.

Pragmatic devolution: the TGWU and GMWU

The constitutional development of the two biggest general unions has, not surprisingly, been quite different from that of the AUEW. As noted in Chapter 1, the latter was founded by closely knit groups of craftsmen for whom collective action was an essential method of protecting the privileges and customs of their trade. The general unions, by contrast, owed their growth to vigorous leadership and organization by full-time officials. There was no reason why the membership of these unions should be suspicious of strong central authority – on the contrary, in many ways it was precisely this kind of structure which kept the organization in existence during the years of high unemployment and falling membership. Consequently with these organizations we do not encounter the typical craft union's reliance on branch and district institutions, nor do we find the same attachment to the elective principle. To this extent it could be said that the general unions are less overtly democratic than the AUEW but this does not mean that their leaders are not subject to checks and balances. As Clegg has pointed out, 'the separation of the powers depends on decentralization of authority to independent institutions with separate representation in the central decision-making bodies', and in the TGWU and GMWU this has been achieved, respectively, through industrial and regional devolution.[13]

The TGWU conforms to Clegg's simple model of union government in so far as its constitution provides for the election at branch level of delegates to a biennial conference which in turn lays down policy guidelines for the general secretary and the General Executive Council. The Executive Council itself is composed of twenty-six representatives from the eleven geographical regions within the union and thirteen representatives from the union's eleven trade groups. All members of the executive are elected for two years but the council meets only four times a year, which suggests that there are more important foci of power elsewhere. One key source of authority is the general secretary himself. Another is the unique blending of regional and industrial (or 'trade group') representation which has always characterized this union. The sub-division of the union into trade groups is particularly important in so far as it has given the organization the necessary flexibility to absorb so many other trade unions. Each trade group represents an amalgamation of industrial and occupational interests which can always absorb new acquisitions and which in practice enjoys considerable operational

Table 11 *Distribution of union members among trades, 1976*

Trade groups	*Membership*
Vehicle building and automotive	175,860
Power and engineering	268,956
Chemicals, rubber and oil refining	138,025
Docks and waterways	56,231
Commercial services	213,804
Passenger services	148,832
Public services and civil air transport	169,379
General workers	243,532
Food, drink and tobacco	209,272
Building, construction, civil engineering	84,787
ACTSS	118,912

autonomy. At the end of 1976 the trade group structure was as shown in Table 11. Each national trade group is administered by its own committee and secretary who in turn are responsible to conferences of lay delegates. Local, regional and national trade group secretaries are, however, appointed by the General Executive Council and are usually excluded from conference proceedings. As a result there is relatively little scope within the union for organized opposition and this has obviously reinforced the position of the general secretary.

This does not mean, however, that the TGWU general secretary is the 'boss' of his union, despite a popular impression to the contrary. Up to the 1960s the predominance of industry-wide bargaining structures within the various trade groups which comprise the union inevitably conferred a good deal of influence and status on the trade group secretaries. The inevitable tendency for major decisions to be taken in Transport House by senior officials was also in accord with the wishes of the two general secretaries who were in office during the pre-war and post-war years, Ernest Bevin and Arthur Deakin. From the 1960s onwards, however, plant and company bargaining became more important in several of the industries in which the union had a major interest. Under Frank Cousins and more vigorously under Jack Jones, the structure of decision-making within the union changed in sympathy with the decentralization of bargaining. Two important initiatives were taken. First, shop stewards were encouraged to participate in local negotiating bodies. Second, full-time officials were instructed to use 'reference back' procedures, whereby stewards, members or conference delegates could have the opportunity to discuss, accept or reject proposals for a collective agreement prior to any settlement being made. In the eyes of full-time officials who had hitherto been accustomed to a centralized structure of accountability and thus to a large measure of autonomy, the new emphasis on lay participation at local level must have seemed revolutionary.[14] But it must be remembered that the change was a response to the realities of collective bargaining as well as the result of Jones's genuine philosophical commitment to workplace democracy.

The fact that Jones could initiate and implement such a radical change in itself illustrates the strength of the position of general secretary within the union. But now that the lay members and activists have been given more scope to participate in those decisions which affect them directly, it may be that future general secretaries will find their authority more circumscribed. Jones himself became a conspicuous casualty of the new system when, in the summer of 1977, he found his advocacy of continued wage restraint repudiated by the biennial delegate conference. He was then placed in the embarrassing position of having to argue for a return to free collective bargaining at the 1977 TUC conference when only a year before he had vigorously advanced the case for an incomes policy. It could, however, be argued that these changes seem more radical than they are. Internally, it would appear that, while lay involvement in collective bargaining and the use of 'reference back' procedures has strengthened the position of the minority of shop stewards and activists, the membership as a whole is no more involved in union affairs than it is in most other major unions. While the current trend towards the establishment of branches based on the workplace rather than on geography may encourage more participation, it seems unlikely that branch business *per se* will ever appeal to the mass of ordinary members. Externally, the power of the general secretary to use the union's block vote at TUC and Labour Party conferences remains undiminished. Whoever occupies the post has, by virtue of his position, considerable influence both on the TUC General Council and in the corridors of Whitehall. It is difficult to envisage any further changes within the union which could alter this situation.

Structural changes have also occurred within the GMWU with broadly the same end in view – the strengthening of rank and file commitment to the union through increased participation. Up to the early 1970s the GMWU was popularly identified with an authoritarian, right-wing style of leadership which had been established by successive post-war general secretaries. The union had never embraced the dual concept of regional and trade group organization favoured by the TGWU but instead relied on an exclusively regional structure of representation. All branches were grouped into ten regions and elected a defined number of members to sit on a regional council. The branches and regional councils together elected delegates to the union's annual delegate conference. The full-time regional secretaries, however, were appointed for life by the National Executive Committee which was itself composed partly of regional secretaries and partly of regional council members. All other full-time officials were similarly appointed for life by the NEC. This committee exercised its powers under the general authority of the union's General Council, on which all ten regions were represented by their full-time secretaries and by a slightly larger number of regional council members. Even the delegates to the annual conference sat and often voted as regional representatives. In these circumstances it is hardly surprising that the regional secretaries tended to operate as quasi-autonomous 'bosses' on whom the union's general secretary depended heavily for support. This regional structure also provided a legitimate channel of opposition to the national leadership and at annual conferences some regional delegations advocated policies which were to the left of the prevailing right-wing orthodoxy. Nevertheless, as in the TGWU, the position of the general secretary, being elected for life, was (and remains) constitutionally strong and regional opposition was never sufficiently widespread to change the union's right-wing stance on major issues of national and industrial policy.

During the early 1970s, however, several significant changes occurred.The Pilkington dispute of 1970 'shook the union to its foundations' in so far as it represented a revolt by a large group of rank and file members against the remoteness of the union's hierarchy.[15] The election of David Basnett as general secretary in 1973 was also something of a landmark. Since then the union has become more attuned to the need for expansion. Its rigid, regional structure may well have deterred potential partners from amalgamation, Certainly its failure to hold out the kind of umbrella for smaller unions which the TGWU's trade group structure provides cannot have helped it in the struggle for members. The need to expand was, therefore, a major factor behind the constitutional changes of 1975. The old two-tier Executive Committee structure was replaced by a single Executive Council, comprising the general secretary, the chairman, the treasurer, and three representatives from each region, two of whom are lay members and the third is the regional secretary. In 1969 the union decided to set up a series of industrial conferences, composed of lay delegates, for purely consultative purposes. In 1975 the system was strengthened in order to encourage national officers to 'sound out' the lay delegates on proposed agreements and on general developments in industry. Regional industrial conferences were also introduced for the same purpose. Another step which was taken in order to strengthen the link between the branches and the union hierarchy was the introduction of a new tier of full-time officers at district level. The emphasis has changed from traditional administration to the provision of a more professional negotiating and recruitment service for each branch within a given district.

These changes clearly do not equal the decentralization which has occurred within the TGWU. The regional secretaries still occupy a very strong position within the union and a formal trade group structure has yet to be created. Perhaps this development must await a major amalgamation with another large union which has diverse industrial interests. Despite the recent constitutional changes the union has not been conspicuously more successful in expanding its membership base than it was in the 1960s. On the credit side, it may be said that under Basnett's leadership the union has rejoined the mainstream of thinking within the TUC and has succeeded in projecting a more dynamic, forward-looking image of itself to potential partners. It has also been more willing to spend money on research, training and educational facilities than many other unions. Its future growth prospects, however, are limited by the fact that nearly half its total membership comes from the engineering industry, from public service industries (gas, water and electricity) and from local government – all of which are likely to contract in manpower terms over the next few years. In these circumstances, the need for one or more major amalgamations will become increasingly acute if the union's rate of growth is to match its projected image.

Constitutional decentralization: the NUM

The National Union of Mineworkers furnishes a more extreme example of area autonomy than the GMWU. Its predecessor, the Miners' Federation of Great Britain, was little more than a loose alliance of area and regional unions, each of which enjoyed almost total autonomy from the federation's head office. The formation of the NUM in 1946 did not radically change the position and the area organizations are still quasi-autonomous bodies with their own constitutions, elected officials and financial resources. The senior officials of the area organizations occupy most of the seats on the union's National Executive Committee and lead their own area delegations at the annual conference. As in the GMWU, it is accepted that each area is free to oppose the policies of the national leadership at both conference and within the NEC and in recent years some areas, notably Yorkshire, Scotland and South Wales, have consistently done so. Consequently the area officials occupy a powerful constitutional position *vis-à-vis* the president and general secretary of the union, both of whom are subject to the decisions of conference and the NEC.

Although the miners have not adopted the elective principle to the extent that the engineers have, there is an organized ideological struggle within the NUM which is in some respects similar to that of the AUEW. Critical factors are the tradition of active participation at branch level within the NUM and the close ties which exist between the branches and the area organizations. Every colliery has its own branch (or 'lodge') which elects by ballot the area officers and sends delegates to an area council. There is considerable scope within this structure for organized electioneering and the past decade has witnessed significant changes in the ideological stance of certain areas through the election of outspoken 'militants'. Within each area and thus within the NEC, the main division is between Labour Party loyalists (or 'moderates') and a faction of communists, Marxists and left-wingers (or 'militants'). The split is reflected in the national officers of the union, with the president (elected for life) traditionally a 'moderate' and the general secretary (also elected for life) a 'militant'. In recent years, however, the left has gained ground within the NEC, largely because of the conspicuous success of the two national strikes called by the NUM which appear in turn to have vindicated the left's general strategy. How long the moderates will succeed in retaining their tenuous majority on the NEC remains to be seen.

In recent years two factors have enabled the current president of the NUM, Joe Gormley, to retain control of the NEC on most major issues. First, it is within the power of the NEC to bypass resolutions of the annual conference by appealing directly to the membership by means of a pithead ballot. This tactic can be very important in national wage disputes since it enables the NEC to adopt a more flexible negotiating position than would be the case if the union's officers were tied to the letter of conference resolutions. On two occasions, of course, a pithead ballot has been used to strengthen the negotiating position of the NEC in so far as a decisive majority of the members have voted for strike action. A ballot does not necessarily strengthen the moderates either. In 1974, for example, the Coal Board's proposed plan for pit-based productivity payments was rejected by the membership despite the active support of moderate members of the NEC. The calling of a ballot, with appropriate recommendations from a majority of the NEC, still allows the opposition in each area to campaign actively against these recommendations. Nevertheless, the fierce internal debate which frequently precedes a decision by the NEC to call for a ballot and the emphasis which the left normally places on the sanctity of conference resolutions suggests that a slight majority of the membership will more often than not support the moderate line.

The second source of support for the moderates on the NEC is, ironically, the conspicuously undemocratic structure of the committee itself. Since 1944 every area within the union has been entitled to at least one representative on the NEC, but this principle has been overtaken by the dramatic contraction in the industry's workforce which occurred in the 1960s. As a result, the smaller areas which (with the exception of Kent) tend by and large to support the moderates, are now over-represented on the NEC. Table 12 shows the 1974 pattern of representation. In addition, the GMWU has one seat on the NEC in respect of its 2000 members in coking plants. In these circumstances it is hardly surprising that left-wing members of the NEC have been campaigning for many years in favour of changes in the constitution which would almost certainly give them a built-in majority. If they succeed, it will be interesting to see the reaction of those who, from a right-wing perspective, argue that unions should be made 'more democratic'.

The growing strength of the left within the NUM is primarily attributable to the way in which certain area representatives have effectively harnessed the dissatisfaction of many ordinary miners with the consequences of the lack-lustre policy which the union pursued in the 1960s. The moderate leadership of the day presided over a precipitate run-down of the industry's manpower and in 1966 agreed to a major reform of the industry's wage payment system which discriminated heavily against the better-paid miners in the

Table 12 *Representation on the National Executive Committee of the NUM*

	Members	*Seats on the NEC*
Cokemen	5,543	1
COSA	17,481	1
Cumberland	1,151	1
Derbyshire	11,820	1
Durham	18,505	2
Kent	2,774	1
North West	10,263	1
Leicester	3,101	1
Midlands	15,201	1
Northumberland	8,904	1
North Wales	1,073	1
Nottingham	33,640	2
Scotland	19,026	2
South Derbyshire	3,037	1
South Wales	29,608	2
Yorkshire	63,328	2

more productive areas. The first symptoms of rank and file dissatisfaction appeared in 1969 and 1970, when major unofficial stoppages occurred in Yorkshire. Gormley, paradoxically, was elected president in 1971 on a platform that presaged vigorous action to restore the miners to the position in the earnings league table which they had occupied before the abandonment of piece-work in 1966. The success of the national strikes of 1972 and 1974 and, in particular, the part played in these strikes by secondary picketing, strongly endorsed the militant strategy. Having witnessed the effects of their bargaining power when used to the full, it seems inherently unlikely that the membership as a whole will in the forseeable future elect area and national officials who are not prepared in principle to employ the weapon of a national stoppage. It could therefore be said that the general direction in which the union has moved over the past decade is attributable to the existence of channels within the union whereby the wishes of rank and file members can be brought to bear on the national leadership. The conclusion would seem to be that, if one measure of the efficiency of a trade union is a successful bargaining strategy, then the recent history of the NUM suggests that the claims of efficiency *can* be reconciled with a reasonable degree of popular control.

The role of conflict

The discussion so far has concentrated on the way in which individual unions have sought to reconcile the conflicting pressures of efficiency and democracy. An alternative way of looking at the problem, however, is to proceed from the assumption that a trade union is a pluralistic organization and that a degree of internal conflict is therefore inevitable. The most familiar manifestation of such conflict is, of course, the clash of interests and priorities between full-time union officials and radically minded lay members. The full-time official is popularly regarded as a 'manager of discontent' whose main task is to harness rank and file support for defined bargaining objectives and achieve those objectives within the established framework of procedures and negotiating conventions. His main interest is said to lie in preserving established bargaining relationships with employers and in conditioning his members to accept the 'realities of life'. As such he has been seen as a vital part of the mechanism of social control which integrates workers into the existing (capitalist) power structure of industrial society.[16] Some rank and file members, however, may take a more radical view of society, or at least of what their union should be seeking to achieve, and may become profoundly dissatisfied with the caution of their full-time negotiators. Not being involved in collective bargaining, they may attach less importance to the maintenance of established procedures, which they may, in any case, regard as a self-imposed limitation on their bargaining power. Full-time officials may therefore be seen as simply part of the structure of *managerial* control. Unofficial strikes and low levels of participation in union affairs could therefore appear as symptomatic of a general alienation from the formal structure of union government.

Conflict is, however, a much more complex phenomenon than the above perspective would imply. As Hemingway has pointed out, within most unions there are certain structural factors which generate conflict.[17] Most of the larger unions contain a variety of different occupational interests which create *vertical* divisions within the organization. One can observe these at work in, for example, the conflicts which have arisen within the TGWU between dockers and lorry drivers over the issue of container handling, and also in the threatened breakaway of toolroom workers from the AUEW. It may be inferred, therefore, that there is a limit beyond which a large, multi-occupational union will find it increasingly difficult to weld together diverse interests. External expansion may ultimately be discouraged by a growing problem of internal control. Moreover, the larger a union becomes, the more likely it is to generate *horizontal* divisions between leaders and members. Such divisions encompass more than the familiar divergence between full-time officials and lay activists. There may, as in the case of the NUM, be conflict between area leaders and national officials or, as in the GMWU, between regional secretaries, branch activists and national officials. In industries where there is a well developed system of plant and company bargaining there may be a significant divergence of interest and outlook between shop stewards and their own constituents as well as between stewards and full-time officials. The picture is further complicated by the fact that conflict may be latent as well as manifest. A situation in which there is apparent unanimity of interests can soon disappear if external circumstances change to the extent that the parties are compelled to recognize that their interests are in conflict and therefore begin to articulate them. We therefore need to examine the way in which the parties subjectively define conflict in a given set of circumstances.

Hemingway's model of union government rests on the crucial proposition that manifest *conflict* between leaders and members reveals how *control* is exercised within the union. He suggests that the parties have three resources at their disposal through which the conflict can be resolved. These are, first *institutional* resources flowing from participation in the organs of union government; second *alliance* resources involving the formation of opposition groups; and third *action* resources involving some outright expression of dissent. The use of all resources occurs within a framework of internal *bargaining* between the groups who are in conflict. The implication is that the use of institutional resources will be the preferred line in most cases since this involves the 'respectable' processes of debate and voting. If this fails, however, then one or both parties will resort to the formation of an organization which can contest elections and get its representatives into positions of influence within the union. If this strategy is constitutionally difficult or if the leadership remains unwilling to change its stance despite the presence of an organized opposition, there may be a resort to coercion. This might involve, on one side, the staging of unofficial strikes, the disruption of official meetings and, as a last resort, the formation of a breakaway union. On the other side, disruptive opposition may be countered by expulsion from the union. If this stage is reached, it does not necessarily mean that the bargaining process has come to an end and that no compromise is possible. In Hemingway's words: 'However grudgingly the parties cease to do battle, they must sooner or later reach an outcome as they exhaust their energies and resources.'[18] Coercion may therefore be as essential an element in the process of union government as voting in elections or participating in conference debates.

If we accept the proposition that conflict is the normal state of affairs within a trade union and that specific clashes of interest are resolved through the process of bargaining, a new dimension is added to the debate on union democracy. This suggests that the formal, constitutional aspects of union government need to be seen in the context of how leaders and members define their respective interests and how they see the issues that divide them. Hemingway's case studies emphasize that the use of constitutional machinery and the mobilization of electoral opposition do not necessarily imply greater control by the members. A change in leadership achieved through the ballot box may simply replace one oligarchic faction by another. The latent dissatisfaction of the silent majority may be mobilized by a relatively small group of activists and focused on a specific issue for electoral purposes. But when the electoral process has elevated the dissidents to positions of authority within the union and the catalytic issue has been removed, the membership may relapse into its traditional apathy. Union leaders may be genuinely committed to the concept of membership involvement and may seek to encourage this through constitutional change. But having opened the door, they cannot force their members to walk through it.

Leaders and members alike view the processes of control in the light of their respective definitions of the situation in which they find themselves and also according to their perception of the needs of the organization as a whole. In a union where the leadership group is divided into two ideologically opposed factions, each group will tend to emphasize the legitimacy of those constitutional or 'democratic' procedures which strengthen its own bargaining power. In the NUM, for example, the left faction stresses the need to reform the NEC and the sanctity of conference decisions; the right stands by the traditional principle of 'one man, one vote' and looks more favourably on the pithead ballot. In the AUEW the left or 'progressive' faction strenuously opposed the introduction of postal ballots whereas the right favoured it. In such situations both sides are likely to appeal, no doubt sincerely, to the democratic principle. By the same token, outside observers will define what *they* mean by democracy according to how they perceive their own interests as well as those of groups such as employers, consumers and governments. Greater control of union leaders by the membership is advocated if it is believed that this will result in a more moderate or responsible pattern of union behaviour. Otherwise the need for leaders to control their members is emphasized. Outsiders are being neither more nor less hypocritical than union members themselves in defining democracy in a way which accords with their own interests and values.

The amateur tradition

A cynic might argue that the vast majority of union members only begin to think about the way in which their organization is being run and implicitly question the quality of their leaders when the union conspicuously fails to meet their legitimate aspirations. Although Moran's argument that the mass of rank and file members consciously trade off their union's performance against participation in its affairs needs to be treated with caution as a general explanation of non-involvement, it is not unreasonable to suggest that many members are more likely to judge their union by *what* it actually achieves for them rather than *how* it goes about it. The practical effects of union policy, measured in terms of real take-home pay, are normally likely to be of greater interest to most members than the problems of how the policy is or should be made. What any union achieves for its members is largely a function of its bargaining power, and this will be determined partly by factors which are outside the control of union officials or their members. But it is also possible for a union to enhance its bargaining power by making the optimum use of the resources at its disposal and this in turn raises several questions about the way in which different unions organize themselves for bargaining purposes and 'service' their members.

It is a commonplace that British trade unions rely heavily on voluntary workers. Without the efforts of shop stewards and other lay officers at branch and workplace level, most unions would simply cease to maintain an effective 'grass roots' organization. While practices differ from one union to another, it seems clear that the vast majority are still influenced by the old suspicion of centralized bureaucracy. In most unions the number of full-time officials is such that the level of dependence on local volunteers and shop floor

Table 13 *Ratio of full-time officials to union members in largest unions, 1976*

TGWU	*Officials*	*Ratio of officials to members*
TGWU	483	1:3995
AUEW (Engineering section)	187	1:6251
GMWU	282	1:3249
NALGO	191	1:3575
NUPE	122	1:5332
ETPU	150	1:2800
USDAW	133	1:3102
ASTMS	72	1:5500
UCATT	170	1:1726
CPSA	21	1:10,979
UPW	12	1:16,758
T&GWU	22	1:2506

activists is inevitably high (see Table 13). Traditionalists would of course defend this arrangement on the ground that it ensures that the union hierarchy is never allowed to lose contact with the rank and file members. In the light of the foregoing discussion, however, it would seem that membership control depends on much more than merely keeping the number of full-time officials as small as possible. Nevertheless, the tradition persists and indeed further manifests itself in the recruitment and payment of full-time officials.

The most important qualification for a full-time post seems to be practical experience as a shop steward or lay representative in the workplace. Educational qualifications and administrative ability are, by contrast, relatively unimportant. Indeed, one might almost say that many unions display profound hostility towards 'intellectuals' and outside experts who are, by definition, likely to have been contaminated by managerial and other alien influences. This potential weakness is aggravated by a general reluctance to provide full-time officers and shop stewards alike with adequate training for their jobs. A one-week course at a union educational establishment is still regarded as an adequate preparation by many manual trade unions, although white collar organizations appear to be taking a more progressive view. The assumption is that practical experience will provide the officer with most of the training he requires. Moreover, most unions take a notoriously conservative approach to remuneration. Full-time officials are expected to devote themselves to the business of the union, very often on a seven-day week basis, for salaries which may be less than the earnings of some of their own members. This approach has been justified by Flanders in the following terms:

Men and women may work for a trade union for either love or money, but British trade unions have always assumed that money would not and should not be the main inducement. They are strongly disinclined to pay their full-time officers salaries in any way comparable with what they would achieve outside the movement. . . . The ultimate logic of purely business unionism is the logic of business itself – that no one is ready to work for it unless he is paid his full market rate. There may be a case for trade unions becoming better employers than they are today . . . but it is inconceivable that they will ever be able to compete with business on a market basis for the recruitment of talent. Unless they continue to tap the love as well as the money motive in recruiting both their full-time and their lay officers, they are bound to be faced with a progressive decline in their standards of performance.[19]

The argument is even less convincing today than it was when Flanders expressed it nearly twenty years ago. It seems to assume that a state of relative personal poverty is the *sine qua non* of unsullied proletarian virtue and that once an official is paid the 'market rate' he will be vulnerable to the evil influences of the market place. There is, however, no *inherent* contradiction between the preservation of a high moral commitment to trade unionism and the payment of salaries which more accurately reflect the responsiblities of full-time union officers. To deny the validity of this proposition is to accept that the modern trade union movement can be managed according to the normative standards of the Victorian craftsman.

Another symptom of the amateur tradition is the conspicuous reluctance of trade unions to charge realistic fees for membership. As Table 14 shows, in 1975 most union members paid less than 20 pence per week in subscription fees. A cynic might argue that even if the unions doubled their current membership fees they would not know what to do with the money. But it may be that the real reason for keeping subscriptions low is the simple fact that many unions are in actual or potential competition with other unions for members. The fear of getting too far out of line with competitors tends to depress the general level of fees and the acid test of success becomes that of who can offer the most services for the least amount of money.

Table 14 *Union membership fees, 1970–5*

	1970	*1975*
Membership covered	9277	9984
Income per member		
Contributions	£4.72	£8.25
Investments	.77	.86
Other sources	.14	.41
Total	£5.63	£9.52
Expenditure per member		
Administration	£3.26	£6.60
Dispute benefit	.39	.29
Unemployment benefit	.06	.07
Accident/sickness benefit	.42	.33
Superannuation	.30	.30
Death/funeral	.15	.16
Total	£4.58	£7.75
Excess income over expenditure	£1.05	£1.75

The level of membership income is particularly important to white collar unions, most of which are of relatively recent origin and receive relatively little income from investments. But the older manual unions have in general been reluctant to invest their funds in the most profitable outlets, confining themselves instead to fixed-interest stocks in central and local government. Most of their assets are not in a form which could easily be liquidated in the event of a prolonged strike or other financial crisis. In 1975 the fund which unions could call upon to finance official stoppages amounted in total to £190 million, or roughly £16 per member. Sustained aggressive action by even the largest unions is not normally possible without substantial borrowing from other organizations. A change in government policy which shifted the financial burden of strike action entirely on to the shoulders of the unions would obviously cause a major upheaval. Unions would either have to reappraise their traditional approach to subscriptions or simply avoid calling any prolonged official stoppages. While such a move would be strongly resisted by the unions, it may seem strange to the outside observer that a trade union movement which has traditionally professed so much faith in voluntarism should be so ill-prepared to absorb the full financial effects of free collective bargaining. The answer probably lies in the fact that traditionally the strike weapon has been generally regarded as a weapon of last resort, to be used (officially) only when all other methods of reaching agreement have failed. Nevertheless there does seem to be a contradiction between the unions' emotional attachment to voluntarism and their unwillingness to provide themselves with resources adequate to ensure that the full range of voluntary activities can be sustained.

From a Marxist standpoint one can explain the limited resources which unions have at their disposal in terms of the limited objectives which they pursue. The principal function of union officials is, according to Hyman, 'the negotiation and renegotiation of order within constraints set by a capitalist economy and a capitalist state'.[20] Consequently we would expect that much of a union official's time would be devoted not to the struggle against capital but, on the contrary, to the control of rank and file aspirations and activities which threaten to disrupt the established framework of order. It follows that the more power a union official is able to exert *over* his members, the less forcefully he will use it *for* them. Vigorous, direct action by the rank and file is the only way of preventing a trade union from becoming totally integrated in the structure of managerial control. From this standpoint, control by the membership is seen as something quite distinct from and even in conflict with control by the union.

The relationship between leaders and members is much more complex, however, than the Marxist interpretation would imply. Conflict within trade unions cannot be explained solely in terms of 'officials' *versus* 'rank and file members'. As we have noted in the course of this chapter, there are potential sources of conflict between different groups at every level within a trade union. When conflict is articulated, it may be resolved by a range of methods, each of which entails some kind of bargaining. If opposition to a leadership group is to be effective it must result either in a change of policy by the group or in its displacement by an alternative group. But this in turn requires systematic organization and the exploitation of all the available constitutional avenues. Consequently, while spontaneous rank and file insurgency is by no means unknown, it would be wrong to assume that this is the normal method by which members exert control over their leaders. It would be equally misleading to assume that such insurgency, whether organized or not, is usually directed against 'collaborative' union officials and constitutes an incipient revolt against capitalism. In recent years we have in fact witnessed several disputes in which 'militant' leaders – officials and stewards alike – have been repudiated by their own members, a situation which tends to reinforce the popular belief that the 'silent' majority is the 'moderate' majority.

The fact that 'moderate' and 'militant' leaders alike have found their authority successfully challenged from within does not support the once popular view that most trade unions are dominated by small groups of lifelong office-holders. But more importantly it suggests that conflict is an omnipresent characteristic of trade union government, as indeed it is of any pluralistic organization. Indeed, it may be that rank and file members have in recent years become more disposed to criticize their officials and lay representatives, from whatever ideological standpoint, for what they consider to be an unacceptable standard of performance. If this is so – and as yet there is insufficient evidence to make a judgement – then not only are the sources of internal conflict likely to grow but the formal distribution of power within a union may increasingly diverge from the real pattern of decision-making. In these circumstances the familiar question of whether a union's internal power structure is 'democratic' or 'oligarchic' misses the point. A more appropriate starting point for analysis is to ask how union leaders and officials seek to reconcile the various conflicts of interest within the organization and thereby preserve its cohesion as both a combative and a regulatory body. This in turn underlines the importance of the relationship between 'power over' and 'power for'. The varying constitutional characteristics of trade unions together with their corporate traditions are obviously relevant in this context, but they need to be seen in the light of the informal social processes through which the conflicts between leaders and members are commonly resolved. It is at this point, however, that value judgements tend to colour our analysis. For the view we take of how much power union leaders have *over* their members depends very much on what they are likely to use this power *for*. To say that they will use this power in pursuit of their members' interests takes us no further since it begs the questions of *how* these interests are defined, *who* defines them, and what the wider effects of achieving them will be. Those who, for example, criticize the amateurism of the unions' approach to collective bargaining often appear to assume that increased efficiency in this field is synonymous with the development of strong central control by managerially minded professionals. If this assumption is valid, these critics need to ask themselves what the effects on collective bargaining would be if the unions were to adopt their recommendations and whether, on balance, the benefits to society as a whole would outweigh the costs.

The view which external critics take of the balance between efficiency and democracy within a given trade union is, in any case, less significant than the perception of the members themselves. If we focus exclusively on the role and behaviour of union leaders and officials, we shall overlook what is arguably the most important dimension of union activity, namely the workplace itself. If the majority of members seem disinterested in the internal workings of their union and show little disposition to discuss the problem of reconciling efficiency and democracy, the answer may be that in *their* eyes the question has already been settled at that level which has most meaning for them. Perhaps they see little or no conflict between *their* interests, however these are defined, and the interests of the union to which they belong. This does not mean that no conflict exists, but simply that many members do not perceive it. This issue will be discussed in the next chapter.

5 Activity in the workplace

Trade unionism began in the workplace and, in the eyes of many union members, it is at this level that the rationale of collective organization is most easily understood. Individual trade unionists may well view with misgiving the activities of their organization when these are considered from a 'national' perspective. They may believe, for example, that trade unions have exerted too much influence over governments, that 'irresponsible' pay claims have driven up the cost of living and that unnecessary strikes have inflicted severe damage on the economy. But when they consider the role of collective action in the context of their own work situation they may well adopt a very different view; organization then becomes an essential defence mechanism against arbitrary management decisions. Collective action is frequently seen as the only way in which established working practices and customary standards of living can be protected against the growing pressures of technological change and falling profitability. In simple terms, it is only by organizing themselves in the workplace that employees can exert countervailing power, the object of which is usually to ensure that the employer behaves in accordance with accepted standards of 'fairness'. The conventional method of imposing a degree of order on this underlying conflict betwen managerial objectives and worker norms is, of course, collective bargaining.

Students of industrial relations know that one of the most significant developments, both in Britain and in other industrial countries, over the post-war period as a whole is the growth of collective bargaining at workplace and company level. Some observers have broadly welcomed this development in so far as it marks a significant move towards the 'democratization' of decision-making at that level where workers themselves are most likely to be directly involved. Others, however, have seen workplace bargaining as an overt challenge to the authority of managers and trade union officials alike and thus as a potential source of disorder within the industrial relations system. On the face of it, the critics would seem to have a good case. Organized resistance to managerial decisions which are felt to be unfair sometimes leads not only to unofficial strikes but, more importantly, to the preservation of old-fashioned and costly working practices. Bargaining over wages at workplace level can undermine the authority of national agreements, push up the 'going rate' for pay settlements, and frustrate the implementation of incomes policies. Hence over the past twenty years policy-makers at national level have devoted much time and effort towards the object of *controlling* workplace bargaining and imposing *order* on workplace activity. This objective has, however, been frustrated by the behaviour of managers, shop stewards and ordinary workers who do not in general share the same definition of 'order' and 'disorder'. What seems disorderly behaviour from outside may well be an eminently rational form of activity of those who are most intimately involved. To understand why these contradictory perspectives have arisen, we need to analyse the nature of workplace bargaining and examine the aspirations and problems of the bargainers themselves.

The origins of workplace organization

Workplace organization is an integral feature of industrial society: 'Industry brings men and women together to work, they naturally associate in groups, and it is natural that these groups should try to exercise some control over their working conditions.'[1] The concept of *control* is central to workplace organization. In its simplest terms control means having the power to achieve certain desired objectives and resist the undesirable objectives of others. Clearly all the principal 'actors' in the industrial relations system – managers, trade union officials, shop stewards, workgroups and governments – seek to exert some measure of control over workplace activity. The extent to which they succeed in a given work situation is likely to tell us something about the balance of power and influence in that situation. The scope of control, therefore, extends beyond the scope of a collective agreement.[2] Although collective bargaining has become more important in many workplaces over the past twenty years, the struggle to exert control is not confined by the formal contents of a plant or company agreement. Many of these agreements are still essentially informal in nature; they may contain a number of formal, written rules but still leave a great many issues to be resolved by the parties on an informal, day-to-day basis. In many workplaces procedural rules have yet to be formalized and written down, while many substantive rules are the result of custom and practice. In other workplaces there is little bargaining in the formal sense of two sides sitting down on a regular basis to negotiate on matters of mutual interest. Yet the absence of formal bargaining between managers and union representatives does not mean that shop stewards and the workgroups they represent have no control over their immediate environment on the shop floor. On the contrary, there may be an unwritten code of rules through which each side influences and, to some extent, controls the behaviour of the other. But if workgroups and their representatives are to exert control over the decision-making process some form of organization is essential.

It is worth recalling at this point that Victorian craftsmen sought to control their working environment by imposing terms and conditions *unilaterally* on their employers. They did not seek to negotiate directly on these matters for the simple reason that the customs and rules of their craft were held to be of concern to themselves alone. The extent to which they succeeded in maintaining unilateral regulation was determined by the market conditions of the time – that is, the employer's ability to stand a prolonged stoppage and the level of demand for their skills. In the engineering industry, for example, the district committees of the ASE regarded themselves as the ultimate arbiters of the terms and conditions under which their members would work. Within each engineering works or 'shop', however, the craftsmen tended to elect a 'steward' whose primary task was to see that the customary practices of the trade were observed. The introduction of both new machinery and incentive payment systems in the pre-1914 period and, above all, the employers' insistence that craft rules should be subject to collective bargaining intensified the struggle for control and thereby strengthened the position of the shop steward. The unprecedented shortages of skilled labour during the first world war and the resulting pressure on the ASE to accept 'dilutees' gave the steward additional scope for negotiating directly with managers in the workplace. Labour shortages had similar effects in other manufacturing industries, so that by 1918 shop stewards had become a major force in workplace relations.

This embryonic organization was confined largely to those workplaces where skilled men occupied a dominant position. There were, of course, many other industries – notably the docks – in which workgroups sought to regulate their immediate environment by adhering to a body of customary rules and devices (emotively described by employers as restrictive practices), but this group regulation seldom developed into the kind of organization for bargaining purposes which characterized the engineering workshops. In any event, all forms of workplace organization were weakened by the onset of heavy and prolonged unemployment after 1920. Many trade union leaders sought to discourage any tendencies towards autonomous workplace activity, while the general slackness of the labour market made employers much less willing to engage in bargaining with shop stewards. But when the economy moved back into almost continuous full employment after 1939, workplace organization began to revive. In some manufacturing industries, the establishment of joint production committees during the war years provided an institutional base from which regular joint consultation could develop in the post-war period. In conditions of full employment many managers found it impossible to prevent joint consultation from gradually and almost imperceptibly developing into collective bargaining. Labour shortages, the operation of piece-work systems and the application of mass production technology all combined to enhance the bargaining power of workgroups and their elected representatives. As workplace payment systems were made to produce *ad hoc* increases in earnings, so an increasing proportion of take-home pay was attributed to workplace bargaining. Not surprisingly the status of the shop steward gradually rose and the activities of full-time officials appeared less and less relevant to the conduct of workplace relations.

Full employment obviously provided the initial impetus behind the growth of workplace organization in so far as it changed the balance of the bargaining power within individual workplaces. But the sharp rise in the average level of unemployment which began in the late 1960s and has continued up to the present time does not appear to have slowed down the underlying trend in favour of workplace bargaining. This suggests that more intangible factors have been at work, the effect of which has been to produce a new level of *expectations* among workgroups. Flanders observed in the mid 1960s that an increase in unemployment could well augment the challenge of workplace bargaining because it would frustrate these expectations:

These are partly expecations in regard to income, including stability of earnings: they look forward to a continually rising standard of living and have entered into various commitments as a result. But equally they have new expectations as producers about the conditions of their working life. They are no longer willing, for example, to suffer individual or collective dismissal at the discretion of management or to accept its orders in a spirit of blind obedience. In many ways they are claiming a greater influence on management decisions, particularly in matters that affect their own welfare and status.[3]

The spread of mass-production technology in the post-war period gave workgroups new opportunities to bargain with management in so far as it increased the vulnerability of the production process to short, localized stoppages and other forms of industrial action. But it also intensified the struggle for control over the immediate working environment as management sought to increase the productivity of expensive capital equipment and workgroups tried to maintain their own influence over the pace and volume of work.[4]

The way in which workplace relations have developed in the motor car industry, however, should not be regarded as typical of what has happened elsewhere. The history, technology and organization of the car industry have combined to give its workplace relations a uniquely disputatious character. In other manufacturing industries the development of workplace organization has by and large been more gradual and, in managerial terms, less disorderly. There are in fact some large areas of employment, particularly in the growing service sector, where workplace organization for bargaining purposes is still largely non-existent. This does not necessarily mean that changes in behavioural norms and expectations have left some workgroups untouched, but rather that there are some work situations in which employee organization has, for various reasons, been inhibited. We must therefore analyse briefly the factors which are responsible for these conspicuous variations in workplace organization.

The structure and pattern of organization

The strength of a given workplace organization may be judged in the light of two criteria – first, the extent to which collective bargaining in the workplace is influenced by external institutions and, second, the substantive and procedural characteristics of the bargaining itself. At one extreme there are workplaces in which a hierarchy of shop stewards negotiates with management within a well-established procedural framework on a wide range of issues, with little or no reference to the full-time officials of the union or unions to which the stewards themselves belong. At the other extreme there are workplaces in which bargaining is entirely in the hands of full-time officials, in which the shop steward organization is weak or non-existent and in which the range of negotiable issues is narrow. Between the two, however, lies an immense range of situations about which it is difficult to generalize.

Recent research suggests that the *size* of the workplace is a crucial influence over the sophistication and autonomy of the steward organization: 'The larger the workplace organisation, the greater the resources at its disposal and the more independent its behaviour.'[5] In establishments with more than 500 employees, size seems to be more important than any other factor.[6] But the influence of size may be weakened if the workgroups themselves do not have a particularly strong sense of unity or lack commitment either to their union or to their workplace representatives. In a large, newly organized white collar establishment, for example, there may be relatively little feeling of collective identity among the workforce; they may still see their grievances from an individual perspective and may thus be unwilling to give much support to their elected representatives when collective action is needed. But even in a predominantly manual establishment where the workers have a long tradition of collective action, it does not necessarily follow that the steward organization will be either well developed or autonomous. The potential influence of several other factors must therefore be considered.

The attitude of *management* is likely to be of considerable significance. An employer who, for example, insists on dealing with a full-time union official whenever an issue of substance arises will obviously tend to discourage the development of workplace autonomy. Successive surveys of workplace relations, however, suggests that most managers prefer to consult or negotiate with shop stewards rather than involve full-time officers, although the level of acceptance varies from industry to industry. The reasons for this preference are not difficult to appreciate. As employees of the firm, stewards know the situation on the shop floor and are in close daily contact with their members. An experienced steward often acts as a 'filter' for grievances and problems, nipping trouble in the bud and only taking up those claims which have real substance. He may actively assist managers and supervisors to maintain standards of performance and conduct provided that customary rules are observed and agreed procedures followed. Indeed, where managers have established an effective relationship with their stewards, the latter tend to acquire a quasi-managerial role. While this does not, of course, exclude the possibility that stewards may on occasion ignore procedure or pursue unrealistic demands, research suggests that in many workplaces the stewards' involvement in day-to-day bargaining with managers has a strong socializing influence on their behaviour. The 1972 Survey of Workplace Relations, for example, disclosed that the overwhelming majority of senior managers and supervisors thought that stewards' demands were always, or at least usually, reasonable, and that they made a significant contribution towards resolving problems in the workplace.

There is, of course, a great deal that management can do to integrate the steward organization within the framework of managerial control. They can, for example, establish joint consultative committees in the workplace in which matters of mutual interest can be discussed with shop stewards over and above their normal negotiating activity. Facilities such as the right to call meetings during working hours, an office and telephone, adequate time off to pursue union duties, and reasonable access to senior management are all likely to have a considerable impact on the way in which the steward fulfills his role and thus on the strength of the steward organization. Where the steward's role is fully accepted by management, there is likely to be far more continuity and stability in the steward organization than in workplaces where hostility is still experienced. Where, by contrast, stewards feel that their role is not accepted and that managers are continually seeking to undermine their authority and weaken their influence over the workforce, they will almost certainly feel obliged to stress the adversary elements in their relationship with management. An atmosphere of perpetual conflict is unlikely to encourage the formation of a stable, autonomous organization; on the contrary, it is apt to lead to a high level of dependence on full-time officers while the scope of bargaining probably will not be wide. Furthermore, in multi-union establishments, managerial resistance to the steward's role will seriously weaken the prospects for inter-union cooperation.

The influence of external trade union organization can also be important. A shop steward directly represents the workgroup that has elected him but he is also an accredited representative of his trade union and must not only pay due regard to the nearest point of contact with the union hierarchy (namely, the local branch) but must also develop an effective working relationship with his full-time official. In some cases, of course, the branch is based upon the workplace itself and as such constitutes the workplace organization.

Where branches are based on the members' places of residence, one would assume that their influence on individual workplaces is in general likely to be less significant, especially where geography makes regular contact between branch officials and shop stewards difficult. In fact, however, this is not always the case. Research suggests that in the public service sector there is a high level of dependence between individual workplace representatives and their local branch, almost regardless of the size of their employment unit and the geographical characteristics of the branch. This may in turn be due to the concentration of wage and salary bargaining at national level. In industries where a large proportion of earnings are determined by bargaining at plant or company level, stewards are likely to be more independent of the local branch than in those where most of the wage bargaining function is performed at national level by full-time officials.

Relationships between stewards and full-time officials are also influenced to some extent by the structure of collective bargaining. The more issues that are determined at plant and company level, the more expertise the stewards' organization is likely to have at its command and the less dependent they will be on the guidance of full-time officials. Since trade unions do not unilaterally determine bargaining structures, it could be said that the relationship between stewards and officers is partly outside the scope of union control. It would, however, be misleading to ignore completely the influence of union policy and structure. In the case of the TGWU, for example, the policy of encouraging workplace bargaining has been accompanied by changes in the role and duties of full-time officers which have tended to make them less available to deal with workplace issues. In other unions the number of full-time officers and the responsibilities they have to carry may be such that stewards are forced to rely on their own resources, even if they themselves would like more contact with their officers. Conversely, it may be that stewards who *could* have more contact with officials deliberately choose to keep them at arm's length.

Another significant influence on workplace organization is multi-unionism. In a workplace where two or more unions are actively competing for members and there is considerable friction between them, the stewards' organization may be fragmented and weak. In general, however, multi-unionism seems to act as a stimulus to workplace organization, even if there is no formal co-operation outside the workplace between the unions involved. A fairly standard response is the formation of a joint shop stewards' committee, on which the various unions are represented, for the purpose of developing a common approach to bargaining issues. In a multi-plant company, the stewards at each plant may form a central 'combine committee' covering the organization as a whole. The main function of these bodies tends to be the exchange of information and the co-ordination of claims. They are seldom recognized by management, however, and have no bargaining functions. At plant level, a joint stewards' committee may or may not be recognized by management, but its activities are likely to have important implications for the conduct of collective bargaining. Where a joint committee exists there is, for example, more likelihood that one steward will be recognized as the overall leader and that regular meetings between the stewards will take place. The larger the workplace, the more sophisticated the steward hierarchy is likely to be. There may, for example, be a full-time convenor, an executive committee and elections to administrative posts within the organization. In this way, inter-union co-operation at national level may be institutionalized in the workplace, and inter-union rivalry restrained by the practical needs of day-to-day bargaining with management. Where only one union is present in the workplace there is, conversely, a tendency for the steward organization to be less well-developed.

Every shop steward does not, of course, have the same *scope* to negotiate with managers – irrespective of the willingness of the managers themselves to negotiate with him. Clearly much depends on the structure of collective bargaining in the industry to which the establishment belongs. In the manufacturing sector as a whole there has been a general trend away from industry-wide bargaining over the past decade but there are still wide variations between different industries within this sector. Even in an industry where national agreements seek to impose some basic uniformity on individual workplaces, the extent to which they succeed depends first on the co-operation of managements and union representatives and second on the influence and cohesion of employers' association officials and trade union officials. Where, by contrast, there is considerable scope for workplace bargaining, the extent to which it actually takes place will be influenced by the structure of the company itself. In multi-plant undertakings, for example, management has some discretion to decide what issues shall be resolved by *workplace* bargaining and those which shall be determined by negotiations at *company* level. Company agreements may, in turn, be 'loose' or 'tight', with important implications for workplace organization. In public employment, by contrast, there is a long tradition of comprehensive bargaining at national level, leaving only interpretative issues and certain 'domestic' arrangements for local negotiation. But even here there are considerable variations between, say, a government department, a local authority and a nationalized industry. The size of the employment unit is always important. A large public undertaking is likely to have *some* discretion in the application of nationally agreed terms and conditions, and there is thus likely to be some scope for domestic, local or regional bargaining.

It does *not* follow, however, that wherever national or company agreements are 'loose', workplace bargaining flourishes and shop steward organizations are well developed and autonomous. Boraston *et al.* found that workplace organizations in building, footwear and hosiery were highly dependent on the external union organization despite the fact that their industry agreements allowed wide scope for workplace bargaining. Conversely, there was some evidence to suggest that within the limits imposed by 'tight' industry agreements, workplace organizations may achieve considerable autonomy. In coal mining, where the reform of the industry's payment system has made national negotiations far more important than they once were, it would appear that, while lodge officials have become more dependent on their area officials in the field of wage bargaining, they have retained their traditional autonomy in respect of all other substantive issues which arise at pit level. The more formal and comprehensive a national or industry-wide agreement is, the more likely it is that those issues which can be resolved in the workplace will actually be spelled out. In these circumstances a 'tight' industry (or company) agreement may in fact encourage the development of organizational autonomy in the workplace.

The degree of bargaining autonomy which a given workplace enjoys has so far been explained as a function of the interrelationship between three major variables – the attitude of management, the policy and structure of the trade unions, and the structure of collective bargaining. We have, however, neglected the contribution of what is arguably the linchpin of any workplace organization – the shop steward himself. The three variables discussed above throw light on why some workplace organizations have acquired more bargaining power than others. We must now analyse the way in which workplace representatives exercise and augment the power which collective organization has given them.

The role of the shop steward

The foundation-stone of a shop steward's power is his ability to represent effectively the interests and aspirations of the workgroup which has elected him for this purpose. In practice, of course, most stewards represent and are accountable to several workgroups, the cohesion of which may vary enormously. Some groups are easily identifiable, others are not. Some, because of their strategic position in the production process, have considerable bargaining power at their diposal; others have no such advantage and must be organized into an effective bargaining force. Whatever their differences, however, workgroups need a spokesman – someone who will articulate their interests and grievances and negotiate on their behalf with representatives of management.

It would be surprising if, given the total number of stewards and the diverse circumstances in which they work, there were no variations in the way in which stewards perceive their role. A major study by Batstone *et al.* has in fact distinguished three different roles. First, there are 'leader' stewards who not only represent their members but seek to shape their interests and aspirations so that they accord with trade union principles. Second, there are 'cowboys' who see their task in terms of maximizing short-run gains for their own constituents to the exclusion of wider collective principles. Third, there are 'populists' who also lack commitment to union principles and act primarily as delegates, uncritically voicing their constituents' opinions and claims. The distinguishing characteristic of effective representation is that stewards 'shape the majority of issues which they deal with, either by initiating issues themselves or by amending or squashing issues raised by others and . . . tend to handle issues themselves without resort to the convenors or other experienced stewards'. Similarly, stewards are said to be pursuing union principles 'if their systems of argument to all audiences more frequently refer to the norms of steward leadership than to members' wishes'. The authors found, not surprisingly, that 'leader' stewards were conspicuously more successful than the other types in using their power to further their members' interests. They also found, again not surprisingly, that in the plants they studied 'populists' outnumbered both 'leaders' and 'cowboys'.[7]

The leadership role is, of course, fraught with difficulty. First and foremost it involves adherence to certain broad principles which individual constituents may regard as irrelevant or even hostile to their own immediate interests. These principles include the pursuit of *unity* and *equity* among the constituent workgroups, both of which require the individual to subordinate his own interests to those of the collective. In all but the most tightly-knit workgroups, however, there is likely to be some conflict between the steward's perception of the interests of his constituency as a whole and the individual members' definitions of their own interests. 'Leader' stewards are also likely to seek to maintain a good bargaining relationship with managements. The problem here is that regular contact with management tends to introduce a quasi-managerial element into the steward's role. We have already noted the tendency for experienced stewards to act as a 'filter' for grievances and to pursue only those issues which they themselves think are worth pursuing. The quasi-managerial aspects of the steward's role are reflected in the large majority of employees who, in the 1972 Survey of Workplace Relations, thought their stewards normally took a 'fifty–fifty' view between management and workers' opinions. Less than one third of the sample thought that he normally expressed the workers' view. The obvious danger is that a 'leader' steward may become too remote from his members, particularly in workplaces where the steward organization is well developed and full-time posts are provided. The 1972 Survey, for example, disclosed that a significant minority of stewards often have difficulty in carrying their members with them. Some 46 per cent of the stewards in the sample said that they were unlikely to get their members to agree with them on a wage issue; 33 per cent said that they could not get their members to accept a management proposal; 23 per cent said that they were unlikely to get their members to agree with them on an hours of work issue; and 16 per cent said they could not get the support of their members to raise an issue with management. Sometimes this lack of support may be due to the fact that the steward's view of a given issue is more 'militant' than that of his constituents, but at other times he may find himself urging caution and 'moderation' upon them, only to have his advice rejected.

These and other findings suggest that a crucial constraint on the power of any shop steward is the extent of the collective *awareness* among the workers he represents. If a steward is to receive the full and active support of his members, they themselves must have at least some awareness of those issues which divide them from management and must also grasp the opportunities for advancing their interests through collective action. Awareness implies both a recognition that real conflict exists and a willingness to take some kind of action. A shop steward can do a great deal to stimulate such awareness and it is in this role that 'leaders' are likely to distinguish themselves from 'populists'. But awareness is also a function of other factors, notably the organization of the work itself and the behaviour of management. In some workplaces the technology, the reward system and the pattern of social relationships all combine to produce an environment in which collective consciousness evolves from and is reinforced by the experience of work. In others, by contrast, work may be organized in such a way that employees are more aware of themselves as individuals and do not instinctively identify with their fellows, Batstone *et al.*, for example, found such a contrast between on the one hand, manual workers in machine shops and assembly shops and, on the other, white collar staff in non-manufacturing workplaces.

Management may also influence bargaining awareness simply by the extent to which it allows conflicts to arise which are then resolved by collective bargaining. A failure on the part of management to diagnose and remedy a grievance may well both heighten the workers' sense of dissatisfaction and increase their determination to do something about it. If the grievance is then resolved through collective action, the bargaining awareness of the group will be permanently enhanced. If the steward has taken the lead in bringing his members' claim to the attention of management and negotiating an acceptable solution, his authority as their representative will be strengthened. Consequently when the next issue arises they may be more prepared to follow his guidance. If, by contrast, he raises their expectations, takes the claim to management and is then compelled to accept a settlement which falls short of what he started out to achieve, not only will his personal authority be weakened but the collective awareness of his constituents may decline. If the steward himself lacks an awareness of what can realistically be achieved through collective bargaining, he is unlikely to be able to control his members and maintain consistent pressure on management. He may also be 'caught napping' by management and fail to challenge managerial decisions which threaten the interests of his members. A workgroup which ultimately discovers that one or more of its interests has been 'sold down the river' may then react explosively.

The main conclusion to be drawn from recent research is that most shop stewards do not conform to the popular stereotype of the aggressive, strike-happy, barrack-room lawyer. More than a decade has elapsed since the Donovan Commission asserted that:

> Trouble is (often) thrust upon them. In circumstances of this kind they may be striving to bring some order into a chaotic situation, and management may rely heavily on their efforts to do so. . . . Thus shop stewards are rarely agitators pushing workers towards unconstitutional action. In some instances they may be the mere mouthpiece of their workgroups. But quite commonly they are supporters of order exercising a restraining influence on their members in conditions which promote disorder.[8]

Subsequent investigations have developed and refined these conclusions but their substance remains the same. Stewards have a vital interest in negotiating with management a framework of rules which will influence managerial behaviour in the immediate work situation. By imposing a measure of predictability on managerial behaviour and stabilizing the frontier of joint control, they also seek to control the behaviour of their own members. Where they are successful, 'order' prevails. But it is also clear that many stewards must encounter and dispose of several obstacles before they succeed in imposing their authority over their members.

The steward's authority is a function first of his awareness of the issues which are important to his members, second of his skill in pushing those issues to a successful conclusion in negotiations with management, and third of his commitment to a body of principles which in turn legitimize his activities in the eyes of his members. Awareness depends partly on the quality of the day-to-day communication between the steward and his members and partly on the steward's instinctive sense of what can and what cannot be achieved through collective bargaining. The effective steward is far more than a mere delegate. Occasionally he may be obliged to tell his members that what they are seeking cannot be achieved. Conversely, in certain circumstances he may need to shape and direct the feelings of his members so that an opportunity to advance the frontier of joint control is not allowed to slip by. The task of persuading workers to do something that they would not otherwise do, or accept something that has hitherto seemed unacceptable, is never easy. Without some ideological points of reference, however, the steward is likely to find the task virtually impossible. Ideology means far more than a simple belief on the steward's part in the policies and objectives of his own trade union. It involves adherence to the principles of unity, equity, mutuality and predictability, without which the steward has nothing to guide him but the immediate wishes of his members at any given moment. A steward's authority is, therefore, a function not only of the role he performs but also of his own personal characteristics, beliefs and skills. It follows that when one steward is replaced by another, whatever authority the former had does not pass automatically to the latter. Authority has to be achieved, primarily by winning the confidence of the steward's constituents and also of management. Once leadership has been achieved, a heavy responsibility rests on the steward. In the eyes of his members he *is* the union, and the continuing strength of the workplace organization depends very much on his efforts.

The closed shop

Two important elements in the strength of any workplace organization are the level and the stability of union membership. The most effective way in which a union can achieve both high and stable membership in a given workplace is to maintain a closed shop. This may take the form of a 'pre-entry' arrangement whereby a worker must be a paid-up member of a specified union *before* commencing employment; alternatively the closed shop may be of the 'post-entry' kind, under which a worker is required to join a specified union within an agreed period of time after starting his employment. Recent research suggests that the vast majority of existing agreements are of the post-entry variety. Only in industries where traditional craft skills are still significant (as, for example, in printing, shipbuilding and steel) or in those where there are special circumstances (as in entertainment and merchant shipping) are pre-entry closed shops commonly encountered. In the engineering industry, pre-entry arrangements are relatively common in those departments (for example, the toolroom) which are composed exclusively of craftsmen, whereas unskilled and semi-skilled workers are much more likely to be covered by post-entry agreements. Elsewhere, however, pre-entry closed shops are relatively rare. Another significant difference between pre-entry and post-entry agreements is that the former are likely to be unwritten and informal whereas the latter tend to be formalized and documented.[9]

In Chapter 2, we noted that over the past decade there has not only been a significant growth in closed shop agreements but also that many customary, unwritten arrangements have been formalized. In the early 1960s McCarthy estimated that while approximately 3.7 million trade unionists were covered by a closed shop arrangement of some kind, only one fifth of this number were subject to a formal agreement.[10] By the end of the 1970s the closed shop probably covered about 5 million workers with well over half this number being subject to formal arrangements. We must account, therefore, both for the physical growth of closed shops and for the recent tendency to formalize customary practices. In each case the main causal factors are not difficult to identify. The spread of post-entry closed shops into new areas of employment, particularly those in which white collar workers are dominant, reflects the growing competition between unions for members and bargaining rights. A union which has a closed shop agreement has a strong institutional defence against attempts by a competitor to invade its territory. Managements also have an obvious interest in avoiding inter-union competition and there is no doubt that many have responded positively to union pressure for a closed shop with the threat of multi-unionism in mind. In this sense the closed shop can act as a powerful stabilizing influence in the workplace and can thereby strengthen the framework of union and management *control.* It gives branch or workplace officials an effective sanction against individual members who refuse to observe collectively agreed rules or follow the accepted norms of behaviour in the workplace. It ensures that procedures cover all the workers within the bargaining unit and helps to remove the administrative anomalies which might otherwise result from the presence of a sizeable non-union minority. Finally, it removes what may be an underlying source of irritation in the workplace, namely the resentment felt by the majority of union members against the 'free-riding' minority of non-members who benefit from the efforts of the union but refuse to accept the obligations of membership. For all these reasons, the introduction of a closed shop may be associated with the planned improvement of industrial relations in a given workplace.

Despite this element of growth, it is generally recognized that many of the agreements which have been negotiated since 1974 represent the formalization of *de facto* closed shops dating back to the 1960s or earlier. This formalization is partly due to the intervention of the law, which has in general encouraged the parties to become more conscious of the need for careful drafting and explicit terminology. In the famous 'Ferrybridge Six' case (1976), for example, an industrial tribunal held that a decision to dismiss an employee in order to enforce a closed shop agreement would be legally valid *if* the membership requirement was imposed consistently on all employees to whom the agreement applied.[11] The decision reminded employers that it was very much in their interest first to commit closed shop agreements to writing, second to define explicitly which groups or grades were covered by the agreement, and third to ensure that one hundred per cent membership was actually maintained in those groups. But some formalization would have occurred regardless of the law, if only because post-entry closed shops are administratively more difficult to operate than the pre-entry variety.

The first problem is for the parties to agree on how much time new employees should be given to join the union and what grounds should be allowed for non-membership. The most common time limit within which a new entrant must either join the union or claim exemption seems to be one month, while the majority of exemption clauses follow the prevailiing legal requirements. Under the terms of the Employment Act 1980, however, a large number of exemption clauses follow the prevailing legal requirements. Under the terms of religious objections. Other grounds for exemption which are not mentioned in any statute but often appear in union membership agreements are designed to accommodate employees who have part-time or temporary status, those who are apprentices or trainees, those who belong to unions which are not specified in the agreement and, finally, those who occupy managerial or some other key or specialist posts. In practice, therefore, the requirement to join the specified union tends to be interpreted more flexibly than is often supposed by outside observers.

The second problem arises from the presence of employees who are members of trade unions which are not specified in the closed shop agreement. This is more likely to arise in the case of manual workers than in that of white collar staff and often involves individuals with long service. The general tendency is for the parties to take a tolerant view of non-specified union members where they are already employees but to be much less tolerant of new entrants who belong to non-specified unions. Some agreements also make provision for those employees who subsequently cease to be members of the specified union by recognizing their right to invoke the religious or 'conscience' clauses. In such cases, however, it is generally accepted that a considerable onus of proof rests on the individual concerned.

Third, the parties must resolve what is potentially a much more serious problem – namely that of existing employees who are not members of any trade union when the closed shop comes into force. The general response at first glance seems surprisingly liberal in so far as the right of existing non-members *to remain* non-members is frequently recognized. In fact, however, many union representatives take the view that, so long as management encourages non-unionists to join, they themselves are prepared to forego 100 per cent membership in the short term in the expectation that, as non-members retire or leave, this objective will gradually be realized. Finally, the parties must decide whether to establish special machinery through which disputes arising over the interpretation of the agreement can be resolved. Clearly much will depend on the size of the establishment and the complexity of the agreement, but the evidence suggests that there is a trend towards providing for independent arbitration.[12]

If injustices are to be avoided, closed shops must be consistently enforced by both managements and trade unionists. Neither side can turn a blind eye to some non-members and simultaneously dismiss (or, in the union's case, press for the dismissal of) others. Since the most common way in which an employee ceases to be a union member is to fall into arrears with his subscriptions, more and more employees and union representatives have in recent years negotiated 'check-off' agreements. According to the TUC, some 50 per cent of all union members are now covered by check-off agreements, under which the subscriptions of union members are automatically deducted from their pay packets by the employer. A check-off system can operate whether a closed shop exists or not, and unions frequently press for one as part of the initial recognition agreement. There are advantages to both sides in having a check-off system. From the union's point of view, it saves a great deal of time and trouble in so far as it enables stewards and branch officials to devote themselves to more important matters. From management's point of view, it removes a potential source of conflict on the shop floor, especially where a closed shop exists.

In summary, there is no doubt that, despite all the twists and turns of the law, the closed shop has become a more widespread and deeply rooted feature of workplace relations over the past decade. It is certainly misleading to regard the law as the critical factor in this development, although it may well have encouraged the formalization of existing arrangements. The real causes must be sought in the need to strengthen the institutional framework of joint control in the workplace and in the need for predictability in union-management relations. This does not necessarily mean that the closed shop will continue to grow at the same rate over the next decade. The provision in the Employment Act that the introduction of a closed shop must be approved by 80 per cent of those to whom it applies will undoubtedly slow down its expansion. The closed shop also continues to arouse deep emotional opposition not only among many employers but also within large sections of the workforce. Nevertheless, in those workplaces where union organization is relatively advanced and high levels of membership are customary, there may well be strong pressure for a closed shop which management will find difficult to resist.

The substance of workplace control

Our analysis has so far concentrated on the sources of control in the workplace and on the institutional framework through which control is exercised. Control is, of course, the outcome of a process involving the use of power. Managers and workgroups seek to apply the power they have at their disposal in order to influence the outcome of the rule-making process in the workplace. The power which each side has, however, is determined by factors such as the technology employed in the workplace, the size of the establishment, the nature of the labour market in which the establishment operates and the way in which pay levels are determined. The changes which have occurred in the balance of control in the workplace over the past half century or so have been seen as the outcome of technological, market and structural changes which have in turn influenced the expectations and attitudes of workers and managers alike. These developments in themselves, however, do not provide a comprehensive explanation. One can certainly quote them in support of the proposition that the *scope* for enhanced control by workgroups over the rule-making process has increased. The extent to which this scope has in practice been realized, however, depends on a range of factors which are more specific to individual workplaces. Under this heading we have briefly discussed the importance of workplace organization and the role of the shop steward. The general point which needs to be emphasized is that, in a given workplace, the extent to which workgroups actually use the power at their disposal depends on their awareness of how it might be used and on the effectiveness of the way in which they organize themselves for the purpose of using it. It is in this context that the role of the shop steward, the sophistication of the steward organization and institutions such as the closed shop need to be seen.

We must now examine in more depth the kind of issues which workgroups and their representatives in practice seek to control. It would be useful to remind ourselves at the outset, however, that control may be exercised either unilaterally or jointly. A workgroup may, for example, determine its own level of output and speed of work within whatever system of incentives and controls management has imposed on the group. These work norms will be informal and unwritten and will be maintained by social sanctions which emphasize the need for every group member to conform to the group's customary standards of fairness and reasonableness. Assuming that management is aware of these norms, it can either tacitly accept them or seek to change them. In organized workplaces where some form of joint regulation has been established, it is likely that management will be obliged to approach the problem of changing these informal, unilateral rules through the process of bargaining. Whatever emerges from this process will carry the status of a jointly determined rule or set of rules which are likely to be more formal in nature than those they have replaced. Alternatively, the focus of the bargaining process may be a rule which has traditionally been determined and imposed unilaterally by management and which workgroups no longer find acceptable. Either way, the issues determined unilaterally by both sides are brought within the scope of joint regulation and, through the negotiating process, are changed in ways which reflect the resolution of conflicting interests and aspirations. In simple terms, therefore, the growth of workplace bargaining over the post-war period may be regarded as symptomatic of the gradual displacement of unilateral rule-making by joint regulation.

In our previous discussion of this topic, however, considerable emphasis was placed on the influence of employee attitudes and expectations over the character of workplace control. We therefore need to analyse those issues over which employees and their representatives actually exert a measure of control. Following on from this, we must ask whether employees are broadly satisfied with the degree of control they currently exert over these issues and, in addition, whether there are issues over which employees have little or no control but aspire to gain it.

One of the most significant developments in the post-war period was the growing popularity among semi-skilled and unskilled workers of the idea that the performance of a job establishes certain 'property rights' in it for the job-holder. In a major study of strikes in the motor car industry, Turner *et al.* observed that many stoppages represented an attempt by workgroups to impose more control over their immediate environment. Some strikes occurred in protest against the unstable levels of both earnings and employment in an industry which was unusually vulnerable to sharp fluctuations in consumer demand; some occurred in reaction to the inequities and anomalies of the incentive payment systems commonly used in the industry; others arose in defiance of managerial decisions to dismiss or suspend individual employees.[13] The significance of this development may be fully realized when set against the traditional right of management to determine the 'work' side of the wage–work bargain. As the Webbs observed:

> When an additional 'hand' is taken on in a manufacturing establishment, practically the only point explicitly agreed upon between him and the foreman is the amount of weekly wage, or possibly the scale of piece-work rates. How many hours he shall work, how quickly or how intensely he is to exert himself, what intervals will be allowed for meals, what fines and deductions he will be subject to . . . the noise, the smell and the dirt, the foreman's temper and the comrades' manners – all this has to be taken for granted, it being always implied in the engagement that the workman accepts the conditions existing in the employer's establishment and obeys his lawful commands.[14]

The experience of full employment in an assembly line industry, reinforced and articulated by an increasingly sophisticated shop stewards' organization, enabled non-craft workgroups to challenge the tradition of unilateral regulation by management in that industry. The reluctance of management to recognize the legitimacy of this 'challenge from below', however, prevented any agreement on where the sphere of unilateral regulation ended and that of joint control began. Thus the Donovan Commission concluded that the frequency of unofficial strikes in the motor industry over issues such as working arrangements, rules and discipline, redundancy, dismissal and suspension 'indicates that there is considerable confusion as to what management does and does not have the right to do; or, where it is conceded to have the right, whether it is or is not making reasonable use of it'.[15]

At the time of the Donovan enquiry it was widely believed that the best way of recognizing and defining the frontier of joint control lay in the extension and formalization of collective bargaining at plant and company level. A blueprint for action was already to hand, namely the well-publicized productivity agreements negotiated in the early 1960s between management and union representatives at Esso's

Fawley refinery. The Fawley agreements suggested that even craftsmen could be persuaded to change their customary work rules if the frontier of joint control was formally extended to include the work side as well as the wage side of the effort bargain. The central theme running through these agreements was that radical improvements in pay and job security could be achieved only if the productivity of the labour force, particularly that of craftsmen, was significantly raised.[16] Higher productivity, however, was in turn dependent on the acceptance of rule changes designed to intensify the use of manpower, such as reductions in manning levels and the removal of traditional demarcation barriers. The concept of *quid pro quo* bargaining on working practices assumed that workgroups in general and craftsmen in particular would be prepared to 'sell' their customary, unilateral controls over their work if the price was right. This, it was argued, would open up a whole range of customary rules to managerial influence while formally conceding the right of the workforce, acting through their representatives, to determine rules jointly with management. The outcome would be a strengthening of managerial authority and an attack on workplace 'anarchy':

> The paradox, whose truth managements have found it so difficult to accept, is that they can only regain control by sharing it. . . . Co-operation demands first and foremost the progressive fusing of two systems of unilateral control – which now exist in conjunction and frequently in conflict with each other – into a common system of joint control based on agreed objectives.[17]

In this way productivity bargaining in the Fawley style was seen as a means of reconciling management's need for greater efficiency with the workers' desire for more democracy.

In the event the arguments so fervently marshalled in favour of productivity bargaining failed to generate the anticipated momentum in the workplace. To some extent, of course, the concept of productivity bargaining was devalued by its close association with the various phases of incomes policy between 1967 and 1970. It soon became accepted practice for shop stewards to 'trade' relatively minor concessions on working practices in return for above-the-norm wage increases. The comprehensive, 'package deal' approach which characterized the Fawley agreements was relatively rare after 1967. But this was due not only to the pressures of wage restraint but also to a fundamental flaw in the logic of productivity bargaining itself. Advocates of the extension and formalization of collective bargaining in the workplace usually perceived the existence of unilateral worker controls in wholly negative terms. Incentive schemes which had slipped out of management's control were seen as 'inflationary' and 'chaotic'; customary rules on manning standards and demarcation were labelled 'restrictive practices'; overtime enjoyed by workgroups on a custom and practice basis was held to be 'unnecessary' and 'inefficient'; informality was seen as a breeding ground for uncertainty and conflict. Surely, it was argued, workers would realize how much their general terms and conditions could be improved once these out-dated practices had been abandoned? Would they not be open to persuasion by rational argument? Unfortunately for the reformers, many workers are guided by a different rationality. Seen from a shop floor perspective, many 'disorderly' and 'inefficient' practices are an eminently sensible response to a hostile environment. The only source of intrinsic satisfaction which is open to many employees lies precisely in the informal, unilateral controls which they exert as a matter of habit over their work and their immediate working environment.

Another fundamental error made by reformers of the Flanders–Donovan school was to assume that workers would willingly abandon the informal, 'non-legitimate' controls which they had hitherto exerted as individuals in favour of the formal, 'legitimate' controls which would henceforward be exercised by their own union representatives on their behalf. As we noted above, the norms and aspirations of shop stewards do not necessarily represent the sum total of what each of their constituents needs and wants as an individual. The way in which stewards, especially 'leader' stewards, perceive problems is often significantly different from the perception of the workers they represent. The 'reform' of a decadent piece-work system, for example, often throws these differences into sharp relief. Brown observed that piece-work systems which have degenerated to the point where they are controlled largely by the informal customs and practices of the workforce 'breed and nurture the inequities, the disunities, the uncertainties and the poor bargaining relationships which are anathema to the steward's implicit principles'.[18] Yet what may appear to be a source of disunity and inequity when considered from a collective viewpoint may also be the principal means through which individual workers can improve their effort bargains and expand their personal control over their work. Indeed, Brown reported that as piece-work systems become subject to custom and practice, so the individual worker is more able to reduce fluctuations in his earnings and increase his own bargaining power. This finding no doubt helps to explain why so many attempts to replace piece-work with 'orderly' and 'rational' time-based payment systems have failed to live up to the expectations of managements and academic reformers alike.

The reform of custom and practice rules and their formalization in written agreements is in fact a much more complex process than the Donovan Commission envisaged. Donovan, it will be recalled, advocated the formalization of unwritten understandings and customs on the grounds that this would extend and legitimize joint regulation and thereby remove uncertainty about the rights and obligations of both sides. Yet the commission also conceded that there was widespread satisfaction on both sides of industry with the tradition of informality. It did not explore the reasons behind this paradox nor did it examine the implications for the management of change on the shop floor. It specifically failed to realize that conflict may occur between shop stewards and their constituents when customs and practices are formalized. The concept of formalization is likely to appeal strongly to many stewards since in practice this usually involves an extension in the substantive scope of manager–steward bargaining. The more sophisticated the steward organization the more committed it is likely to be to formalization. In Brown's words:

> An integrated shop steward body develops a predilection for explicit negotiation with management. In doing this it can engage in the creation of fresh rules of job regulation in a deliberate, intentional way and can deploy its sanctions economically and with maximum effect. By formalizing plant level negotiations, management effectively deepens the recognition it gives to its employees' trade union organisation. It reinforces the procedural position of the stewards and, if any plant agreements negotiated between them are written down, the stewards' position is reinforced further.[19]

But while formalization may enhance the stewards' bargaining relationship with management, it may also weaken their position *vis-à-vis* their own members. When formalization comes about through management–steward negotiation, the rules themselves may not change very much but the focus of the *authorship* will move away from the workers themselves. They will in future be regarded as 'management–steward rules' and the workers' commitment to them will be weaker. But since the process of formalization is itself a bargaining process, requiring a degree of compromise on both sides, it is more than likely that at least some of the rules *will* be changed.

This will tend to weaken the commitment of rank-and-file workers to the formalized rules. It is hardly surprising, therefore, that in workplaces where significant formalization has occurred, informal rules either have never really disappeared or have soon begun to creep back again.[20]

The post-Donovan enthusiasm for formalizing workplace rules and extending joint control at the management–steward level has been replaced in recent years by a growing interest in the needs and aspirations of the individual worker. Much of this interest has, of course, been motivated by the debate on worker participation and by the need to 'prove' that most workers are simply not interested in the more ambitious schemes for power-sharing in industry advocated by the TUC and the Bullock Commission. Nevertheless, the results of recent investigations are relevant in the present context. They suggest that most workers want to extend their control over the work situation only in those areas where this control is already well developed. They also suggest that workers regard control as relevant and desirable only when it closely relates to their own jobs. Not surprisingly, researchers have found relatively high levels of worker influence over substantive issues such as payment systems, hours of work, the pace of work, grading and seniority arrangements and work study methods, as well as a strong interest on the part of workers in strengthening their influence in these areas.[21] This apparent desire to extend worker autonomy does not necessarily imply a rejection of management's 'right to manage' nor does it suggest that there is a widespread demand for unilateral control by trade unions. What is does indicate, however, is that many workers would like more direct consultation, and perhaps some negotiation with management on those issues which are closely bound up with their own jobs and on which they feel have a contribution to make. The authors of a recent study of participation in the British Steel Corporation, for example, found that many workers and indeed shop stewards regarded 'participation' as a means of improving efficiency in the sense that workers should be given more freedom to exercise their skills and abilities, based as they were on a level of knowledge and experience which they regarded as superior to management's.[22] By the same token, no recent survey of worker opinion has indicated that there is much interest in extending shop floor control to issues such as pricing policy, investment and profit distribution, all of which are regarded not only as remote from the work situation but also as the proper and sole responsibility of management.

An equally significant conclusion which emerges from recent research is that the growth and assertion of worker control over job-related issues has been fundamentally *reactive* in character. The notion that most British managers are bound hand and foot by union rule books and restrictive practices simply has no basis in fact. In many workplaces, the vast majority of managerial decisions on the work side of the wage–work bargain, such as the determination of output targets, the flow of work, the introduction of new production methods and the hiring and firing of labour, are rarely if ever challenged directly by workgroups or their representatives. Even where some kind of formal resistance is organized, the focus of the conflict is more likely to be the effects of a management decision or the possible alternatives to that decision rather than the reasons behind it or the right of management to take it. The general pattern is rather one of *adaptation* by the workforce to rules which are determined predominantly by management. In workplaces where the shop steward organization is relatively advanced, where the bargaining awareness of the workforce is well developed, and where the technology enables workgroups to exert a measure of coercive power in a direct and immediate way, collective resentment may take an overt form. But, as Marchington has observed,

> . . . even in well-organised plants, reaction can be no more than adaptation; for a steward it is very much a case of accommodating decisions and manipulating them to the extreme so as to protect the interests of his members. . . . Work priorities become adapted to the possibilities available and, for most individuals, priorities centre around effort and reward, good working relations and a satisfying job. When we have written of an employee 'controlling the line', this does not mean that he can decide whether there should be a line or not, but rather that he exerts greater control over the line than his immediate superior(s). Control, therefore, has always to be used as a relative term.[23]

By adapting managerial rules to suit their own needs and priorities, workgroups gradually develop for themselves a web of customs and practices which in total represent a measure of control over the work situation.

Procedures and workplace control

The argument so far suggests that workgroups and their representatives are more likely to react against the effects of a managerial decision than they are to challenge the decision itself. When open conflict does occur, the main causal factor is often the *way* in which a decision has been taken. Shop stewards may well be consulted by management before a final commitment is made to a particular course of action but find themselves ignored or bypassed and therefore feel obligated to stage some kind of protest. Workers themselves may react spontaneously to a managerial decision which arbitrarily interferes with an established norm or practice on the shop floor. It is at this point that the argument will focus on the observance of the existing framework of procedural rules in the workplace.

It will be recalled that a major theme in the Donovan Commission's strategy for restoring 'order' to workplace relations was the formalization of procedures covering areas such as collective disputes, individual grievances, discipline and redundancy. Formalization was advocated in the belief that it would compel managers and stewards to negotiate an agreed framework of rules at workplace level in which the rights and obligations of both sides were clearly articulated. Each procedure agreement would define precisely the scope of joint control and would thus remove the uncertainty which allegedly lay at the root of so many unofficial and unconstitutional strikes. The commission's recommendations, however, have not evoked the kind of response from managers or union representatives which was initially anticipated. It is certainly true that the pressures of legal regulation have encouraged many managements to negotiate formal procedures in areas such as union membership, discipline, redundancy and grievances. It is also the case that union recognition agreements are now much more likely to be written down than they were in the pre-Donovan years. But successive surveys of workplace procedures since the late 1960s have revealed a continuing and widespread attachment to informality in their use. It is also evident that the mere act of formalizing and clarifying procedural rules does not in itself make a breach of those rules by either side any the less likely.

The fundamental purpose of any procedure is to provide an orderly framework within which disputes can be resolved. It requires both sides to accept a code of 'Queensberry rules' in their day-to-day relationships. Consequently we may regard a system of procedures as a distinct social organization based on shared values and norms:

The desirability of peaceful settlement; the importance of observing the other party's expectations in respect of procedure; the restraints and conventions of social interaction which maintain an environment favourable to compromise; these are at once the pre-conditions and the consequences of successful conflict-regulation. In so far as there is normative agreement about these behaviours, it embodies a recognition by both sides that any immediate tactical advantage resulting from the violation of shared expectations would be outweighed by damage to the system within which they had hitherto accomplished satisfactory results.[24]

It was noted earlier that employers and trade union officials in Britain have traditionally attached overwhelming importance to the need for effective procedures for the resolution of collective grievances and disputes at industry level. It was also noted, however, that the extension of formal procedures within the enterprise itself to cover both collective and individual issues has been a very different proposition in so far as it has raised a number of unpalatable questions about the structure of power at this level.

The prerequisite of effective procedural relations is a recognition by both sides that their power to take action unilaterally must be voluntarily held in check. In other words there must be a moral commitment to a *shared* system of authority. For management, this raises the fundamental problem of control in so far as it implies that the right to manage the business is subject to the consent and co-operation, not simply the passive acquiescence, of the workforce and its representatives. For trade unions, there is also a problem of control, in the sense that officials and stewards must persuade their rank and file members that 'going through procedure' is as much in their interests as in management's. Two important influences on employee attitudes to procedure are, first, the *level* at which the rules are decided and, second, the degree of *involvement* which employees both directly and through their representatives have in deciding them. The Donovan Commission was, of course, quite right in pointing out the empty formality of industry-wide procedures, such as that in engineering, which assumed that those issues which remained in the workplace would be resolved unilaterally by management. The commission therefore concluded that the moral commitment of ordinary employees to procedure would be greatly strengthened if procedural rules were negotiated directly between managements and union representatives at plant and company level. In theory the strategy seems plausible. In practice, however, there remains a problem of ensuring that ordinary employees become involved in the rule-making process. As a social organization, a system of procedures at any level, whether industry, company or workplace, can develop its own set of values and loyalties. In Fox's words: 'The norms and values shared by the representatives of both sides in this social organisation may become almost as important in moulding their thought and behaviour as the requirements of their managerial or collectivity role.'[25] In other words, even where the parties are managers and shop stewards rather than employers' association and trade union officials, there is an inherent tendency for them to become immersed in the conventions and rituals of their procedural relations. It is hardly surprising, therefore, that on occasion, shop stewards, let alone full-time officials, may have great difficulty in persuading their members to observe the rules of the game.

The problems which union representatives may encounter in maintaining the moral commitment of their members to formalized rules have already been noted. It therefore comes as no surprise to find that some stewards are very reluctant to accept the formal limitations on their own discretionary power which are implicit in a jointly agreed procedure. In the case of disciplinary procedures, for example, many stewards still take the view that the maintenance of discipline is a managerial prerogative, and that for them to become directly involved in enforcing an agreed system of rules and penalties would be to compromise their own freedom to challenge a particular decision which their members regarded as unfair. Where collective issues are at stake, however, and especially where management is seeking to change a customary rule or practice, stewards may be more anxious to constrain managerial power in a formal way.

One of the most effective constraints is represented by the insertion of a *status quo* clause into the negotiating procedure. Broadly, a *status quo* clause commits management not to change a substantive rule affecting the interests of one or more workgroups until either the disputes procedure has been exhausted, or agreement has been reached with union representatives or, alternatively, the matter has been referred to third-party arbitration. At the time of writing it is probable that only a small minority of procedure agreements incorporate a formal *status quo* provision. The absence of such a clause, however, does not mean that management in practice has *carte blanche* to act, even if the relevant procedure agreement appears to give management wide discretion. In the engineering industry, for example, the national procedure agreement which was negotiated in 1898, and lasted up to 1972, contained a sweeping clause to the effect that the federated employers would tolerate no interference by trade unions in the management of their business. Yet, in a study of the way in which the engineering procedure operated during the 1960s, Hyman found that the formal rights assigned to management by the national agreement were often impossible to uphold in practice:

> A wide range of alterations in workshop practices can in reality be affected only by mutual consent; and the more powerful and self-assured the workers' organisation within the factory, the wider this range is likely to be. In consequence, the principle of *status quo* may operate even where the doctrine of managerial functions in theory applies. A company which is unable to obtain employee co-operation in an alteration will commonly refrain from exercising its formal rights for fear of provoking a stoppage or other sanctions.[26]

Both sides may in fact prefer to let *status quo* arrangements remain informal if only because formalization requires precise definition.

The extent to which a *status quo* clause actually restricts the power of management to act unilaterally depends to some degree on the precise wording of the clause. If the management is merely required to exhaust the established disputes procedure before implementing a substantive change, the only sanction which could ultimately prevent implementation is, of course, strike action. But even if a strike does take place, it may not be effective. If an arbitration clause is written into the *status quo* arrangement, each party must accept that the arbitrator's decision may go against its own interests. If, however, union representatives demand that management must reach *agreement* with them before an established rule is changed, then obviously management's freedom to innovate is considerably restricted. Consequently both sides may well prefer to avoid the problem of defining what *status quo* actually means for fear of having to accept a rule which reduces their freedom to manoeuvre. As long as there is a general understanding to the effect that customary practices will not be changed without some form of prior consultation or negotiation, the parties may prefer to judge every issue on its own merits and frame their responses accordingly. There will be some issues, for example a major reduction in the size of the workforce, on which shop stewards may well seek to impose a veto on management action, and others on which they may be content with only a ritual protest. A precisely defined *status quo* clause can therefore be seen as a threat to this flexibility. It must be reiterated, however, that *status quo* arrangements, whether formal or informal, merely enable the workforce and its representatives to react more effectively to managerial initiatives; in themselves they do nothing to extend the frontier of joint control into the formulation of policy options and initiatives by management.

Direct action

In conclusion, we need to discuss briefly the role of direct action by individual workgroups and the workforce as a whole in changing or maintaining the existing frontiers of control at workplace level. Direct action includes not only strikes but also the banning of overtime, 'working-to-rule', 'sit-ins', and threats to apply any of these sanctions. Popular reportage of industrial relations often infers that when workers take action, they almost invariably go on strike. Nothing, however, could be further from the truth. The 1973 Survey of Workplace Relations, for example, suggested that overtime bans are the most common form of industrial action and that both working to rule and threatening to strike are as common as striking itself. More recent research by the Department of Employment has underlined the uneven distribution of recorded strike activity and confirmed the belief that even in manufacturing industry many establishments are almost entirely strike-free. It would clearly be naive, however, to infer from the mere absence of recorded stoppages either that stoppages never occur or that other forms of direct action are not encountered in apparently strike-free establishments from time to time. Nevertheless, the focus of the present discussion is on the overt withdrawal of labour, on the grounds that this constitutes the most extreme and in certain circumstances the most effective form of direct action. A more comprehensive analysis of strike activity in Britain is offered in Chapter 6, but the following characteristics of stoppages are relevant to the present discussion of workplace relations.

A strike has traditionally been represented in popular reportage as a breakdown in the union–management relationship. A failure to settle a dispute by negotiation through the recognized procedure was – and to some extent still is – seen as a reflection on the parties themselves, and especially on the union representatives who call the strike. Shop stewards who lead a withdrawal of labour are particularly likely to attract general disapprobation if such action occurs before the relevant disputes procedure has been exhausted (that is, if the strike is 'unconstitutional') and the appropriate full-time officer has not formally signified the support of the union to which the strikers belong. The Donovan Commission shared this traditional perspective. The frequency of unofficial and unconstitutional strikes was attributed by the commission to the *absence* of formal, agreed rules. Once the appropriate rules had been negotiated, it was envisaged that only 'eccentrics or subversives' would seek to act in defiance of them. From what has already been said about the difficulties of formalizing custom and practice rules, it should be clear that the traditional view of the sanctity of procedures is extremely superficial. When issues arise on the shop floor, work-groups will tend to define them in their own terms, rather than those of a formal procedure, and take whatever action seems appropriate to them in those circumstances.

> Workers are involved in a developing situation which is, from their perspective, primarily parochial. They perform particular limited tasks in association with others whom they know, and they have a number of persons whom they know as individuals who represent, for them, management and union. The niceties of agreements and union constitutions are much less real or meaningful to them than, say, the fact that a machine is dangerous, one of their colleagues has been victimised, or a member of management is 'taking them for a ride'.[27]

In these circumstances the rules embodied in union–management procedures may simply be irrelevant.

This does not mean, however, that most of the strikes which occur on the shop floor are totally spontaneous outbursts of indignation or resentment against some aspect of the work situation or a particular management decision. Some undoubtedly do fall into this category. Recent research, however, has emphasized the importance of the shop steward's role in determining the way in which a particular grievance is processed. Stewards of the 'leader' variety share with full-time union officials the characteristics of 'managers of discontent'. As in normal day-to-day bargaining with management, 'leader' stewards will often seek to ensure that when a dispute occurs their members do not stumble into strike action or embark upon it frivolously without regard for the prospects of success. Even in relatively well-organized workplaces, strike action often requires a considerable degree of organization, and the task of mobilizing the necessary commitment on the shop floor falls to the steward hierarchy. The process of winning support may well involve a sustained attempt by the stewards to increase the bargaining awareness of their members, which may in turn involve the subordination of both individual and group interests to the perceived needs of the workforce as a whole. An issue which is of great significance to one particular group, and which the group itself is determined to resolve through direct action, may be of little apparent interest to the rest of the workforce. In the eyes of the stewards, however, the overriding trade union principles of unity and equity may be in jeopardy if the aggrieved group is allowed to take action unilaterally. Consequently the 'leader' stewards will be faced with the task of either dissuading the group from taking action or marshalling the support of other groups for such action. The course which is ultimately followed will therefore be decided first by the stewards' own perception of the importance of the disputed issue in relation to the other bargaining objectives that they happen to be pursuing, second by their estimate of the strength of feeling within the aggrieved group, and third by their assessment of the potential support for action among the rest of the workforce.

This argument assigns the dominant role in initiating strike action (and, by implication, all the other forms of direct action) in a given workplace to the shop stewards' organization. It is, of course, conceivable that those who believe in the 'agitator' theory of strikes will feel vindicated by the evidence that stewards can and occasionally do steer their members towards strike action. In reality, however, the stewards' ability to act as a 'manager of discontent' is subject to certain constraints. First, much depends on the strength of the workplace organization itself. Where the union plays a salient role in the work experiences of its rank and file members and effective leadership by the stewards has built up a strong collective consciousness, it may well be possible for the stewards to initiate, control and terminate industrial action in pursuit of certain agreed objectives. In other workplaces, however, a totally different set of circumstances may apply. Where organization is relatively weak, or where workgroups are accustomed to pursuing their own sectional interests regardless of the wider implications, or where the quality of steward leadership is poor, it may be difficult for the stewards either to initiate action or to control it once it has begun.

Second, much depends on the attitudes and aspirations of the rank and file members themselves. Contrary to popular belief (except perhaps in the small minority of workplaces where the strike has become endemic), most workers do not respond like Pavlov's dogs to calls for strike action by their stewards. If stewards seek to raise their members' bargaining awareness and win commitment to strike action, they may also be obliged to raise their members' aspirations and convince them that certain concrete objectives can only be achieved if direct action is taken. If, however, the substantive outcome of the strike falls a long way short of these targets, the credibility of the stewards may be seriously damaged. Alternatively, the collective consciousness and aspirations of the members may be raised to such a pitch that once the strike has begun the stewards lose tactical control over the course of events. The stewards may then find it difficult to persuade their members to return to work when their own experience tells them that the action has achieved its maximum effect in terms of management's response. Moreover, there are likely to be occasions when stewards would much prefer to resolve a dispute through negotiation with management, but a hard line by the latter leaves them with no alternative but to initiate some form of direct action. Even when such action has started and the steward is hoping for a more reasonable response from management, the latter may still refuse to make concessions. This will in effect force the steward to choose between trying to get his members to resume work and escalating the conflict. Alternatively, a group may feel so aggrieved over a particular issue that they take immediate action without even consulting the appropriate steward. Whether a dispute results in strike action and, if it does, the duration and size of such action therefore depends as much on the behaviour of workgroups and management alike as on that of shop stewards.

It follows that when we are considering the nature and extent of worker control over the rules of the workplace, and the action which workgroups can take in order to defend or increase their control, we cannot confine our attention to 'structural' factors and ignore the attitudes and behaviour of the individuals concerned. Technological and market factors no doubt determine the potential for collective action and help to explain why some groups have more scope for action than others. But structural variables do not explain differences in the extent to which bargaining power is actually used. Published studies of workplace relations indicate that the use of power is subject to a complex web of rules, traditions and understandings – mostly unwritten – which in general tend to restrain both aspirations and action. Workplace organization reflects the traditional structure of authority in industry in the sense that its purpose is reactive. Stewards and rank and file workers alike spend most of their time accommodating themselves to managerial decisions. The steward's perception of how best to adapt to managerial control may, however, differ from that of his members. He may think primarily in terms of negotiating more and more rules with management and thereby extending the scope of joint regulation in the workplace. His members may regard such rules as remote and irrelevant or perhaps even a threat to their own customary norms and practices. In their eyes the most effective method of adapting to managerial control may be simply to extend the scope of their own unilateral control over the job. It follows that we should be very sceptical of general blueprints for the 'reconstruction' of workplace relations which emphasize the need for formal, collectively negotiated rules covering every matter of substance. Informal, customary rules usually constitute a more effective check on management than any written procedure because these rules are the outcome of the workers' own day-to-day experiences on the shop floor. But even at their most effective, such rules only tend to affect managerial behaviour at the margins; they do not challenge the existing structure of power in industry. The *raison d'être* of collective activity in the workplace is the same as it has always been – to change, adapt and 'socialize' the rules and conditions laid down by management.

6 Collective bargaining

Collective bargaining has long been regarded as the principal activity, indeed the *raison d'être* of trade unions in Britain and elsewhere. Despite all the changes that have occurred in the economic and political context in which collective bargaining has been conducted over the past thirty years, the ideological commitment to it within the trade union movement remains extremely strong. The traditional assumption is, of course, that collective organization is essential if terms and conditions of employment are to be improved to a level which workers themselves regard as fair and reasonable. In the absence of collective bargaining, employees would be wholly reliant on the benign working of market forces and the good intentions of their employers. This deep-seated belief in voluntary organization and self-help encompasses all aspects of the wage–work bargain. Alternative systems of rule-making such as compulsory arbitration have been consistently rejected by trade unionists and employers primarily because collective bargaining permits both sides to retain the maximum degree of autonomy. In essence, a collective agreement, whether written or unwritten, represents a recognition by the parties that their interests are in conflict and that such conflict is best regulated by a system of jointly agreed rules and understandings. As the Donovan Commission observed, collective bargaining as practised in Britain provides 'a very high degree of self-government' in industry: 'Not only do managers and shop stewards have a considerable freedom from outside interference, but all work groups are given scope to follow their own customs and take their own decisions.'[1]

Why, therefore, has the voluntary principle been the target of so much criticism over the past two decades? The fundamental reason lies in the growing dichotomy between the style, structure and outcome of 'free' collective bargaining and the policy objectives of successive governments in their role as managers of the economy. Since 1945 all governments have sought in varying degrees to improve the underlying performance of the economy by direct intervention. Such intervention, however, has frequently foundered on the system of pay determination. In most industries outside the public sector wage and salary decisions are taken at more than one level, and in some industries the most important level of decision-making is the workplace itself. Governments, employers' associations and national union leaders may use all the moral authority at their command to influence the conduct and outcome of collective bargaining but the focus of power effectively lies beyond their control. Thus, while recognizing the benefits of the traditional system of voluntary regulation, the Donovan Commission asserted that these were increasingly outweighed by

> . . . the tendency of extreme decentralisation and self-government to degenerate into indecision and anarchy; the propensity to breed inefficiency; and the reluctance to change – all of them characteristics which become more damaging as they develop, as the rate of technical progress increases and as the need for economic growth becomes more urgent.[2]

In short, the commission argued that the traditional justification for the voluntary principle – the preservation of industrial peace through self-regulation – was no longer appropriate in the context of a 'managed' economy.

The commission pinpointed three characteristics of collective bargaining which it felt should be changed. First, the *style* of bargaining, especially at workplace level, was overwhelmingly informal and this, it was felt, tended to generate uncertainty. Second, the *structure* of bargaining was becoming increasingly decentralized and fragmented and was thus beyond the control of either managements or union officials. Third, the *autonomy* of the bargaining system reflected a deep-seated reluctance on the part of the bargainers themselves to recognize their responsibilities to the rest of the community. These defects should be remedied, said the commission, in a way which restored managerial control over the process of pay determination while recognizing the legitimacy of the demand for extended joint regulation from shop stewards. With the wisdom of hindsight we may now perceive the limitations of the commission's analysis and its prescription for reform. Nevertheless, the themes mentioned above provide a useful peg on which to hang an analysis of collective bargaining as it has developed since the Donovan era.

Bargaining styles

It was noted in the previous chapter that the Donovan Commission attached great importance to the contrast and indeed conflict between formal and informal bargaining in British industry. Britain, said the commission, had two systems of industrial relations – a formal system of official institutions and industry-wide agreements and an informal system of *ad hoc* bargaining in the workplace. The traditional system of bargaining over a narrow range of substantive issues at industry level assumed that all other employment rules in the workplace would be determined unilaterally by management with perhaps a limited degree of joint consultation. This assumption, however, was no longer valid. The rules embodied in many industry-wide agreements were being supplemented by a growing body of informal understandings and agreements negotiated by managers and shop stewards in the workplace. Moreover, said Donovan, the two systems were actually in conflict:

> The informal system undermines the regulative effect of industry-wide agreements. The gap between industry-wide agreed rates and actual earnings continues to grow. Procedure agreements fail to cope adequately with disputes arising within factories. Nevertheless the assumptions of the formal system will still exert a powerful influence over men's minds and prevent the informal system from developing into an effective and orderly system of regulation. The assumption that industry-wide agreements control industrial relations leads many companies to neglect their responsibility for their own personnel policies. Factory bargaining remains informal and fragmented, with many issues left to custom and practice. The unreality of industry-wide pay agreements leads to the use of incentive schemes and overtime payments for purposes quite different from those they were designed to serve.[3]

The only remedy lay in persuading both sides to stop pretending that they controlled behaviour in the workplace through the formal system and recognize the need for an extended and formalized system of collective bargaining at plant and company level.

The commission's faith in the efficacy of formalized, negotiated rules covering all matters of substance was criticized in the preceding chapter. The point which emerges from more recent research is that while there has undoubtedly been some formalization of procedures at plant and company level, reliance on informal methods and understandings remains widespread. Even in workplaces where the parties are well disposed towards formalization, it has been noted that informal arrangements are an integral part of procedural effectiveness.[4] Informality obviously meets a practical need, namely to achieve workable solutions to particular problems in the shortest possible time. It is also likely to be an essential factor in the development of a strong bargaining relationship between managers and 'leader' stewards, since this is likely to involve a great many off-the-record discussions and exchanges of confidential information which can never be recognized in a formal procedure. Stewards are likely to find it easier to raise issues which management may consider 'sensitive' (that is, a matter of prerogative) in an informal context than through the formal procedure where both sides will feel obliged to adopt more rigid positions. Even the operation of formal, industry-wide disputes procedures is characterized by a web of informal understandings which are essential to its effectiveness. In Hyman's words: '. . . the formal processing of issues through procedure is intimately connected with the far less formal aspects of bargaining; the use of procedure may provide the arena for off-the-record dealing, may be a bargaining gambit, or may provide a substitute for settling issues'.[5] In so far as it equated formality with industry-wide bargaining and informality with plant and company bargaining, the Donovan analysis grossly over-simplified the position. One cannot draw a clear distinction between formal and informal bargaining and imply that there is a simple choice between the two.

Does this mean therefore that the notion of two systems *in conflict* is erroneous? In manufacturing industry, where Donovan felt that the formal–informal dichotomy was most acute, the continual upward drift in earnings and the growth of unofficial, unconstitutional strikes may be viewed with grave concern by government policy-makers but not, apparently, by the parties themselves. In industries where national agreements establish only basic terms and conditions, neither managements nor shop stewards see anything untoward or illegitimate about 'filling in the gaps' through a mixture of formal and informal bargaining. Problems are more likely to arise in those industries and services (mainly in the public sector) where national agreements seek to impose comprehensive or standard terms and conditions on all establishments and workplaces. In these circumstances there is a strong possibility that the terms of a particular settlement at national level will conflict with the needs and priorities of one side or the other at local level. If this happens, the dissatisfied party may well try to adapt the rules and persuade the other party to accept modifications. Whether the bargaining or consultative process in which the parties engage is formal, informal or a mixture of both is of no great significance.

Bargaining structures

The 'two systems in conflict' theory has also been criticized on the grounds that it over-simplifies the structural characteristics of collective bargaining in Britain. The commission conceded that the formal system had more obviously ceased to apply in private manufacturing industry, especially engineering and motor vehicles, than elsewhere. It almost completely ignored those sectors in which national agreements had retained their authority and workplace bargaining was virtually non-existent, except for a passing reference to a few instances where industry-wide bargaining 'can and does establish effective pay structures'.[6] This analytical weakness clearly showed itself in the commission's failure to distinguish between multi-employer and single-employer agreements at national level – a distinction which has become increasingly significant since the Donovan era. This superficial approach produced the somewhat trite observation that henceforward industry-wide agreements should be confined to the regulation of standard hours, holidays and minimum wage rates. Consequently the commission's strategy envisaged that formal bargaining at plant and company level would and indeed should become the main focus of pay determination.

What, then, has happened to bargaining structures since the Donovan era? If we focus first on *levels* of bargaining within the manufacturing sector alone, it seems fairly clear that, while the significance of national agreements on pay between trade unions and employers federations (that is, multi-employer bargaining) has declined, the majority of workers are still affected by bargaining at more than one level. A survey by Daniel in 1975 of 250 manufacturing establishments with over 200 employees found that, while national bargaining still affected earnings levels in 49 per cent of workplaces, only 17 per cent of managers thought that this was the *most important* level as far as the earnings of their workers were concerned. Company or divisional bargaining occurred in 34 per cent of the sample and 20 per cent of the managers regarded it as the most important level, whereas plant or establishment bargaining occurred in 72 per cent and was considered to be the most important level by 55 per cent of the sample.[7] The survey may have understated the significance of industry-wide bargaining by excluding plants with less than 200 employees since dependence on nationally determined pay rates tends to diminish as the size of the establishment increases. It should also be emphasized that the extremely low levels of dependence on national bargaining which Daniel noted in engineering and metal-working may well have been changed by the agreement of 1979 which set a new national minimum rate for skilled men. Data from the New Earnings Survey suggests that in 1973, 24 per cent of male manual workers in manufacturing industry were affected by national agreements *only*, whereas 45 per cent were affected by various combinations of national, company, district and plant agreements.

An equally important aspect of bargaining structures, however, is the *scope* of the bargaining itself and here micro-studies have

Table 15 *Percentage of full-time adult employees in various public sector industries affected by a national collective agreement only, 1973*

Industry	*Full-time male manual*	*Full-time female manual*	*Full-time male non-manual*	*Full-time female non-manual*
Coal mining	98.1	—	100.0	65.7
Steel and iron	7.0	—	30.9	27.3
Gas, electricity and water	73.9	—	80.3	76.2
Railways	94.2	—	88.6	87.0
Port and inland water transport	23.1	—	17.3	—
Air transport	70.1	—	62.3	69.6
Postal services and communications	99.8	—	99.9	98.9
Education	55.5	57.5	82.8	85.7
Health	87.6	93.0	91.1	92.0
National government	70.4	75.7	98.0	98.6
Local government	63.8	72.9	83.1	77.1
All industries and services	40.6	36.4	39.6	48.1
All manufacturing industries	24.1	29.4	12.5	13.5
All non-manufacturing industries	57.3	48.5	52.0	55.7

thrown more light on structural change. It will be remembered that the Donovan Commission was particularly concerned with the steady upward drift in earnings which resulted from the operation of decadent incentive schemes and institutionalized overtime payments. The commission made the point that many workplace payment systems were out of control and not subject to collective bargaining between managers and shop stewards. Since the Donovan era, however, there seems to have been a pronounced move within the engineering industry away from piece-work and towards job-evaluated pay structures. One estimate suggests that the number of manual workers in manufacturing generally who are covered by job evaluation schemes doubled between 1968 and 1975, so that by the mid 1970s approximately half the manual workforce in this sector was so covered.[8] This negotiating activity has obviously occurred at company or plant level and represents a significant extension in the scope of collective bargaining between managers and shop stewards. It may also help to account for the fact that between 1966 and 1976 the number of full-time manual stewards in manufacturing rose from 1000 to 5000.[9] The structural importance of this development lies in the increased tendency for managers to protect their reformed pay structures from the potentially disruptive effects of multi-employer bargaining at national level.

Outside the manufacturing sector, however, national bargaining in general assumes far more importance. In the public sector (with the exception of the steel industry and the docks), national agreements on pay tend to determine a very high proportion of employees' earnings (see Table 15). Since the late 1960s an important shift has occurred towards local bargaining for manual workers in sectors such as local government. The initial impetus was provided by the former Prices and Incomes Board (1965–71) which urged the negotiation of local productivity agreements and work–study-based incentive schemes. As a result, in the local government sector, domestic bonus payments now contribute a very significant proportion of manual workers' earnings. In electricity and the railways, however, the trend has been in the opposite direction in so far as local incentive schemes have been abolished and workers are now almost totally dependent on national bargaining. Industry-wide bargaining on pay in the public sector, however, is fundamentally different from that in, say, engineering and metal-working in the sense that the unions negotiate with a *single* employer rather than an employers' federation, and the agreements made are both comprehensive in scope and 'tight' in construction.

There does not appear to be any desire to change this system on either side:

> . . . most public services are provided by large, centralised undertakings operating under parliamentary scrutiny with standardised administrative arrangements and accounting procedures, thus limiting the scope for local bargaining of both a formal and informal kind. . . . A few attempts have been made in recent years to break down the dominance of these industry level agreements but these have been fiercely resisted by management, with the tacit approval of the unions concerned.[10]

Not surprisingly, public sector bargaining is dominated by a relatively small number of large bargaining units which in turn means that the negotiators do much of their work in the full glare of national publicity.

In most public sector industries and services there is a long tradition of joint consultation at local level, although the formality and general effectiveness of this practice seems to vary considerably. As in the private sector, there has been a significant increase in the number of workplace representatives and it is reasonable to assume that joint consultation frequently shades imperceptibly into *de facto* bargaining. Consultation and bargaining, whether formal or informal, covers a wide variety of non-wage issues, including discipline, which are left to local discretion by the appropriate national agreement. There may also be consultation and perhaps some bargaining over the application of national pay agreements, while the operation of both domestic and national grievance and grading procedures provides ample scope for lay representatives to negotiate directly with management on issues affecting individual employees. Over the past decade the volume of this activity has almost certainly increased.

Turning back to the private sector, as a whole, we must note that some significant changes have occurred since the Donovan era in the way in which multi-employer bargaining is conducted. Brown and Terry have pointed out that most multi-employer agreements are of either the 'floor' or the 'safety net' variety.[11] Agreements of the 'floor' type establish minimum wage rates which, when increased, are passed on to all employees regardless of any additional earnings which the latter receive through company or plant bargaining. There has, however, been a tendency for employers to reduce the cost-inflationary effects of 'floor' agreements by transforming them into 'safety nets'. Where nationally agreed rates are regarded in this way, workers whose earnings are already well above the minimum do not necessarily receive the periodic increases in these rates. Indeed, in some industries employers have traditionally been free to implement or ignore increases negotiated at national level.

Another significant development is the tendency for very large employers in a variety of industries to break away from multi-employer bargaining. As a result of the rapid concentration which has occurred within many industries over the past twenty years, some companies have grown in size to the point at which the case for adopting a completely independent approach to collective bargaining has become very persuasive. At the other end of the spectrum there appears to have been an increasing tendency for small firms to join an employers' association. This development may be explained at least partly in terms of the growth in union membership in small firms, and may in turn account for the fact that, between 1950 and 1972, the density of coverage of manual workers by national agreements in both the public and the private sector increased from 48 per cent to 65 per cent.[12] The growing tendency for multi-employer bargaining to reflect the needs and interests of relatively small firms will probably encourage more large enterprises to establish their own autonomous bargaining arrangements in the future. The emergence of single-employer bargaining in the private sector is therefore likely to be a self-sustaining process.

Once a large firm has decided to break away from multi-employer bargaining, senior management must decide how they will organize themselves for bargaining purposes and, more specifically, what kind of bargaining structure will be appropriate to the needs of the organization. Many factors are likely to influence the final decision. Clearly the structure of the company itself, including the number, size and location of its establishments, the technology and payment systems employed, and the degree to which management decision-making is centralized or decentralized will be of considerable importance. Some large firms have developed most of their bargaining activity to the level of individual establishments while others have sought to negotiate comprehensive 'national' agreements covering all locations. There seems, however, to be a gradual movement away from quasi-autonomous plant or workplace bargaining towards more centralized structures in which the company itself is the dominant level of rule-making. Daniel, for example, noted that 'the only level which threatened to usurp plant bargaining was company or divisional negotiation'.[13] The potential significance of company-level regulation was underlined by the Donovan Commission in the following terms:

> Boards of multi-plant companies may prefer to negotiate company agreements rather than allow each factory manager to negotiate separately on his own. A company agreement will be more effective than a series of factory agreements in ensuring that the company's collective arrangements with the union is square with its personnel policies. The agreement will have to permit some scope to subordinate negotiating committees in each factory, especially since work practices are to be a subject of negotiation but . . . there is a fundamental difference between factory negotiations within the scope of present industry-wide agreements and factory negotiations within a company agreement.[14]

The trend in favour of developing company-wide pay structures and negotiating wage and salary agreements at this level is, of course, consistent with Donovan's declared objective of strengthening managerial control over earnings. Other issues of substance which tend to be included in company agreements are hours, holidays, fringe benefits and disciplinary rules. Clearly, however, there will always be a range of issues which are peculiar to the workplace and will no doubt continue to be resolved by a mixture of formal and informal bargaining at that level.

The pattern of strike activity

The structure of collective bargaining is largely responsible for the various changes in the pattern of strike activity in Britain which have occurred over the past few decades. Strikes should not normally be interpreted as a breakdown in collective bargaining, nor do they necessarily indicate procedural weaknesses. They are, in Clegg's words, a means of exerting pressure to achieve bargaining objectives, and bargaining structure 'determines where pressure is effective'.[15] As we noted in the previous chapter, strikes are by no means the only form of pressure which union negotiators bring to bear on management. The Donovan Commission, for example, observed that overtime bans were as frequent as strikes and that both threats to strike and working to rule were hardly less common. Daniel found a very similar pattern of multiple action, with strikes only marginally more common than other sanctions. The use of all kinds of collective sanctions should therefore be regarded as an integral part of the bargaining process, although in many workplaces they may still be virtually unused.

Before we examine the various factors which determine the pattern of strike activity in Britain, the main features of this pattern must briefly be described. Workplace surveys present a much more accurate picture of the real frequency of strike activity than do the statistics issued by the Department of Employment. The department attempts to record all 'stoppages of work due to industrial disputes' which involve ten or more workers and which last for at least one day. This definition, however, may well exclude about half the strikes which occur in manufacturing industry, when managers may for various reasons decide not to report stoppages to the department.[16] The Donovan Commission's conclusion is therefore likely to be as valid now as in the mid 1960s;

> . . . industrial disharmony manifests itself in overt action on the shop floor more frequently than the official statistics imply. Presumably the larger a stoppage is, the more likely it is to be reported and included in the official statistics . . . small stoppages, and the use of the various other forms of industrial pressure, occur a good deal more frequently than one might otherwise suppose.[17]

The pattern of recorded strike activity in Britain over the period 1958–78 is given in Table 16. The apparent stability of the number of recorded stoppages (with the exception of the sharp rise in 1968–70) masks an important change in the industrial pattern of strike activity. In 1958 the mining and quarrying industries accounted for about 75 per cent of all recorded strikes; by 1978 this proportion had fallen to just over 13 per cent. Over the past two decades almost every manufacturing industry has experienced an increase in strike activity. There is, however, no discernible trend in the number of working days lost. The sharp annual fluctuations in this figure reflect the incidence of large-scale disputes and these tend to be influenced by short-term factors.

When other indices are used, the apparent change in the industrial distribution of strikes looks rather less significant. Strike *frequency* may be measured by the number of strikes per 100,000 employees, and strike *incidence* by the number of working days lost per 1000 employees. Recent research by the Department of Employment suggests that over the period 1966–76, five industries (coal mining, docks, motor vehicles, shipbuilding and steel) accounted for about 25 per cent of stoppages and 33 per cent of working days lost, although

Table 16 *Strike activity in Britain, 1958–78*

Year	*Number of stoppages beginning in year*	*Number of workers involved in stoppages beginning in year*		*Aggregate number of working days lost in stoppages*
		directly ('000s)	*indirectly* ('000s)	('000s)
1958	2629	456	67	3,462
1959	2093	522	123	5,270
1960	2832	698	116	3,024
1961	2686	673	98	3,046
1962	2449	4297	123	5,798
1963	2068	455	135	1,755
1964	2524	700	172	2,277
1965	2354	673	195	2,925
1966	1937	414	116	2,398
1967	2116	551	180	2,787
1968	2378	2073	182	4,690
1969	3116	1426	228	6,846
1970	3906	1460	333	10,980
1971	2228	863	308	13,551
1972	2497	1448	274	23,909
1973	2873	1103	410	7,197
1974	2922	1161	461	14,750
1975	2282	570	219	6,012
1976	2016	444	222	3,284
1977	2703	785	370	10,142
1978	2471	725	276	9,405

they covered only 6 per cent of employees. In terms of both frequency and incidence, private manufacturing industry seems markedly more strike-prone than either the public sector or the private service sector, although major disputes involving public employees obviously have a considerable impact on the total number of working days lost.[18]

Within manufacturing industry, however, strike activity is very uneven in its distribution. In the period 1971–3, the department found that in manufacturing as a whole, strike activity was concentrated in a very small proportion of the 60,000 or so establishments employing eleven or more workers. In an average year, strikes were reported in only 2 per cent of establishments, although these accounted for 20 per cent of the manufacturing labour force. In three-quarters of manufacturing industries, at least nine out of ten establishments seem to have been strike-free. Even in the minority of establishments which reported strikes, some were obviously more strike-prone than others. Some 5 per cent of the establishments which experienced strikes accounted for 24 per cent of the total number of strikes and 67 per cent of the days lost. This concentration may well vindicate Donovan's view that in a small number of establishments an 'endemic' strike situation exists. The likelihood of strikes appears to be associated mainly but not exclusively with establishments of over 1000 employees. According to the department's survey, strike incidence rose from 15 days per 1000 employees in establishments employing 11–24 workers to 3708 in those employing over 5000 workers.[19] The relationship between establishment size and strike frequency, however, is less clear-cut. Bearing in mind the tendency for the department's figures to understate the number of stoppages and, in addition, the prevalence of other forms of action short of a strike, it would perhaps be misleading to assume that 'small' is invariably 'beautiful'.

The final and perhaps best-known characteristic of British strikes is that the vast majority of them – on average 95 per cent – are unofficial. In popular discussion, the term 'unofficial' has often been used in a way which implies that the workers involved in such stoppages have either broken the rules of their own union or ignored the advice of their full-time officers. In reality, however, the situation is much more akin to the Donovan Commission's description:

> Most [unofficial strikes] can concern issues arising at plant level which are not dealt with at all in agreements negotiated by union leaders. . . . In most cases trade unions adopt no official attitude to individual unofficial strikes, since the question seldom arises whether they should be treated as official or not. They commonly take place before any full-time union official at district level, let alone at headquarters, is aware that the problem exists and indeed . . . even senior shop stewards may have no forewarning. . . . In many trade unions there is no rule under which members are expressly forbidden to go on strike without prior authorisation. What the official attitude of the union should be to a strike begun without prior authorisation is a question which has to be considered only if the strike lasts long enough to make intervention by full time officials necessary or if there is a question of paying dispute benefit.[20]

The payment of strike benefit, however, does not arise in the case of the many stoppages which are too brief to be recorded and, of course, where the action taken falls short of a stoppage. The use of sanctions in workplace disputes is almost entirely in the hands of shop stewards and workgroups, and in all except serious and prolonged stoppages the question of official authorization is irrelevant. The trade unions which tend to be most involved in strikes are those which predominantly organize male, manual workers and are relatively large in size. Very few of the 400 unions with less than 10,000 members seem to get involved in strike action, and although the involvement of white collar unions has increased in recent years it is still at a much lower level than that of the large manual organizations.

Explaining the pattern of strikes

It would appear that the main purpose of striking is to bring pressure to bear on managements, employers' associations or governments in order to achieve one or more bargaining objectives. It is hardly surprising, therefore, that since 1966 disputes over pay have accounted on average for more than half of all strikes and about 80 per cent of working days lost, as Figures 1 and 2 show. It is always possible, of course, that many strikes have more than one cause and that the reason most commonly given for striking – pay – only masks a much more complex motivation. In Hyman's words:

> Since managerial control is legitimised in our culture, it is not surprising that acceptance of a wide area of managerial prerogative is one of the foundations of collective bargaining. Workers, too, cannot formulate explicitly those grievances which stem from the exercise of managerial control without questioning their very subjection to this control. The basic necessity that every strike must be settled means, moreover, that workers are obliged to specify their grievances in a form which permits resolution in *negotiation with employers.* Where workers' deprivations derive from their very status as employees, the requirements of the strike situation prevent this grievance from receiving articulation.[21]

These vaguely felt dissatisfactions are crystallized by shop stewards, as managers of discontent, into a set of precise, negotiable demands which both employers and their own members can understand.

Another reason why it may be unwise to draw too clear a distinction between wage and non-wage disputes is that many of the former are concerned with relatives and differentials. As we note later in this chapter, relativities are intimately bound up with social and

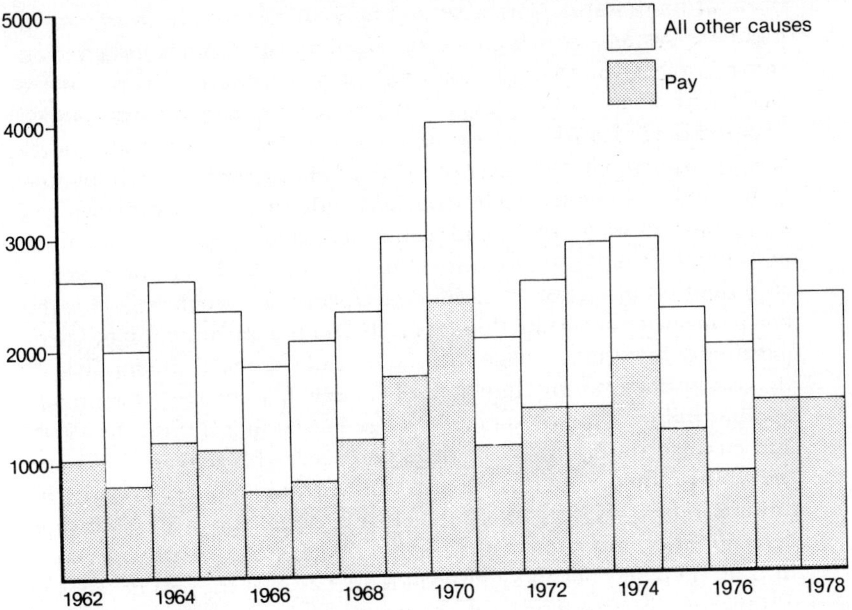

Figure 1 *Number of stoppages*

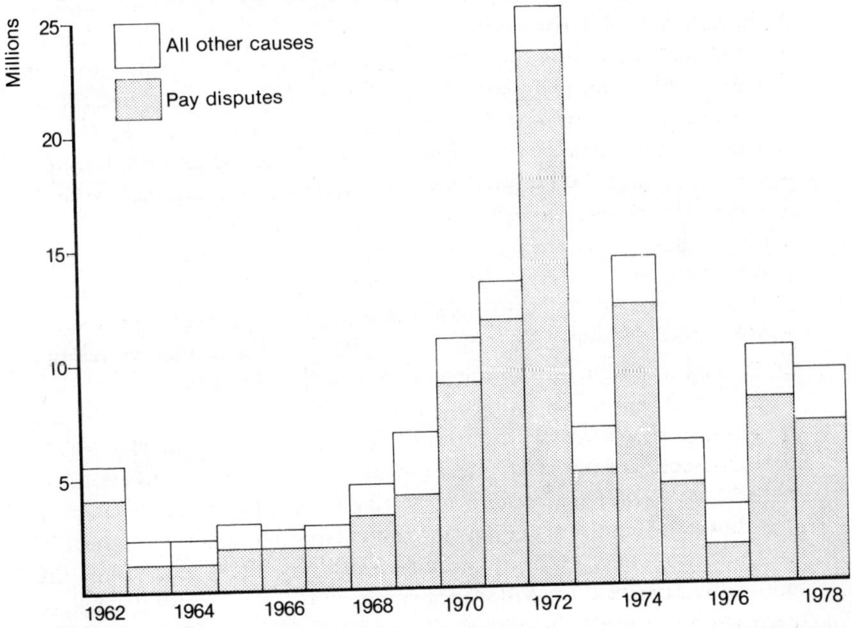

Figure 2 *Working days lost*

occupational status. The abandonment of piece-work in favour of payment systems which guarantee stability of earnings has enabled some groups, for example coal miners, to compare their pay more easily with that of other groups. In the mining industry the main focus of wage determination up to the 1960s was the colliery itself. Piece-work prices were settled according to the characteristics of individual coalfaces – a system which produced wide fluctuations in earnings and a pattern of strike activity which reflected the dissatisfaction of individual groups at particular pits. During the 1960s, however, a combination of factors including the closure of uneconomic pits, the mechanization of production methods and the introduction of fixed, nationally negotiated wage rates drastically reduced the number of strikes in the mining industry. The new payment system made comparability a major theme in wage bargaining during the 1970s and enabled the NUM to organize two successful strikes embracing the whole industry. In this sense it could be said that the change in the mining industry's bargaining structure brought the process of wage determination more into line with that of the public sector as a whole. Indeed, there has been a significant tendency over the past decade for groups of hitherto non-militant public sector employees to take industrial action in pursuit of grievances over pay relativities. Although strikes in the public sector are still far less common than in private manufacturing industry, when they do occur the structure of collective bargaining ensures that they involve large numbers of employees and a correspondingly large total of working days lost.

There can be little doubt, however, that since the late 1960s many pay disputes have originated not so much from dissatisfaction over relativities as from a more fundamental frustration with the failure of *real* incomes to grow in line with expectations. While this may be attributed in part to the tendency of a low-productivity economy to generate a wage–price spiral, an increasingly important factor since the late 1960s has been a *wage–tax* spiral. Under a progressive tax structure there is an automatic tendency for tax liabilities to rise more than in proportion to earnings – a process technically known as 'fiscal drag' – and all groups of employees have experienced a sharp increase in the effective rate of deductions from their earnings. For most manual workers, fiscal drag is a relatively recent experience. Turner *et al.* have shown that, whereas the typical manual worker was hardly liable for income tax until the late 1950s, by 1974 nearly half his income was taxed at the full standard rate.[22] But non-manual workers have also felt the effects of the falling threshold at which earnings are liable for income tax (see Table 17).

Table 17 *Relationship between earnings and income tax liability, 1971–9*

	1971–2	*1972–3*	*1973–4*	*1974–5*	*1975–6*	*1976–7*	*1977–8*	*1978–9*
Percentage of earnings[1] *taken in direct tax:*								
Quantiles of earnings[2]								
highest decile	19	18	20	21	25	25	23	23
upper quartile	16	15	17	18	22	22	20	20
median	12	11	14	15	19	19	17	18
lower quartile	8	7	10	10	15	15	13	14
lowest decile	3	2	5	66	11	11	9	10
Income tax threshold[3] as a percentage of median earnings	61	64	56	57	48	48	52	47
Median earnings (£ per week)	29.8	33.4	38.4	43.8	55.9	65.8	72.3	82.0

1. Of a married man with two children, aged 4 and 6, and with no income other than his earnings from full-time employment and family support

2. The earnings figures are derived from the *New Earnings Survey* (see Appendix, Major Surveys: New Earnings Survey). They relate to manual and non-manual workers in April at the start of each financial year.

3. Taking account of the effects of earned income relief where appropriate.

The wage–tax spiral was accelerated by fiscal drag during the 1970s once union negotiators realized that if the money wage increases of their members merely kept pace with the cost of living, the tax system would still cause a reduction in their real incomes. The obvious lesson was that money wage targets should be pitched at a level which ensured both a post-inflation and post-tax improvement in real terms.

In these circumstances it is hardly surprising that between 1965 and 1979 every government sooner or later found it necessary to resort to a formal incomes policy in order to restrain the inflationary 'push' of collective bargaining. Incomes policy undoubtedly has a short-term effect on both pay settlements (and therefore real incomes) and the level of strike activity. In those years when an incomes policy has been rigorously imposed (for example 1966–7, 1973 and 1975–6), the absolute level of strike activity measured by the number of working days lost has been comparatively low and the relative importance of disputes over pay has declined. Incomes policies, however, have succeeded in 'holding down the lid' on pay settlements for periods of one, two or exceptionally, three years only to be blown apart in the inevitable period of readjustment.[23] Since the 1960s there have been two periods, 1966–9 and 1975–7, in which incomes policy may well have reinforced the depressing effect of fiscal drag on real disposable incomes (see Figure 3). Union members who have felt increasingly dissatisfied with their real take-home pay have, not unnaturally, tended to blame incomes policy. The tax system lies beyond the reach of collective bargaining; incomes policy does not. Consequently the restraining effect of incomes policy on both strikes and real incomes sooner or later results in a major upsurge of strike activity over pay issues as union members and their representatives seek to make up the lost ground and, for a time, appear to be successful in doing so.

Two other variables may have an influence on short-term fluctuations in the level of strike activity, although the evidence is less clear-cut. An increase in aggregate union membership may lead to an increase in strike activity, especially if (as in 1969–70) union growth is itself the result of growing dissatisfaction with real take-home pay. We noted in Chapter 3 that economic factors were largely responsible for the upsurge in union membership among white collar workers and some groups of lower-paid manual workers which occurred at the end of the 1960s. It would therefore be surprising if this growth had not resulted in some increase in strike activity among these groups, however temporary this may have been. We also noted that

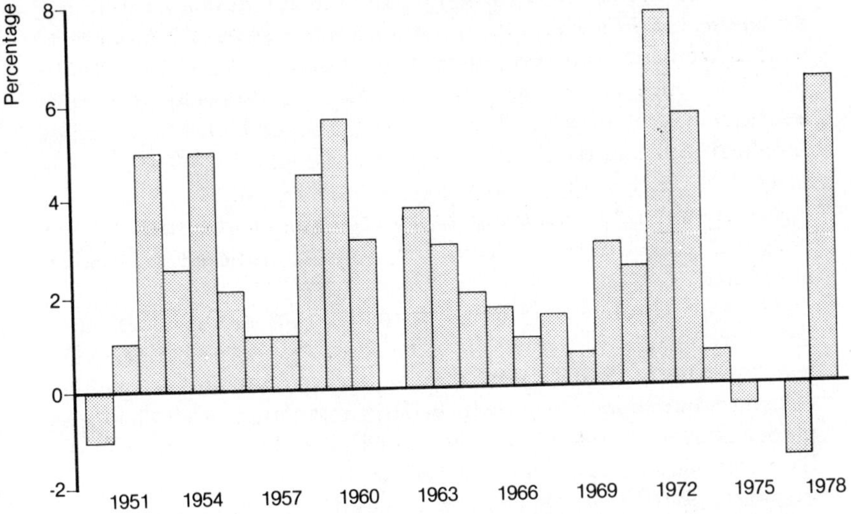

Figure 3 *Year by year percentage changes at constant 1975 prices, in personal income after allowing for tax and inflation*

rising unemployment may have a dampening effect on union growth and it is not unreasonable to suppose that this may in turn have a short-term effect on strike activity. It is conceivable, therefore, that the sharp increases in unemployment which occurred in 1971 and 1975 deterred groups of workers who felt themselves vulnerable to redundancy from going on strike. But once unemployment has stabilized itself, albeit on a higher plateau, the 'threat' effect on strike activity is likely to diminish.

To summarize the argument so far, the pattern and level of strikes over pay issues has been explained in terms of both long-run and short-run factors. In the private manufacturing sector, bargaining at plant and company level has become an increasingly important determinant of earnings levels. It is hardly surprising, therefore, that strikes and other forms of action have become more common in industries which were once largely strike-free. In the public sector, earnings are still determined predominantly at national level, so that while strikes over pay are relatively infrequent, when they do occur they tend to be of major significance. The pattern of strikes over non-pay issues such as manning levels, discipline, union recognition and redundancy can also be explained primarily in terms of bargaining structures. In the public sector such issues are likely to be the subject of detailed regulation by formal bargaining at national level. In the private sector, however, they are not normally covered by industry-wide agreements and regulation at plant and company level is still extremely uneven. It follows that when strikes do occur over these issues 'they are much less likely to be contained by procedure than similar disputes in the public sector'.[24] These gaps in the coverage of workplace bargaining, reinforced by the continued reliance on informal, unwritten procedures, help to explain why such a large proportion of strikes in Britain are 'unconstitutional' as well as unofficial.

When the Donovan Commission analysed the nature of Britain's strike problem, it was able to look back over a fifteen-year period in which the long-term relationship between strikes and bargaining structures had remained undisturbed by short-term factors – hence its preoccupation with private manufacturing industry. Since the Donovan era, however, the relative significance of factors such as incomes policy, sharply rising inflation, the wage–tax spiral, expanding union membership and rising unemployment has increased. While the relationship between bargaining structures and strikes has not disappeared, the sharp annual fluctuations in the level and distribution of strikes are now determined largely by the interplay of other variables, the significance of which may change considerably from one year to the next. Consequently the pattern of strike activity has become much more unpredictable since the Donovan era and the commission's strategy for reducing the number of strikes is much less relevant in current circumstances than it was in the mid 1960s.

Before leaving this topic, we must consider briefly an alternative explanation of British strike trends – namely that strikers have been encouraged to stop work and stay out longer by the comfortable financial cushion which is allegedly provided by state welfare benefits and tax rebates. It is generally accepted that union strike pay is in most cases well below 10 per cent of average male earnings and that even this modest benefit is paid only in a tiny minority of strikes.[25] Some unions, notably the NUM, do not pay dispute benefit even in official strikes. Indeed, as noted in Chapter 4, the vast majority of British unions simply do not have the financial strength to pay realistic levels of benefit to strikers for any length of time. In these circumstances it is no doubt tempting to conclude that many strikers are in effect being subsidized by the state, especially as the average duration of strikes has steadily increased over the past two decades.

In 1960, 82 per cent of recorded stoppages lasted for four days or less; by 1978 this proportion had fallen to 50 per cent. It follows that the financial hardship entailed in striking must have diminished.

The 'state subsidy' theory, however, does not stand up to close analysis. A striker who has dependants may claim supplementary benefit for those dependants after a week and in most cases two weeks of being on strike. This immediately excludes the 66 per cent or so of strikers who are back to work within two weeks of taking action. If there had been an increase in the value of supplementary benefit payments relative to average earnings, the 'subsidy' theory might hold good for the minority of strikers who stay out for more than two weeks. In reality, however, no such increase has occurred since the mid 1950s. In most cases the amount of benefit paid is likely to be modest in relation to average earnings. When supplementary benefit is being calculated for individual families, union strike pay, child allowances, tax rebates, and the striker's wife's earnings (if any) are all offset against the amount payable. The relative importance of supplementary benefit is difficult to judge because each claimant is assessed individually. Nevertheless it has been estimated that during the nine-week strike at the Ford Motor Company in the autumn of 1978, of the 57,000 workers involved, only 15,527 actually received supplementary benefit, and the average weekly payment per recipient was slightly more than £13. Tax rebates may be a significant source of income for single strikers or those with few dependants who are paying relatively large amounts of tax, but since the single men and married women cannot claim supplementary benefit and the rebates due to strikers with dependants are offset against benefit, this can hardly provide a large cushion. Consequently, while benefits and rebates may have had a marginal effect on the duration of stoppages, it seems highly improbable that they have had any effect on their frequency or motivation. Unless a strike is seen as a short-lived demonstration of anger (and many unrecorded stoppages probably fall into this category), most workers withdraw their labour in the knowledge that both they and their families are likely to experience a serious loss of income and reduction in living standards.

Strikes will occur as long as employers and trade unionists are free to negotiate terms and conditions of employment. They are, however, more likely to occur in some work situations than in others. The importance of bargaining structures in general and the level of pay determination in particular has been emphasized in this brief analysis. But differences in strike activity between industries are also associated with differences in *economic* structure. Factors such as a large average size of establishments, high labour intensity, high average earnings and a large proportion of male manual workers have all been positively associated with relatively frequent strikes. The character of the technology in use may also be important. Assembly-line production methods, for example, are more closely associated with stoppages than those which permit a higher level of individual control over the job. Under certain conditions, therefore, the pattern of strike activity in the workplace may be an amalgam of 'calculative' stoppages designed to put pressure on management in the normal bargaining process and spontaneous outbursts of resentment against working conditions or production methods which the strikers find alienating. Differences between industries and workplaces must also be related to the impact of short-term macro variables such as incomes policy and the rate of inflation. The structure of collective bargaining alone, therefore, is now only one element – albeit an important one – in the overall pattern of strike activity. In addition it must not be forgotten that strikes are usually called in reaction to the behaviour of management. Some strikes may be consciously provoked by managers who are pursuing their own bargaining objectives and have estimated that a stoppage will be less damaging to them than a concession to the union. In order to put the strike 'problem' in perspective, therefore, we need to examine the process of pay determination more closely.

Principles of pay determination

So far we have confined our attention to the institutional framework within which collective bargaining takes place and the sanctions which may be invoked. We noted earlier that, while the earnings of the majority of workers are still determined by bargaining at more than one level, there appears to be a long-term movement in favour of single-employer bargaining. The public sector model, characterized by relatively formal, fixed-term comprehensive agreements, is gradually being adopted by negotiators in the larger enterprises in the private sector. We must now move on, however, to consider the arguments which management and union negotiators commonly use when bargaining in a formal way on wages and salaries, whether the bargaining itself takes place at industry, company or plant level.

Those who believe that pay bargaining is a no-holds-barred

struggle in which principles and arguments are used merely to camouflage the application of coercive power do grave injustice to the bargainers themselves. This does not mean, of course, that there are no ritualistic elements in collective bargaining nor that crude force plays no part in the process. There are many examples in recent years of unions, especially in the public sector, who have been compelled to resort to vigorous industrial action before the employer has made what they consider to be a realistic offer. To the extent that this happens, it introduces an air of weary cynicism into the bargaining climate and undermines commitment among ordinary employees to the conventions of the bargaining process. In general, however, the tendency for both sides at all levels to devote more and more time and professional expertise to the preparation of claims and responses suggests that the quality of the arguments used and the skill with which they are deployed play a major part in determining the final outcome.

Contemporary theories of pay determination tend to emphasize the interaction of bargaining principles and bargaining structures, assigning only a subsidiary role to the operation of supply and demand in labour and product markets. If market factors *were* the dominant influence, there would presumably be little point in any worker joining a trade union and collective bargaining would be nothing less than a gigantic hoax. In fact Daniel's 1975 survey suggests that in manufacturing industry the state of the product market is a major influence on management's approach to wage bargaining. When demand is rising, management's main concern, apparently, is to avoid interruptions to output associated with collective bargaining; when demand is falling, however, they are much more anxious to prevent inflationary wage increases from weakening their firm's competitive position.[26] In general terms we would therefore expect trade union negotiators to encounter less resistance from management to pay claims during economic upswings than in recessions. It rarely happens, however, that all product markets move into and out of recessions at the same speed or to the same degree, so that at any given point in the economic cycle some markets will be considerably more buoyant than others. Consequently, if demand factors actually influenced the outcome of collective bargaining, we would expect to find them reflected in differential pay settlements. Daniel, however, found no such differences:

> Those [workers] in situations of rising demand received no more than those in situations of falling demand. Similarly, the level of the establishment's labour intensity, and the cash flow implications of pay rises, were not reflected in the level of the settlement . . . this would suggest that 'social' or 'institutional' factors had more influence on the outcome of negotiations than did 'economic' ones.[27]

These institutional factors are reflected in the emergence of a 'going rate' during the initial stages of every annual bargaining round. Daniel found that the prospects of reaching a settlement without strike action were relatively poor in those enterprises whose market situation made it very difficult for management to match the going rate. Conversely, workers appeared quite satisfied when their pay settlements equated with the going rate even if management could have afforded more. The inference is that workers' expectations from collective bargaining are influenced more by social pressures than by economic facts.

This does not, of course, mean that the argument across the bargaining table revolves exclusively around the concepts of fairness and social equity. In the private sector at least the employer's *ability to pay* will usually have a major influence on his response to a union claim, especially where the firm is operating in a stagnant or declining market. It would appear from Daniel's survey, however, that the argument rarely carries much weight with union negotiators. One reason for this lack of impact is, of course, the unions' refusal on principle to accept that their members, in a particular establishment, should receive less than the going rate merely because management alleges that it cannot afford to pay this rate. Another reason, however, appears to be connected with the unwillingness or inability of most managements to supply union negotiators with detailed information on profits, prices and cash flow which would validate their response. Ability to pay has not – at least until very recently – played a significant role in public sector bargaining. If in the past a nationalized industry has been unable to finance a pay settlement from its own revenue account, the government of the day has usually found the necessary money. The current policy of reducing public expenditure and controlling it through strict cash limits may, however, bring a new and, for the trade unions, wholly unwelcome emphasis on ability to pay into the wage bargaining process.

The *productivity* of the establishment is closely related to the employer's ability to pay and has, from time to time, played an important role in wage bargaining. The first organized attempt to enhance the importance of productivity occurred under the auspices of the Prices and Incomes Board between 1965 and 1970. The incomes policy which was pursued during this period sought to encourage managements and unions to negotiate more efficient working practices and in general achieve a closer relationship between pay and productivity. In practice, however, the parties were faced with the complex problems of measuring the productivity of different workgroups and evaluating the relative contribution of labour to such improvements in efficiency as could be quantified. As the Prices and Incomes Board itself conceded: 'Productivity is a relation between inputs and output. Output may be difficult to measure or a varying product mix may confuse comparisons of productivity over time . . . [but] inputs other than labour may be significant.'[28] Indeed, eventually the board was obliged to admit that the problem of measuring the direct contribution of labour to higher productivity was virtually insoluble and that workers should simply be seen to be 'contributing' towards this objective. In the circumstances, it is hardly surprising that the productivity criterion has in general been flexibly applied to wage bargaining. Where an industry or firm has a relatively good productivity record, union negotiators will emphasize the need to reward workers for their co-operation in accepting new technology or reduced manning levels. Where, by contrast, productivity is relatively low, union negotiators are likely to blame the failure of management to invest in new equipment and to reject any suggestion that their members' earnings should suffer. In many parts of the public sector there is the additional problem of applying the productivity criterion in any shape or form to groups, such as nurses and teachers, whose job is to supply a vital public service but from which there is no measurable output. Indeed, there are many workers in the private sector who are subject to the same constraint, which helps to explain why even in manufacturing industry the productivity-based incomes policy of 1965–70 favoured some groups at the expense of others.

Since 1970 productivity has in general occupied a far less significant position in the arguments advanced in support of pay claims than the *cost of living*. The increasing importance of this criterion clearly reflects the high levels of inflation which Britain has experienced over the past decade. Many trade union negotiators have regularly been able to demonstrate to management that since the last annual pay settlement their members' earnings have been seriously eroded in real terms by the rate at which the cost of living has accelerated. The legitimacy of this argument seems to find widespread acceptance. An ORC poll conducted in the autumn of 1972, for example, when a Conservative government was trying to persuade the TUC to accept a voluntary incomes policy, suggested that the overwhelming majority of the population was prepared to accept an annual pay rise of £2 per week provided that the rise in the cost of living could be kept below 5 per cent. An equally large majority felt that it was more important to control the cost of living than that people should obtain large increases in money wages. The Heath government and its Labour successor both accepted that the success of their respective incomes policies depended primarily on keeping the increase in the cost of living below the official norm for money wage increases. Indeed, the former introduced a general system of index-linking or 'threshold payments', while the latter resorted to cuts in income tax in order to protect real incomes from inflation. Similarly, Daniel found that 'the increase in the cost of living since the last pay rise was by far the most important consideration for the claims of union officers in all circumstances' – a consideration to which management was in general sympathetic. Indeed, there was a general consensus that 'the minimum increase employees should get was compensation for increases in the cost of living since their last pay increase'.[29]

The widespread acceptance of cost-of-living arguments in pay bargaining is indicative of a general concern for fairness and social equity. The mere fact that a worker's earnings keep pace with or even exceed the rise in the cost of living, however, will not in itself ensure that he is wholly satisfied with his pay. He and his group may in fact be doing relatively well in terms of the cost of living, but may still be dissatisfied if a workgroup with whom they habitually compare themselves achieves an increase and so upsets the relationship which has hitherto existed between their respective levels of earnings. Most wage bargains are ultimately bargains over wage *differentials* and *relativities*. Differentials have both a market and a social function. In market terms they can either induce workers to enter a particular industry or occupation or discourage them from doing so. Over the past decade, for example, several groups in the public sector, notably coal miners, policemen and nurses, have successfully argued that conspicuous shortages of new recruits to their respective occupations could only be corrected by a major adjustment in their relative pay. In the private sector skilled engineering workers have used the same argument, though with much less success. The problem for employers is that in general a pay increase which is designed to correct a labour shortage must be a very large one if it is to be effective and must somehow be protected against erosion by external factors. It is also very difficult to measure whether or not a major increase in relative pay has actually increased the supply of labour in a particular occupation since any upturn in recruitment may be the result of several other factors.

The social functions of differentials are less tangible but more influential. In Robinson's words:

> Some differentials indicate society's assessement of the value of a particular job, and they are frequently interpreted by individuals in specific occupations as indicators of status and a general sort of esteem. Indeed, differentials and relativities are the only way in which a worker can decide whether he is fairly paid.[30]

Fairness is, of course, based on comparison. Individuals and groups decide whether or not they are fairly paid by comparing their earnings with those of other individuals and groups. The argument then revolves around the selection of appropriate comparative reference points and on occasion this may prove to be a major stumbling block if management refuses to accept the legitimacy of a particular comparison. In practice, however, the argument tends to be simplified by two factors. First, most reference points are already well established and are therefore sanctioned by tradition. Indeed, on various occasions over the past twenty five years the government of the day has actively supported the principle of comparability in respect of certain public sector groups, while independent commissions of inquiry have indicated the reference points which in their view should apply to such groups. The Priestley Commission on civil service pay (1955), the Guillebaud Committee on railwaymen's pay (1960) and the Phelps Brown Committee on the pay of London busmen (1963) all produced detailed recommendations which helped to fix comparative reference points for their respective groups and occupations. Second, it would appear that most orbits of comparison are geographically and occupationally narrow. Daniel, for example, found that manual workers were likely to evaluate their position relative to some other group of manual workers in either the same plant, company or locality doing broadly the same type of job. He also found that both management and union negotiators tended, if anything, to institutionalize and restrict these orbits of comparison even more than the workers themselves.[31]

Last, but by no means least, the relatively recent movement towards the reform of plant and company payment systems has introduced another important element into the bargaining process. In the Donovan era many firms in the manufacturing sector were using incentive schemes and systematic overtime primarily in order to supplement the low basic rates embodied in multi-employer agreements. Owing to incomes policy and general pressure on costs, a very significant proportion of these schemes have since been replaced by time-based payment systems which enable management to control the movement of earnings more effectively. There are still many establishments, however, in which incentive schemes are still in use. Daniel, for example, found that arguments over the rate for the job under some form of payment by results were still the most common source of strikes in the manufacturing sector and that both incentive schemes and overtime were the most important sources of earnings drift.[32] Employee pressure to make incentive schemes yield higher earnings was particularly noticeable in the engineering and metal-working industries, whereas in other industries the source of this pressure was more likely to be the level of overtime. The larger the establishment, the more management was likely to encounter disputes over inter-group differentials and the more pressure there would be to change differentials through pressure on the payment system. But, while the introduction of more 'orderly' systems based on job evaluation has undoubtedly resolved some of these problems, it has also created new ones for both managements and union representatives.

By definition, a management initiative to replace a 'decadent' payment system with one more susceptible to management control is likely to challenge the position of those workgroups in the establishment who have successfully adapted the system and exerted a large degree of control over both earnings and output. Shop stewards are therefore likely to demand a high price for their co-operation with the new system, which may in turn create problems for management with other, less favoured groups. Moreover, the introduction of job evaluation, like any other rule change, is itself often a matter for bargaining. If the gradings produced by the scheme are unacceptable to one or more groups, there will be pressure for adjustment. Indeed, as we have noted before, the process of formalization may in itself crystallize and activate conflicts which have hitherto remained dormant. As Robinson has noted:

With informal, unwritten bargaining, a set of relationships can be created and can survive for a considerable time, even though the trade unions concerned refuse to endorse them publicly and may even criticise them publicly. The bargainers are not formally responsible for the relationships that result from a set of fragmented bargains in the same way that they are for differentials that are included in the formal agreement. They can, therefore, avoid responsibility for the results and advocate or accept views from their rank-and-file members which advocate a change in relative wages.[33]

Job evaluation may, by increasing the general awareness of other groups' relative pay in the establishment or bargaining unit, compel shop stewards to drop the pretence and challenge those gradings which they and their members regard as unacceptable. It is perhaps significant in this context that Daniel found no evidence that job evaluation resolved problems over differentials. On the contrary, managements in establishments which operated a job-evaluated payment system reported problems with differentials in about the same proportion as those in plants which did not.[34]

Conflict between groups over relativities and differentials will be exacerbated if the groups concerned belong to different unions which are already in competition with each other for members. In the motor industry, for example, there has long been competition between two 'open' unions, the AUEW and the TGWU. The former, representing many craftsmen in the industry as well as other manual grades, must have regard for the need to maintain acceptable differentials. The latter, representing large numbers of semi- and unskilled workers, has in recent years pursued a wage policy based on the principle of 'second to none'. The same pattern of conflict can also be seen in the rivalry which exists between two 'closed' unions on the railways, namely ASLEF and the NUR, and in similar rivalry between two 'closed' unions in the printing industry, the NGA and NATSOPA. In all such cases, the maintenance and elimination of differentials are regarded as acid tests of the respective unions' ability to represent their members' interests:

The adoption of public positions on differentials is not the same as taking up a public position about the size of an increase which a union is seeking from an employer. In the latter case, it is generally recognised that some compromise is to be reached. In the former case, failure to secure the publicly-declared differentials might be seen not as a victory for the employer but for the other union. It may be that 'losing' a differentials argument with another union is considered more serious than 'losing' a wage claim to an employer.[35]

Problems of this nature have been aggravated by the flat-rate, equity-based incomes policies which prevailed in most of the years between 1972 and 1978. Incomes policy has itself helped to determine, to a greater or lesser degree, the going rate for settlements and it is to this topic that we must now turn.

Incomes policy: the union role

At the root of all incomes policies lies the belief that free collective bargaining adds a great deal of impetus to the inflationary spiral by increasing employers' wage and salary bills at a faster rate than productivity. This does not mean that the bargaining behaviour of trade unions is the only or even the most important cause of inflation, but simply that the agreements which employers and unions negotiate on pay eventually have some impact on the price mechanism. The relative importance of collective bargaining as a source of inflation will no doubt continue to be disputed by economists, politicians and trade unionists alike. All we need to note for our purposes is that successive governments, both in Britain and elsewhere, have *believed* that there is a causal link between the processes of pay and price determination and have, as a result, sought to regulate collective bargaining through the medium of incomes policy.

There is not and never has been an orthodox or standard trade union approach to incomes policy. The attitude of the majority of unions as represented by the TUC has in fact varied considerably over the past thirty five years, swinging from active co-operation at one extreme to outright rejection at the other. At any given moment the consensus of opinion within the TUC will be determined by the interplay of several different factors, all of which are discussed below. It would be wrong, however, to ignore the sharp ideological conflict which invariably emerges at the annual conferences of the TUC between, on the one hand, those trade unionists who oppose all incomes policies in principle and, on the other, those who are aware of the grave social injustices inherent in the practice of unregulated collective bargaining. This clash of ideologies was well illustrated in the debate at the 1975 annual conference over the General Council's recommendation that the 'social contract' with the Labour government should be developed and that the limit on pay increases for 1975–6 should be £6 per man per week. For the opposition, Ken Gill of TASS argued that:

> By supporting the social contract we accepted implicitly last year the theory of wage inflation as being the main besetting sin. We warned then that wage cuts were bound to follow. We also said that voluntary restraint provided moral justification for wage control, especially if it did not solve the crisis. And it can and never will solve British capitalism's crisis. . . . Free collective bargaining must not be sold. Workers must not be made to pay for this crisis, which was never their responsibility.[36]

The counter-argument was best expressed by Jack Jones of the TGWU:

> I yield to no one in commitment to strong shop floor organisation to achieve good wages and working conditions. . . . But the union I lead and myself personally have never supported the idea that trade unionism is a licence for any group to look after themselves and to hell with the rest . . . surely our policy is to use our general strength and influence to promote social justice, to bring about economic circumstances which will give all workers protection and the opportunity for economic advancement. Not a free for all but a fair for all – that is our policy.[37]

The same debate probably takes place within most trade unions whenever incomes policy appears on the agenda of an annual conference. The views of the majority of delegates, however, may well change from year to year, depending on a range of factors which must now be mentioned.

Much depends on the content of the policy and the degree of participation in shaping that content which the government has allowed the TUC. In 1965, for example, the TUC evidently had little say in formulating the policy which the Labour government enunciated and pursued for the next five years. The lack of union participation was clearly evident in the policy itself, in so far as its main aim was to tie pay increases much more closely to productivity and weaken those criteria – comparability and the cost of living – to which trade union negotiators customarily attached the greatest importance. After the introduction of a six-month statutory 'freeze' on pay in 1966, the majority of delegates at successive annual conferences of the TUC voted against the continuation of the policy and urged the government to pay more attention to the principle of equity. Ultimately, however, the policy collapsed, not so much under the weight of hostile TUC resolutions but because it lost the support of negotiators at plant and company level. The problems of measuring productivity and applying this criterion to indirect workers and white collar staff have already been discussed. In general, it may be said that the main beneficiaries of the policy were manual workers directly engaged in the production process; many other groups, however, did less well in relative terms and by 1969 felt that they had been unfairly treated.

When the Labour government left office in 1970, it did so in the midst of an 'explosion' in pay claims which marked the collapse of its incomes policy. Its Conservative successor initially refused to adopt a formal incomes policy and relied instead on a strategy of gradually damping down the level of pay settlements in the public sector and exhorting employers to follow suit. The policy had some success against the less powerful groups of public employees but was completely shattered by a national stoppage in the coal industry early in 1972. In the following months, the government reversed its approach and sought to win the support of the TUC for a voluntary incomes policy or 'social contract' based on the principles of equity and fairness. A package of proposals was produced which offered the TUC a target growth rate of 5 per cent for the economy, a ceiling of 5 per cent on the cost of living, protection for the low paid and a system of index-linked payments in the event of the cost of living threshold being crossed. As a *quid pro quo,* the TUC was required to accept a general norm for pay settlements of £2 per man per week and also to give an undertaking that all settlements would be maintained for twelve months. Although the negotiations broke down, their significance must not be underrated. After two years of conflict and bitterness over both wage bargaining and the Industrial Relations Act, a Conservative government was offering the TUC the opportunity to participate along with the CBI in developing a tripartite system of managing the economy. Yet it was precisely on this principle that the negotiations foundered. For in the General Council's view, it was impossible to distinguish between a policy on incomes and all the other social and economic policies which the government was pursuing and which had implications for the living standards of union members. Consequently the government was faced with a list of political demands, including the repeal of the Industrial Relations Act, which it found incompatible with the maintenance of its own credibility as a government. The same problem emerged again under its successor.

When the attempt to win union support for a voluntary approach failed, the government proceeded in November 1972 to introduce its own policy and to give it the full backing of the law. The policy itself, however, was clearly designed to win the support of rank and file union members who, it was hoped, would force their leaders to acquiesce. Following a five-month freeze on pay and prices (phase one), the government introduced a flat-rate norm for all bargaining groups which imposed a ceiling of £250 per year on all individual pay increases (phase two). A new agency, the Pay Board, was established, with power to enforce the norm directly on employers who were found to be exceeding it. The assumption was that the vast majority of workers would be induced to accept the policy if they knew that it was being applied with the same even-handed justice to everyone. As a further inducement, the government imposed legally enforceable restrictions of unprecedented severity on price increases, profit margins and dividends. An elaborate system of policing the behaviour of prices was introduced and placed in the hands of another agency, the Price Commission. Initially the policy met with some success in the sense that very few trade unions openly sought to break through the statutory limitations on pay. Many negotiators had anticipated the policy by rushing through settlements the previous autumn. The miners decided to accept their phase two offer and the small number of groups in the public sector who did resort to strike action made little impact. There was much discussion within the TUC of the desirability of concerted industrial action against the policy but no single union was prepared to lead the attack.

In designing phase three of its policy, however, the government faced a more difficult problem. The NUM had acquiesced in phase two but was unlikely to do so for the second year running. At its conference in July 1973 the union had adopted bargaining objectives for the next pay round which far exceeded anything that was likely to be sanctioned in phase three. Nevertheless, the government believed – correctly in the event – that the miners were the key to the success of phase three and framed its provisions with the peculiarities of the coal industry in mind. Consequently, while the new flat-rate norm was relatively modest and the principle of threshold payments was retained, employers were allowed to pay large premiums to groups who worked 'unsocial' hours. It was known that a large proportion of miners would qualify for payment under this rule, and because no other industry relied on 'unsocial' hours to the same extent, the special position of the miners would be recognized. The problem for the NUM, however, was that, while some of its members would have benefitted considerably from this provision, many others would have received little or nothing beyond their basic entitlement under phase three. Consequently, although the Coal Board exploited phase three to the limit, the offer never proved to be a basis for negotiation. Following the miners' imposition of an overtime ban, the government put British industry on a three-day week and the TUC intervened with its offer to sanction the suspension of phase three for the miners. This initiative committed the TUC to use its moral authority to the full in order to persuade other affiliated unions not to exploit a special settlement for the miners. It also implied that the TUC was tacitly accepting the existence of phase three. The government rejected this offer, however, and subsequently called a general election. It was ironic, therefore, that a government which had offered the TUC a formal role in managing the economy, had based its incomes policy on principles which it knew would appeal to many union members, and had designed the final phase of this policy to meet the needs of one particularly powerful union, should fight an election on the theme of 'excessive' union power.

With the election of a Labour government in March 1974, the TUC acquired an unprecedented degree of responsibility for devising the content of incomes policies and implementing them. It took office with a firm commitment to the idea – first heard in the autumn of 1972 – of a wide-ranging 'social contract' with the TUC. The idea behind the contract was that, in a period when prices were bound to rise due to inflationary pressures throughout the world, union negotiators would be induced to forgo inflationary increases in money wages if their 'social' wage was improved. The government proceeded to implement its side of the contract by repealing all statutory controls over wages (except the phase three threshold payments) and disbanding the Pay Board while retaining strict control over prices and profits. In addition, food subsidies were introduced, pensions were increased, council house rents frozen and the Industrial Relations Act was repealed. The government also committed itself to a radical redistribution of wealth and to a major extension in state control over large areas of private industry. In return, the TUC undertook to persuade its affiliated unions not to attempt to increase the real incomes of their members through collective bargaining. Money wages were supposed to keep pace with but not exceed the rise in the cost of living and the twelve-month interval between settlements was to be strictly observed. Unions were also urged to bear in mind the needs of efficiency and the problems of the low paid. But the TUC refused to establish any kind of internal 'vetting' machinery for pay claims (as had existed in 1965–9) and just confined itself to giving 'pointed advice' to union negotiators.

Experience soon suggested, however, that the assumption which lay at the heart of the 'social contract' – namely that workers would equate improvements in the 'social' wage with higher real earnings – was fundamentally at variance with reality. Faced with a rapidly accelerating cost of living, most negotiators either sought to anticipate future inflation by achieving wage settlements which exceeded the rate of price inflation or caught up with the inflation that had already occurred by breaking the twelve-month rule. The problem was further aggravated by the general tendency to correct the anomalies which had arisen under the previous period of statutory control. Some private employers felt they needed to pay far more than a strict observance of the social contract permitted, and did so. The government itself bowed to the same pressures by conceding major improvements in relative pay to some of its own employees, notably teachers and nurses, who, it was felt, had fallen badly behind. By the spring of 1975, with inflation still accelerating to an annual rate of 25 per cent, unemployment rising rapidly, and foreign confidence in the pound beginning to collapse, both the government and the TUC recognized that the social contract had failed and that collective bargaining must be brought under firm control.

The next phase of incomes policy was again devised and initiated by the TUC, especially by Jack Jones of the TGWU. After some bargaining with the government, a new ceiling on pay settlements of £6 per man per week was announced for the wage round of 1975–76. The policy had, by comparison with its predecessor, much in its favour. As a simple, flat-rate figure it was easy to understand and appealed to the same sense of equity as the policy of 1972–4 had sought to exploit. It was also introduced in response to a particularly severe financial crisis, which in turn helped to create a climate of opinion within the TUC favourable to strong action. For its part, the government retained the instruments of price control and, although some of the recent improvements in the 'social' wage were phased out, there was no radical change in the direction of its economic strategy. The General Council could therefore sell the policy to its members as a temporary response to an exceptionally severe crisis which would otherwise have caused massive unemployment and reduced living standards. Daniel reported that nearly half the union negotiators in his sample saw the policy in precisely these terms.[38] The rapid acceptance of the policy, however, left two major problems on the horizon. First, the government had committed itself to bringing down the rate of inflation to 10 per cent by the middle of 1976 and to reducing the level of unemployment. The General Council accepted these targets and persuaded affiliated unions that, if the £6 limit was observed, this in itself would go a long way towards achieving them. Second, it was recognized that, if the flat-rate principle *was* generally accepted, it would create longer-term pressures for the readjustment of eroded differentials. Union leaders representing white collar workers forcibly expressed this viewpoint and Daniel's survey found widespread support for it among management and union negotiators alike.

The failure of the £6 limit, despite its widespread acceptance, to achieve the agreed targets on inflation and unemployment did not, however, bring TUC–government co-operation to an end. On the contrary, the TUC again took the lead in designing another phase of incomes policy for the bargaining round of 1976/1977. This imposed a ceiling of 5 per cent on total earnings, with a minimum of £2.50 and a maximum of £4.00 per man per week. The twelve-month rule for settlements would also continue to apply. The main *quid pro quo* offered by the government was a marginal reduction in direct taxation which it was hoped would help to maintain real incomes and reduce any pressure for above-the-norm increases. The position of the General Council *vis-à-vis* the small but vocal opposition within the TUC was strengthened by two factors. First, despite some unavoidable slippage, the £6 limit had been generally observed and had helped reduce the annual rate of inflation by about half (to less than 13 per cent) between mid 1975 and mid 1976, Second, all trade union leaders were well aware that, if the voluntary policy collapsed, the government would be forced to resort to statutory control or lose all credibility, with extremely adverse consequences for the Labour movement as a whole. The obvious dependence of the government on the active support of the TUC prompted Sidney Weighell of the NUR to observe that no one could govern Britain without the 'acquiescence' of the trade unions. Nevertheless, the consensus of opinion at the TUC annual conference in September 1976 was unambiguously in favour of an 'orderly return' to free collective bargaining when the policy lapsed in July 1977. There was little doubt in the minds of those union leaders who represented craftsmen and professional workers that their members would not tolerate any further erosion of differentials.

From the middle of 1977 until the government lost office nearly two years later, the TUC officially stood aside from the formulation of incomes policy and left the government to devise and impose the two further phases of the policy unilaterally. The most that the General Council would do was to urge affiliated members to observe the normal twelve-month rule. Why did the TUC retreat from the extremely influential position it had achieved between 1974 and 1976? First and foremost, national union leaders, who might otherwise have been moderately well disposed to a continuation of a jointly agreed incomes policy, were compelled to recognize that many of their own members and negotiators in the workplace were no longer willing to accept it. Dissatisfaction at this level was partly the result of a growing discrepancy between the average rate of earnings growth and the increase in the cost of living during 1976–7, causing a sharp fall in real incomes. But, more importantly, the government's formula of uniform flat-rate or percentage increases linked to reductions in income tax was fundamentally incompatible with the conventional criteria of collective bargaining at plant and company level. By 1977 pressure was building up in the manufacturing sector for much more 'flexibility' in order to correct eroded differentials, adjust relativities, restore incentives and catch up with the cost of living. To some extent the government recognized these pressures when formulating the policy for 1977–8 in so far as it made provision for 'self-financing' productivity deals over and above the 10 per cent ceiling on ordinary settlements. The norm of 5 per cent for 1978–9, however, never had any realistic prospect of success and the private sector was seriously affected by the general upsurge of strike activity which began in late 1978 and continued well into 1979.

The role of trade unions in the public sector was critical to the success or failure of successive incomes policies in the 1970s. The pay 'explosions' of 1969–70, 1972, 1974–5 and 1978–9 were all spearheaded by groups of public sector employees, and during the period when TUC participation in the formulation of incomes policy reached its zenith, the most vocal opponents of co-operation came from the ranks of the public sector unions. The fact that some of the most dogmatic advocates of free collective bargaining represent groups in the public sector is not as surprising as it appears at first glance. For, while it is true that no government since 1945 has refrained from imposing financial limits of some kind on the freedom of public authorities to negotiate, many union representatives in this sector have expressed deep resentment against what they see as discriminatory treatment. The tendency of all governments to 'set an example' to the private sector, by enforcing all incomes policies as rigorously as possible in those industries and services where they are the ultimate paymasters, has been regarded as a violation of the traditional obligation of the state to behave fairly towards its own employees. Both flat-rate and productivity-based incomes policies have disturbed established pay relationships both within the public sector and between public and private sector groups. When governments have refused to recognize the grievances of the more powerful groups, notably the miners, the electricity supply workers and the railwaymen, the latter have on various occasions over the past decade taken direct action. The adoption of a more militant approach to collective bargaining appears to have been effective. Between 1970 and 1976 the relative pay of manual workers in the public sector increased by 10 per cent and, although there has since been a slight movement back in favour of the private sector, the improvement is still very obvious.[39] The success with which some groups have exploited their bargaining power has no doubt inspired some of the less powerful groups to adopt the same tactics, so that 'few public sector groups now regard the strike as a contravention of their obligations to the public'.[40] Militancy may also have been increased by other factors such as reductions in manpower in the case of the nationalized industries and major reorganizations in the case of local government and the health service. Whatever the reason, the days when governments could rely on the passive acquiescence of their own employees have long since gone.

The overriding importance of comparability in the determination of public sector pay has already been noted. As the government itself admitted in a White Paper issued in July 1978, the pay policies of the previous three years had 'inhibited the adjustment of internal pay structures and external pay relativities that would otherwise have occurred'. During 1977–8 the government had in fact conceded the claims of firemen, policemen and servicemen for 'special treatment'. In the following year, however, as pay settlements in the private sector moved far ahead of the government's 5 per cent norm, the pressure for comparability in the public sector broke out in the form of widespread strikes. The extent of the disruption compelled the government to recognize the force of these demands and in March 1979 it established a Standing Commission on Pay Comparability. The commission's task was to compare the pay of public sector employees with that of appropriate groups in the private sector. References to the commission were entirely at the discretion of the parties themselves and the role of existing research and arbitration bodies in the public sector remain unchanged. Despite the long-standing opposition of the TUC to the 'interference' of government-sponsored agencies in wage bargaining, the commission quickly gained the acceptance of the public sector unions. This is hardly surprising in view of the fact that a reference to the commission was almost certain to result in some increase in the relative pay of the group under consideration. In reality, therefore, the commission was nothing more than yet another *ad hoc* safety-valve through which the claims of particular groups could be accommodated. The potential role of the commission or a similar body in a reformed system of wage determination will be discussed in Chapter 7.

At the time of writing, the present Conservative government is committed to running the economy without a formal incomes policy. The government's view is that in the private sector the level of pay settlements should be determined by free collective bargaining which, it is assumed, will be geared to the profitability of individual enterprises. Employers will therefore concede wage increases which they can afford to pay; if they settle for anything more, they will either have to reduce their labour force or go out of business. In the light of our previous discussion of the principles of pay determination, this view of collective bargaining seems unduly simplistic. The employer's ability to pay is but one of the arguments used in wage bargaining and even in a period of economic recession other criteria will continue to shape the outcome of the bargaining process. In the public sector, however, the freedom of management and union negotiators has already been severely constrained by the government's imposition of firm ceilings on revenue expenditure. This in turn implies that a norm for pay settlements, however informal it may be, will emerge in public sector negotiations. If the 'going rate' in private industry is significantly ahead of that in the public sector, the institutional linkages which have long existed between the two will undoubtedly generate considerable pressure for comparability. As long as the Comparability Commission existed, public sector unions had an appropriate institutional forum in which claims for changes in relative pay could be investigated. It was illogical for the government to insist that the criteria of productivity and ability to pay must play the dominant role in wage determination and simultaneously allow a public agency to propagate the principle of comparability. By abolishing the commission, however, the government has denied itself the use of a potentially valuable 'safety' mechanism. Ministers now have no choice but to 'stand firm' against every 'unrealistic' pay claim, with all the disruption to vital services which such a policy may eventually entail. Sooner or later, therefore, they may be driven by the pressure of events to consider alternative methods of ensuring that the outcome of collective bargaining is consistent with what they conceive to be the public interest.

It would be useful to remind ourselves that in its 1978 White Paper, the Labour government envisaged the setting of an annual earnings ceiling as a *permanent* feature of collective bargaining. The approach to pay determination, said the White Paper, should be based every year 'on a broad agreement between government, unions and employers about the maximum level of earnings which is compatible with keeping inflation under control in the following twelve months'. This strategy, derived as it is from the West German 'concerted action' model, may not be ideologically unattractive to a right-of-centre government. It would, of course, encounter the same practical objections at plant and company level as the nationally determined pay norms of 1975–7. These will be discussed in the following chapter in the context of reforming the bargaining system. But if such an approach were to gain the support of the trade unions at national level, the TUC would undoubtedly expect some form of political *quid pro quo* from the government. The involvement of the General Council in the formulation of incomes policy over the past decade, starting with the abortive 'social contract' of 1972 and ending in the achievement of almost total control in 1975–7, implies that any government which seeks to revive the concept of tripartite economic management must be prepared to *bargain* with each of its would-be partners, particularly the TUC. Whether the present government or its successor will feel inclined to make tangible concessions on matters of policy in return for promises of co-operation remains to be seen. Even if such promises are kept, the political price of obtaining them may be unacceptably high. In the final chapter, therefore, we must consider the question of whether or not the present system of pay determination can be changed without recourse to a formal, 'social contract' type of agreement at national level.

7 A giant's strength?

Over the past twenty years or so the belief that British trade unions have acquired too much power has become a commonplace feature of political and economic discussion. Early in 1978, for example, *The Sunday Times* published a series of articles on the subject of 'union power' which began with the assertion that, while working people had done badly under the Labour government in terms of jobs and real wages, the 'powers and privileges' of the unions had 'multiplied'.[1] In Chapter 2 we discussed the popular belief that the legislation of 1974 and 1975 has conferred a range of new and socially dangerous immunities on the unions, and concluded that it does not square with reality. This does not, of course, mean that legal limitations on these immunities would have no effect on the bargaining power of most unions. But the experience of the 1970s suggests that the bargaining power of the trade unions is only marginally determined by the legal framework within which it is exercised. If, therefore, the power of Britain's trade unions has increased, we must look beyond the law to discover why this has happened.

Is it in fact the case that British trade unions *have* acquired more power? If it is, then we ought to be able to find more than one yardstick by which this increase can be measured. We should, for example, expect to find a direct relationship between union bargaining power and the structure of pay relativities. We should also expect to find some evidence that collective bargaining has redistributed income in favour of employees in general. Other measures of union power should logically include the extent to which the unions have caused inflation by increasing money wages faster than productivity and holding down productivity growth in order to preserve employment. If it can be shown that unions *do* play a leading role in the inflationary process, then incomes policy must be regarded as an essential part of a counter-inflationary strategy. The extent to which the unions are prepared to accept restraints on their freedom to bargain must determine the success or failure of an incomes policy, and this may well be conditional on political concessions from the government of the day. We ought, therefore, to be able to show that the TUC has exerted more and more influence over government policy-making on a wide range of economic and social issues.

In the course of this concluding chapter we shall seek to probe these popular beliefs and, in doing so, to arrive at a more realistic evaluation of the limits of trade union power. In the light of this analysis, we shall then proceed to consider the future development of collective bargaining and discuss some recent suggestions for changing the way in which this method of rule-making operates.

Trade union and wage relativities

The effect of trade unionism on relative wages may be defined as the degree to which unions raise the wages of their members through collective bargaining above the level which those same workers would have been paid in the absence of unionization. Indeed, as Mulvey has noted, unions 'would probably go out of business if they were unable to achieve a positive union/non-union wage differential'.[2] Economists tend to argue that the interaction of supply and demand in the labour market continues to affect relative wages independently of collective bargaining but as yet we have no acceptable yardstick by which this can be measured. Since it is virtually impossible to say accurately what the wages of a given group or workers would have been in the absence of trade unions, researchers have attempted to compare the level and movement of organized workers' wages with those of non-unionized workers who are otherwise comparable. In Britain, however, this presents immense problems because of the long-established influence of collective bargaining. There is virtually no labour market in which wage levels are determined without reference either to wage agreements elsewhere or to incomes policy norms or to some other institutional criterion. Statutory minimum wage regulation has existed since 1909 and the Wages Council system was introduced in 1918 with the objective of protecting workers in low-paid industries where union organization was either weak or non-existent. Since Wages Council awards tend to follow the general 'going rate', workers in poorly organized sectors such as retailing benefit indirectly from the efforts of trade unions in other, better-organized industries.

It seems reasonable to assume that the introduction of collective bargaining into a hitherto unorganized industry or company will have a permanent, 'once-for-all' effect on the relative pay of the employees in the new bargaining unit, but it would be surprising if collective bargaining had no subsequent effects on relativities. Indeed, there are certain types of differentials which are almost certainly affected by union activity. Trade unions have, for example, traditionally sought to achieve a standard rate for a given job and, to the extent that they have succeeded, they have eroded or eliminated *personal* differentials. Under collective bargaining an employer is likely to have far less discretion to pay each worker a rate which he believes reflects individual skill, experience, effort or market value. Personal differentials which reflect racial or sexual prejudices, however, may still exist under collective bargaining and for this reason governments have sought to eliminate them through legislation.

It seems equally likely that trade unions have reduced differentials between *firms* which operate in the same product and labour markets. Indeed, the rationale of multi-employer bargaining is that the same basic rates should be paid for a given group of jobs throughout a particular industry. Clearly this leaves considerable scope for actual earnings levels to vary with the profitability of individual firms and the pressures of local labour markets. Trade unions, however, normally seek to reduce the dispersion of earnings between plants and, from what we know of wage determination in the workplace, they have probably had some success. As we noted earlier, comparability is a powerful normative influence over the wage bargaining process at plant and company level and workers tend to compare themselves with other workers doing similar jobs in the same geographical locality. Earnings differentials still exist *between* different geographical areas and, given that living costs and labour market characteristics still vary both locally and regionally, we would expect them to persist with or without collective bargaining. Nevertheless there is evidence that both in Britain and elsewhere trade unions have narrowed geographical differentials.[3]

The effect of trade unions on *occupational* and *industrial* differentials is more problematic. It was once believed that occupational differentials were primarily determined by cyclical movements in aggregate demand, so that when unemployment was high differentials widened and *vice versa*.[4] Recent research, however, has challenged this conclusion and has accorded a much more important

Table 18 *Average hourly earnings (excluding overtime) of full-time adult male skilled workers as a percentage of labourers' earnings in certain industries*

	1963	*1971*	*1973*	*1976*
Time-workers				
Engineering	143	144	138	128
Shipbuilding	134	133	128	119
Chemicals	114	109	108	105
Payment-by-results-workers				
Engineering	146	149	143	131
Shipbuilding	138	148	136	130
Chemicals	111	107	107	108

role to collective bargaining. One of the most significant changes in the structure of occupational differentials during the 1970s was a marked compression of the differential between skilled and unskilled manual workers after a long period of relative stability (see Table 18). If the excess demand hypothesis held good, we would have expected differentials to have moved in the opposite direction in view of the behaviour of unemployment during the first half of the 1970s. The apparent insignificance of the level and rate of change of unemployment – a conclusion supported by Brown's study of pay structures in the West Midlands engineering industry – suggests that institutional factors have been influential.[5] One such factor is the post-Donovan tendency to abandon piece-work and rationalize plant and company pay structures. The amalgamation of hitherto autonomous and fragmented bargaining units of skilled, semi-skilled and unskilled workers has almost certainly helped to compress the traditional differentials between these groups. This compression has been particularly severe in the motor car industry, where some groups of skilled men have expressed considerable dissatisfaction with the negotiating performance of their union, the AUEW. Trade union structure may therefore affect the rate at which compression takes place. In the motor industry skilled men are represented by a union which includes within its ranks large numbers of semi-skilled and unskilled workers, and is in open competition with another union, the TGWU, whose wage policy has emphasized the principle of equity. In electrical engineering, by contrast, unions representing skilled men (principally the EETPU) have retained their grip over bargaining units and here the erosion of skill differentials has been far less pronounced. It has also been discovered that, contrary to popular belief, the differential between clerical and manual workers' pay in the engineering industry was relatively stable during the first half of the 1970s. This again underlines the significance of bargaining structures in so far as clerical and manual unions negotiate in separate bargaining units.[6]

Research suggests, therefore, that compression has occurred *within* rather than *between* bargaining units. The presence of trade unions who are seeking to achieve equity-based bargaining objectives must obviously have some effect over the behaviour of pay relativities, but the objectives themselves and the vigour with which they are pursued are in turn strongly influenced by the general rate of inflation. It has been observed that, in the first half of the 1970s, workplace negotiators in the engineering industry as a whole responded to an accelerating rate of inflation by bargaining to compress differentials.[7] This behaviour may reflect a genuine desire to protect the lower-paid workers in a given bargaining unit from the effects of inflation; but it may also reflect the influence of a 'money illusion'. If workers perceive 'fair' pay differentials in cash rather than percentage terms, as research suggests they do, and if these perceptions are slow to adjust to inflation, then compression may well be tolerated by skilled groups. Conversely, when the rate of inflation begins to fall, concern for social equity declines, workers' perceptions of 'fair' differentials catch up with reality and workplace negotiators bargain to *widen* differentials. Thus the severe compression of the period 1970–6 ceased between 1976 and 1978, and resumed in 1979–80. If this analysis is correct, the popular argument that flat-rate incomes policies are the principal cause of eroded differentials must be open to doubt. Even the most rigid incomes policy can be interpreted at workplace level in a way which accords with changing perceptions of fairness. This 'flexibility' may, however, involve marginal departures from the letter, if not the spirit of an incomes policy. It is this element of 'slippage' which largely accounts for the general belief that concern for differentials eventually destroys incomes policies which are based on the principle of rough justice for all.

The above argument infers that individual trade unions are unlikely to have enough power to effect long-term changes in differentials *between* industries. These differentials reflect not only the bargaining power of the union (or unions) which organize the workforce, but also the characteristics of the labour force (age, sex and skill mix), the method of wage payment, the ratio between labour and capital, and underlying trends in product demand. In Britain and most other western countries, the industrial wage structure shows remarkable, long-run stability. A recent study of earnings differentials by the Department of Employment, for example, has concluded that between 1948 and 1977 most industries 'maintained their long-term position with great consistency'.[8] The vehicles, paper, printing and metal manufacturing industries remained consistently above the average, and textiles below. The two industries whose relative position changed dramatically – coal mining and dock labour – were both subject to sharp contractions in the size of their workforces, changes in wage payment systems and a significant substitution of capital for labour (through increased mechanization). They were also characterized by major outbreaks of direct conflict between unions and management. In coal mining two national strikes were called by the NUM in 1972 and 1974, resulting in wage settlements which sharply improved relative earnings. In the docks the period 1967–72 was marked by frequent strikes, both official and unofficial, over the related issues of decasualization, job security and technological change which again produced a major improvement in relative pay. These awards, coupled with the less dramatic but significant gains made by groups such as electricity supply workers and local authority employees, help to explain the post-1970 change in the relative position of the public sector which we noted in previous chapter.

In general, however, collective bargaining and trade union structure have both had a stabilizing effect on inter-industrial differentials. In those industries where earnings levels are effectively determined by bargaining at national level, particularly in the public sector, the formulation and settlement of pay claims is strongly influenced by the principle of comparability. The use of agreed comparative reference groups is sanctioned by tradition and is likely, therefore, to discourage any long-term change in the differential position of any one industry. The weakness of industrial unionism in Britain has reinforced this stabilizing tendency in so far as the presence of the same unions in several different industries has facilitated comparisons and helped to institutionalize a 'going rate' in every annual bargaining round. Even when it is generally agreed that a group has fallen badly behind in relative terms, any improvement will only be short-lived if other comparable groups move ahead more quickly in subsequent years. This appears to have been the experience of the school teachers in the years following the Houghton settlement of 1975. If a group is to maintain a relative improvement it needs to be able to demonstrate, both to the employer and to other comparable groups, that there has been a change in the nature or importance of the work it performs of such magnitude that its claims to special treatment must be recognized in successive bargaining rounds. In recent years, very few groups have surmounted this obstacle and such cases must, almost by definition, continue to be extremely rare.

Trade unions, inflation and unemployment

We argued above that workers' and union negotiators' perceptions of 'fair' differentials are shaped by the general rate of inflation. This analysis clearly puts trade unions in a reactive role and infers that the union push on money wages is a *dependent* variable in the inflationary process. Some economists, however, have long argued that the money-wage push is a major, independent cause of inflation and that the force of this push has increased in recent years as a result of certain sociological and psychological changes in the characteristics of the labour force. The experience of full or at least high employment and rising real incomes has, it is argued, weakened the traditional pattern of 'deferential' behaviour on the shop floor and encouraged workers to band together and assert their 'right' to higher and higher standards of living. The gap between the expectations of organized labour in Britain and the income levels which a low-productivity, uncompetitive economy can actually sustain has consequently been 'filled' by wage-push inflation. This analysis has been clearly articulated by Phelps Brown:

> . . . collective bargaining today is not between labour and capital, or employees and management, for the distribution of the products of particular industries between pay and profit, but between different groups of employees for the distribution of the national income between them as a whole and the inactive population. Cost inflation appears basically as the process by which particular groups of employees enter and enforce claims to shares in the national product that add up to more than the total product; and the over-subscription comes out as a rise in prices.[9]

The 'old bottle' of traditional collective bargaining structures and negotiating conventions has thus been infused with the 'new wine' of ambitious expectations and assertive behaviour. Changes in aggregate demand which once imposed some discipline on the process of wage and price fixing have thus been overridden and muted.

The socio-political cost-push analysis is, however, ambiguous on the role of trade unions as formal organizations in the inflationary process. The close, traditional involvement of trade unions in the system of industry-wide bargaining infers that they themselves are one of the 'old bottles'. Full employment in the post-war period is seen as the principal factor behind the growth of bargaining in the workplace, a process in which shop stewards have played a far more influential role than full-time officials. Indeed, as workplace organizations have become more sophisticated, their autonomy has increased and the formal control which union hierarchies can exert over them has declined. It is admitted that workplace bargaining on wages is confined largely to the manufacturing sector, but the Aukrust model of wage inflation asserts that high-productivity manufacturing industries which are open to international competition set the pace for wage settlements in the economy as a whole. Whatever 'going rate' emerges from wage bargaining in these industries is then transmitted to the less efficient, more sheltered industries and services in which workplace bargaining may be virtually non-existent. The behaviour of relative wages in the public sector, however, casts some doubt on the relevance of the Aukrust model in Britain, at least since the late 1960s. If it is indeed the case that the growth of earnings in the public sector has set the pace for wage bargaining in the private sector, then the role of trade unions as formal organizations is more significant than the Aukrust model suggests.

Those who take a socio-political view of the causes of accelerating inflation in Britain since the late 1960s usually quote the apparent breakdown of the Phillips curve in support of their position. Phillips, it will be recalled, examined the relationship between changes in money wage rates and the level of unemployment between 1861 and 1957 and found that low unemployment was associated with large increases in money wages and *vice versa.*[10] This analysis appeared to suggest that aggregate demand had exerted a much more powerful influence over the movement of money wages than trade union activity. The main policy implication was that governments should decide the level of demand at which they wished to run the economy, and use the conventional tools of demand management (monetary and fiscal policy) to maintain this level. If inflation rose to a point at which the balance of payments moved into deficit, excess demand would be removed by government action and the level of wage settlements would fall as unemployment rose. Trade unions were therefore seen as purely reactive agencies.

The simple trade-off relationship depicted in the Phillips curve, however, appeared to break down in the late 1960s when unemployment and inflation rose simultaneously. The socio-political school has explained this dramatic change in terms of an autonomous growth in the militancy of organized labour in Britain and Western Europe as a whole. There was a general tendency for real disposable incomes to rise more slowly than productivity in 1966–8, so that the 'wage explosion' which began in 1968 and continued through 1969 and 1970 marked a concerted attempt by organized labour to recover the lost ground. Economists of 'monetarist' convictions, however, have argued that the Phillips curve did not break down but simply shifted upwards. The key variables in their analysis are the level of inflationary *expectations* and the degree of excess demand which governments have generated. By the late 1960s the experience of sustained full employment had generated a rise in inflationary expectations, which were further augmented by the massive increases in energy and raw material prices of the 1970s. The more deeply embedded that expectations of rapid inflation become, the less effect a rise in the level of unemployment will have on the rate of inflation. Moreover, all western governments have tended to maintain excess levels of demand in order to avoid politically unacceptable increases in unemployment. In Friedman's terms, there is a 'natural' rate of unemployment in every economy which represents equilibrium between supply and demand in the labour market. Whatever level of unemployment is implied by the natural rate must be *structural* or *frictional* in character, which means that it derives from labour market rigidities and cannot be removed by simply expanding aggregate demand. If a government seeks to do so and pushes the actual rate of unemployment *below* the natural rate, the result will be accelerating inflation.[11]

This analysis is undoubtedly relevant to the British experience since the late 1960s. The gradual but apparently irreversible deterioration in the relative performance of British manufacturing industry – the reasons for which we cannot analyse here – has prompted successive governments to maintain employment and aggregate demand at a high level by increasing the size of the public sector. Between 1960 and 1975 public expenditure rose from 41 per cent to 58 per cent of GNP and the number of employees in the public sector rose from 24 per cent to nearly 30 per cent of the employed labour force. Bacon and Eltis have analysed the consequences of this growth for the wealth-creating sector of the economy and concluded that the resulting squeeze on resources has initiated and reinforced the downward spiral of 'de-industrialization'.[12] The lack of sufficient industrial plants to provide work for more than a falling proportion of the labour force implies that the rising level of unemployment in Britain has been structural in character. In Friedman's terminology, the natural rate of unemployment has increased but governments have tried to reverse this trend by creating more and more jobs in the public sector. This policy has entailed a massive increase in the public sector borrowing requirement and thus in the money supply, leading to a sharp increase in the rate of inflation. Wages in the public sector have been allowed to play a less reactive role than is implied by the Aukrust transfer model because successive governments have failed to control the volume of public spending, and it has been relatively easy for higher wage bills to be passed on to taxpayers.[13] As we noted earlier, the growing burden of direct taxation has eroded the real incomes of public and private sector employees alike, with obvious consequences for wage expectations and trade union bargaining behaviour.

The effect of trade union activity on inflation and unemployment is, therefore, rather less clear-cut than the exponents of a simple, cost-push model of inflation would assert. Union negotiators at industry, company and workplace level formulate their bargaining objectives in response to factors beyond their immediate control, notably the general rate of inflation and the level of settlements achieved by comparable groups. This does not, of course, imply that particular wage agreements do not *contribute* to the upward movement of money wages by raising the general level of inflationary expectations or by disturbing the established structure of relativities and differentials, thereby provoking counter-active behaviour elsewhere. Indeed, in previous chapters we have underlined the role of union negotiators in shaping the bargaining objectives of their members and focusing their reactions to external events and pressures on specific, achievable targets. But the evidence does not suggest that we can isolate union activity as an *independent* cause of inflation or unemployment. We must remember that it takes *two* parties to negotiate an 'inflationary' wage settlement, and that decisions which appear irrational and self-defeating when viewed from the perspective of national economic management may seem eminently sensible when seen through the eyes of managers and union representatives in the workplace. We must also take heed of the monetarists when they remind us that the wage–price spiral needs an accommodating increase in the money supply if it is to continue. It is, of course, always possible for the trade unions, acting through the TUC, to bring pressure to bear on governments to expand the money supply. The first phase of the 'social contract' (1974–5) represents the most successful attempt which the unions have made to influence government policy in this area. The rapid collapse of the contract and the subsequent reversal of government policy, however, suggests that union influence over demand management is likely to be short-lived.

But is it not possible for the trade unions to frustrate action by governments which is designed to reduce both inflation and unemployment? Turner *et al.* for example, have argued that 'where unions are both important and independent of the state, it is increasingly difficult to control inflation, and impossible to cure it, without a viable and broad union agreement to the appropriate measures'.[14] This conclusion receives some support from the experience of 1975–7, which was discussed in the previous chapter, but it also begs the important question of the political price which an agreed counter-inflationary policy may entail. The balance of opinion within the TUC has always been overwhelmingly opposed to 'monetarist' prescriptions for inflation and is currently against the alternative weapon of incomes policy. Since the trade unions' alternative economic strategy, based as it is on higher public spending and stringent import controls, does not seem attractive to any government, the prospects of achieving the 'broad agreement' which Turner *et al.* advocate are rather remote. In these circumstances the only viable option for policy-makers is to seek to improve the trade-off between inflation and unemployment by reducing the growth rate of the money supply and curbing inflationary expectations. This implies that, in the private sector, negotiators will be faced with a stark choice between excessive increases in money wages and higher unemployment. Negotiators in the public sector will face the same choice, except that their room for manoeuvre will be even more limited by enforced reductions in public spending. The main potential weakness of this approach is, of course, that a relatively small number of unions in the public sector have the power to disrupt vital services and supplies. It follows that any government which seeks to reduce inflation by cutting the public sector borrowing requirement will sooner or later find its nerve tested to the full by one or more trade unions in the public sector. In this sense it can be argued that a few particularly powerful unions *are* in a position to frustrate any counter-inflation strategy.

It is also conceivable that trade unions can help to maintain unemployment at a higher level than it would otherwise be. Keynesian economists have argued that if substantial involuntary unemployment exists, real wages (the real cost of employing labour) must be too high. Consequently if trade unions prevent real wages from falling to their market-clearing level, unemployment will persist. Union negotiators could do this either by insisting on unduly high increases in money wages or by forcing employers to accept working practices and manning standards which hold down productivity growth and thus inflate unit labour costs, or by a combination of both. Since those groups with the most bargaining power tend to be those who least fear the threat of unemployment, it is possible for them to negotiate wage increases which, in a situation of relatively slow monetary growth, will be passed on to less powerful groups in the form of higher unemployment. It is this relationship which has provoked some observers to condemn the 'stupidity' of trade union leaders for seeking to maintain the real incomes of their members above whatever level would be necessary to restore full employment.[15]

Such criticisms, however, border on the fatuous. To condemn any trade union for doing the very thing it is in business to do is to engage in a somewhat fruitless exercise. No individual negotiator, whether at plant or industry level, can possibly be aware of the macro-economic consequences of any wage increase be negotiates. His loyalty is to the members he represents and it is their immediate interests which must inevitably be uppermost in his mind. As Daniel has pointed out:

> Wage and salary earners respond in relation to their own pay according to their particular family circumstances and workplace relations, and the facts of life from their perspective, rather than the facts of life as they appear from a perspective derived from the management of the national economy. For these reasons, concern about the general problem of inflation is relatively remote and abstract. Concern about personal earnings in relation to commitments and the rising cost of living is immediate and specific.[16]

While negotiators and members alike may be prepared in certain circumstances to tolerate a reduction in their real incomes, as indeed many did in 1975–7, they will do so with the intention of making up the lost ground as soon as possible. Any union official or shop steward who conspicuously fails to bargain effectively on behalf of his members is unlikely to last long in office. The main criterion of his effectiveness is the size of the wage increases he negotiates, not the additional unemployment which his activity may ultimately cause elsewhere.

Trade unions and productivity

The argument that trade unions actually hold down the growth of real wages and cause unemployment by compelling employers to tolerate 'restrictive practices' is a very familiar one. It rests, however, on two very dubious assumptions – first that restrictive *labour* practices are the most important cause of low productivity, and second that *trade unions* are responsible for the existence and retention of these practices.

The record of Britain's performance in terms of productivity growth is well-known and needs no repetition. All we need say is that in manufacturing industry as a whole there is a steadily widening gap between productivity levels in Britain and the average elsewhere within the EEC.[17] This explains why, despite the relatively low wages paid in British industry, *unit* labour costs have risen more rapidly in Britain than in most other West European countries. Different explanations have been advanced for this trend. Some observers have emphasized the apparent reluctance of British manufacturing firms to invest in modern, labour-saving equipment. Others have pointed to the low rate of return on the capital which has been invested in manufacturing industry and have adduced that this relative lack of profit deters 'productive' investment. There is persuasive evidence, however, that behavioural and institutional factors have also had a restraining effect on productivity growth. Several micro-studies have emphasized the significance of problems such as overmanning, breakdowns in the flow of production, high fixed overheads, quality faults and high levels of non-productive time.[18] Managerial weaknesses have often been identified as the principal cause of under-used manpower but the potential contribution of workgroups and trade unions cannot simply be brushed aside. Employers tend to argue that they would be more willing to introduce labour-saving technology if the unions would in turn adopt a more flexible approach to manning standards and demarcation. A common trade union reply, however, is that the jobs of their members must, as far as possible, be protected and that the benefits of new technology must be shared equally between the owners of capital and the providers of labour.

It is not difficult to imagine that employees who continually work under the threat of redundancy will be reluctant to give up the various controls which they are able to exert unilaterally over their jobs. As noted in Chapter 5, such controls may be viewed as 'restrictive practices' from a managerial perspective, but may be a rational response to an insecure environment when seen through the eyes of the individual employee. It may also be the case that, while feelings of insecurity breed a reluctance to accept new working practices, resistance to change in itself tends to make insecurity of employment more likely, so that the process is self-reinforcing. As unemployment has risen over the past decade and fears of higher unemployment in the future become more widespread, so resistance to change may in general have hardened. In declining industries such as the docks and newspaper printing, new technology has been introduced only after prolonged strikes. Elsewhere, however, the pattern of initiatives and responses is less clear-cut. Much depends on the circumstances in which change is introduced and on the nature of the benefits which union negotiators and members believe will accrue to them from the proposed changes. In this area the skill and sensitivity of managements may determine the success or failure of a particular initiative.

It must also be remembered that when union officials or shop stewards negotiate changes in working practices, they are seldom concerned with rules which have been incorporated into union rule books. As we noted in Chapter 5, the controls which workers exert over their jobs are usually a matter of informal, unwritten custom and practice which would exist in some form even in the absence of a trade union. Any attempt to dismantle or otherwise weaken these controls is, therefore, a matter of great concern to a union representative and his members. The negotiator must be certain in his own mind that he is not committing his members to changes which they will find unacceptable and that, if they are accepted, the *quid pro quo* from management is sufficient to offset the loss of unilateral control which his members will experience. It is this conflict between the short-term and long-term interests of their members, and the way in which the members themselves perceive this conflict, which often accounts for the apparent ambiguity of union representatives towards new technology and enables their critics to accuse them of 'Luddism'.

Trade unions and income distribution

We argued earlier that a trade union can, through collective bargaining, increase the money wages of its members at a rate which exceeds the general rate of inflation, If, however, other unions follow suit and the money supply is allowed to accommodate the general increases in money wages, inflation will simply accelerate and the real gains to union members will soon disappear. The question, therefore, is whether trade unions can achieve and *sustain* increases in the real wages of their members through collective bargaining, thereby increasing their share of national income.

A conclusive answer is virtually impossible since no one has yet succeeded in relating changes in the distribution of income to changes in union bargaining power. Given the difficulty of finding an objective measure of bargaining power, this is hardly surprising. We can, of course, use the share of employee compensation (total wages and salaries) in GNP as a proxy, and this exhibits a long-term upward trend. In 1860–9 emloyee compensation comprised 45 per cent of GNP; by 1935–8 this had risen to 59 per cent and by 1976 it stood at just over 71 per cent.[19] But this does not necessarily reflect the efforts of trade unions. It may simply be the result of the decline in the relative shares of income from self-employment, rent and foreign investment, and of the steady increase in the proportion of the workforce which is employed in labour-intensive service industries. Obviously there are limits in a capitalist economy to the extent to which employees' compensation, with or without union organization, can be increased at the expense of profits. Firms can maintain profit margins in a 'soft' market by passing higher labour costs on to the consumer in the form of higher prices and in a 'hard' market by reducing employment. If unions press too hard on profits, they will endanger the growth of the capital stock (that is, the level of investment) on which their members' real incomes ultimately depend. The share of profits tends, as one might expect, to vary with the business cycle, falling in recessions and rising during booms. The evidence does not suggest, therefore, that over the past thirty years the expansion of union membership and the alleged growth of union bargaining power in Britain has led to a dramatic fall in the share of profits. Indeed, in 1976 this share was – at 15 per cent – almost exactly the same as in the late 1930s.

Although the share of wages and salaries has risen as a proportion of GNP, the distribution of income and earnings has changed only slowly. In 1976–7, the top 10 per cent of income earners claimed 26 per cent of total personal incomes (23 per cent after tax), which was almost exactly the same as in 1959 and only slightly less than in 1949. The share of the bottom 50 per cent hardly changed at all over the same period, which suggests that, if the various groups of low paid workers who joined a trade union in these years achieved any increase in their real incomes, it was at the expense of some other, probably non-unionized group in broadly the same income band. Changes in the distribution of *wealth* (including property and equities) have apparently been more dramatic. In 1966 the most wealthy 1 per cent of the population owned 33 per cent of total wealth, but by 1974 this had fallen to 22.5 per cent. By the same token, the least wealthy 50 per cent increased their share from 3.5 to 7.1 per cent over the same period. These changes, however, have been attributed to the rapid rise in the market value of all residential property, the sharp fall in share prices in 1972–4, and the tendency towards increased saving by many of those in the lower wealth bands. Indeed, during the period 1974–7 this trend was significantly reversed. By 1977 the share of the most wealthy 1 per cent had climbed back to 24 per cent and that of the least wealthy 50 per cent had fallen back to 5 per cent. Britain, therefore, became an appreciably less egalitarian society under a Labour government which came into office pledged to achieve a 'massive redistribution of wealth and power in favour of working people', and under whose aegis trade union power allegedly reached an all-time peak.

It seems likely, therefore, that, while a trade union can negotiate wage increases which raise its members' real incomes, the effect will fall mainly on some other group of workers whose real wages will decline. A union can restrict entry into a particular trade or profession by means of the closed shop and can use its monopoly power to force up the real supply cost of its members; but this is likely to be a once for all increase and will have adverse repercussions on unorganized or less well-organized workers elsewhere. It is virtually certain that the long-term upward movement in the real wages of the labour force as a whole owes little to the trade union movement. The behaviour of real wages in the long run depends on the growth of real income per head and on the distribution of total income, neither of which appears to be influenced to any appreciable extent by trade union activity. But we must remember, of course, that workers do not join trade unions in the expectation that the share of labour in the national income will be increased. They do, however, believe that collective bargaining will improve their own personal incomes and as long as some improvement follows they will go on believing in the efficacy of collective action. The more that inflation and direct taxation erode their real wage gains, the more likely they are to see collective bargaining as the only method of achieving even a temporary improvement.

Inequality and deprivation

One does not have to be a Marxist or even a socialist to appreciate that the distribution of power within industry itself is, despite a popular impression on the contrary, fundamentally unequal. The main function of trade unionism, both now and in the past, is to impose limits on the power of employers to make *some* of the rules under which employees work without consultation and negotiation. We have argued that the impact of union activity on the wage side of the wage–work bargain has been limited, while the effect of collective bargaining on the distribution of national income has at best been marginal. In these circumstances it hardly seems surprising that decades of organization and activity by trade unions do not appear to have had much effect on the social and occupational status of the bulk of traditional members drawn from the manual working class.

Recent research has confirmed that the occupational hierarchy has been remarkably impervious to collective organization and that there is still a deep division between manual and non-manual work. This division emerges in several ways. First, most manual workers enjoy considerably less security of employment than non-manual employees. Unskilled manual workers are particularly vulnerable to unemployment and are disproportionately represented on the unemployment register at every stage in the economic cycle. This insecurity is an inherent feature of manual employment. As Roberts has observed, 'manual workers do not "join firms", they simply take jobs. Firms do not enrol blue-collar hands as members of the organisation; they are hired to do jobs and remain only as long as the jobs last'.[20] A recent survey by Townshend found that within a five-year period far more manual than non-manual workers had experienced a change of job and that redundancy was much more prevalent among the former. He also found that substantially fewer manual workers had a right to a reasonable (that is, one month) period of notice of dismissal.[21] An additional source of insecurity arises from the way in which manual workers are still paid by the number of hours they work and many depend quite heavily on regular overtime. Consequently manual earnings are much more likely to fluctuate from week to week than most non-manual earnings. Manual workers are also more vulnerable to loss of earnings through ill-health and industrial accidents. They are far less likely than non-manual employees to receive full or indeed any payment by the employer for sickness and injury, and are also less likely to be covered by an occupational pension scheme.

It should also be remembered that, while some manual workers are well paid by white collar standards, their affluence is not based on a progressive career structure. White collar employees, especially those in managerial and professional jobs, can normally anticipate a long-term career in which earnings rise with age and experience, reaching a peak just before retirement. Most manual workers are, by contrast, likely to attain their maximum earning-power much earlier in life and may well see their earnings taper off in late middle-age as their physical capacity declines. Thus, while some manual workers may enjoy a relative advantage in take-home pay during the early years of work, this will have completely disappeared by the attainment of middle-age. Moreover, as a professional or managerial career progresses, so the status and authority of the post-holder increases. The work itself is likely to become more challenging and satisfying, and the various fringe benefits associated with white collar employment are likely to grow in importance. Even low-level non-manual workers, however, tend to enjoy considerable advantages over their manual counterparts. In terms of basic working conditions, such as washing, canteen and toilet facilities, manual workers are much more likely to experience deprivation than non-manual workers. In 1974, for example, the AUEW reported that one in four of its 1.2 million members were employed in factories which were still not equipped with toilets. Holiday entitlements and hours of work also differ considerably between manual and relatively low-grade non-manual employees. Clerical staff are likely to have a shorter working week, longer holidays (which increase with length of service) and more discretion over when to take their holidays than are manual workers.[22]

These inequalities in the workplace have been well summarized by Roberts:

> Manual work is the sale of labour power, little more, for money and little else. It offers no prospects of a progressive career and little security. The

incumbent remains on the receiving end of authority. If the work is intrinsically satisfying, this is an unexpected bonus, not a normal expectation. By the public-at-large the work is accorded little status . . . the vast majority of jobs are clearly on one side of the divide or the other, and most workers know where they stand.[23]

Why, therefore, have manual workers' trade unions failed to bridge or at least narrow this divide? Why have they paid relatively little attention to all those aspects of the employment contract, other than pay, which strongly affect the status, satisfaction and security of their members? The answer lies in the generally observed acquiescence of their members in the *status quo*. In his 1974 survey Daniel, for example, found that most employees were remarkably content with their situation and that they apparently accepted, without question, the existence of traditional differentials.[24] While Daniel's survey was aimed specifically at wage issues, the same conclusions doubtless apply to non-wage aspects of the work situation. The absence of widespread feelings of relative deprivation was attributed by Daniel to the 'very narrow social horizons' which most people have when evaluating their own position. As long as groups of manual workers continue to compare themselves with other manual groups doing similar jobs in the same locality, the existence of profound inequalities between themselves and groups who are further up the occupational hierarchy is unlikely to evoke a strong sense of injustice.

The apparent insensitivity of manual union negotiators to these glaring inequalities and their continuing preoccupation with money wages may also be explained by the slow growth in their members' real incomes. Union representatives in other EEC countries can devote a great deal of attention to the equalization of status, security and fringe benefits in the knowledge that their members' real wages have steadily increased and that additional non-wage benefits can be financed from higher productivity. Their efforts in this field are also legitimized by a powerful tradition of employer paternalism and a strong framework of state regulation. In countries such as France and West Germany, the government imposed restrictions on the power of employers to dismiss long before British politicians became aware of the gaps and weaknesses in the voluntary system. Occasionally an awareness of the gap between British and continental practices intrudes into the conventional process of wage bargaining. One such example occurred in 1976 when the NUM apparently realized that British coal miners were unique in so far as their age of retirement was 65 compared with an EEC norm of 60. The prospects for a general equalization in Britain, however, may have been further reduced by the growth of white collar unionism. There can be little doubt that the desire to protect traditional differentials and the associated trappings of occupational status has given a powerful impetus to white collar union recruitment and explains the antipathy of many white collar employees towards manual unions. It would be realistic to assume, therefore, that in workplaces where white collar workers are well organized, any movement towards the erosion of status differentials will be resisted. We may also predict that a renewed attempt by the government to close the gap by means of legislation, thereby carrying forward the advances embodied in the Employment Protection Act of 1975, will be resisted by employers on financial grounds.

Trade unions and worker participation

Over the past ten years or so, some trade union leaders and academics have expressed dissatisfaction with the limited results of collective bargaining. As a result, within the trade union movement there has been a marked growth of interest in possible methods of extending joint decision-making into areas hitherto reserved exclusively for senior management. The General Council's report to the 1974 Congress, for example, argued that

> there are a number of specific questions of close concern to workpeople which are not being effectively subjected to joint regulation through the present processes of collective bargaining and additional forms of joint regulation are needed, particularly as capital becomes more concentrated and the central decisions of boards of directors seem increasingly remote from any impact by workpeople through their own organisations.

The questions which the authors of this report had in mind obviously impinged on traditional managerial functions such as the allocation of financial resources, the profitability of the enterprise, and plans for the expansion or contraction of employment. Such arguments recognize that, while some rudimentary information on those issues may be extracted from management in the normal course of collective bargaining, the relevant *policy* decisions will already have been made by senior managers and it is these decisions which typically fix the constraints within which negotiations subsequently take place.

Even at the height of the TUC's enthusiasm for extended participation, however, several union leaders expressed strong ideological opposition to any proposal which would place union representatives in company boardrooms and give them the power to decide policy on an equal basis with management. Collective bargaining in its traditional form enables union representatives to oppose and, if their organization is strong enough, ultimately veto policy decisions and initiatives taken by management. The right to *oppose* is therefore seen as the acid test of trade union independence, and many union officials are apprehensive about the loss of freedom inherent in any proposal that their shop floor activists should become closely involved in the formulation of policy. This view is strongly supported by various surveys of shop floor opinion which, as we noted in Chapter 5, indicate that there is little interest in substantive issues which appear remote from the individual employee's own job and work situation. Thus, while a small number of public and private enterprises have experimented with various forms of worker representation at board level, the general level of interest in worker directors seems to have declined since the publication of the Bullock Commission's report in 1977.

While the details of the Bullock report need not concern us here, the general concept of union representation on company boards raises one or two problems which we should note. In a non-union enterprise, the role of worker directors is likely to be fairly straightforward. Management may wish to have an experienced, articulate employee present when policy issues affecting the workforce are being discussed so that the rest of the board can derive some benefit from a 'shop floor' perspective on these issues. In these circumstances the role of the worker director is likely to be purely consultative. In an organized workplace, however, where collective bargaining is well established, worker directors face a more complex task. As members of the board they not only have the same legal responsibilities as the management directors but, more importantly, are likely to develop the same sense of corporate loyalty. Their attitudes to specific issues which come before the board for decision will be strongly influenced by the managerial information which is given to them. They may as a result find it increasingly difficult to maintain effective communication with their own constituents on the shop floor, and indeed, may be seen by the latter as practically indistinguishable from the other directors.[25] Management will strongly resist any attempt by worker directors to *negotiate* on behalf of their constituents, and other union activities will also insist that the established framework of collective bargaining is maintained. Consequently, even in a unionized enterprise, the role of worker directors is likely to be consultative in nature and, as such, may have little if any effect on the overall management of the business.

The Bullock Commission sought to remove this fundamental difficulty by giving worker directors *parity* of representation on company boards. The possibility that this might paralyse decision-making was anticipated in the commission's proposal that a third but smaller group of 'independent' directors should be co-opted by the others – the $2x + y$ formula – which would hold the balance between them. Bullock also recommended that the selection of worker directors should take place solely through trade union machinery and that the unions themselves should hold the initiative in introducing worker directors at enterprise level. Critics of the commission argued that these proposals would in effect bring collective bargaining into the boardroom, with disastrous effects on the decision-making process. In defence of the $2x + y$ formula, however, it could be argued that no real benefit will ever be derived from worker representation at board level unless it is based on the principle of equal responsibility. If worker directors can always be out-voted by the management majority, they will have no incentive to accept any responsibility for whatever decisions are made and thus for the overall success of the enterprise. The Bullock approach can therefore be seen as a strategy for *integrating* union representatives in the process of policy-making, thereby removing the adversary, reactive role which conventional collective bargaining requires union negotiators to assume.

It is precisely this prospective integration, however, which arouses so much apprehension in the minds of many union leaders and activists. European experience in this field suggests that parity of representation is a double-edged weapon. In Batstone's words: 'Parity of representation appears to be an important condition to ensure that worker representatives become integrated into the informal processes of debate and information exchange. But in doing so they tend to become even more integrated into a managerial perspective.'[26] It is by no means obvious that the small group of independent directors proposed by Bullock would be able to weaken the inevitable tendency for managerial perspectives and priorities to dominate the decision-making process. But, above all, the Bullock strategy assumes that union-appointed directors will be as eager to accept the responsibilities of board membership as they will be to grasp the power it entails. The evidence which unions such as the EETPU presented to the commission suggests that many are not. Parity of representation

> . . . could convey the impression that the management has captured or absorbed the trade unions. In particular situations, the workers who held that view might be driven to set up means of alternative representation at the place of work. In a world where state power and management prerogative have become more concentrated, more pervasive and yet more remote from those who are affected by the exercise of those powers, the impression that worker directors represent the absorption of trade unions into this scenario of corporate elitism is even more perilous.

The obvious difficulty facing trade unionists who adopt this thoroughly traditional perspective is how to justify the *status quo* in view of the manifestly limited achievements of conventional collective bargaining. With all its faults, the Bullock report at least gave the unions an opportunity to extend their influence into a sphere of decision-making from which they have traditionally been excluded. The response of the unions themselves, however, varied from lukewarm approval to outright hostility. The force of habit and tradition, strengthened by the limited perspectives of rank and file members, has once again overridden the desire for change.

The reform of collective bargaining

The foregoing analysis implies that union officials and their members have in effect tied themselves to a treadmill. By resisting any change which may prejudice their traditional right to oppose management decisions, they have ensured that any future changes in the structure of power in industry will only come about through the processes of conventional collective bargaining. This means, of course, that such changes will at best be marginal. The negotiation of more *status quo* clauses in procedure agreements, for example, may put a more effective brake on unilateral action by managements. The gradual extension of formal joint regulation over issues which have hitherto been determined by informal and customary practices will also strengthen the idea of management by agreement. To the extent that this happens, however, it will tend to enhance the authority of management by legitimizing the role of union representatives in the system of control.

Of more immediate significance is the possibility of changing the collective bargaining system in a way which recognizes that governments have a legitimate and permanent interest in the process of wage determination. This involves far more than the familiar debate about whether Britain needs or does not need an incomes policy. The problem which must be solved is that of gaining the co-operation of union negotiators at all levels of the bargaining system in implementing reforms which will help them to achieve their primary objective in collective bargaining, namely a permanent increase in the real incomes of their members. While the critics of incomes policies are right to remind us that direct government intervention in collective bargaining has frequently succeeded in increasing the rate of money–wage inflation once the dam has been breached, they tend to ignore the role which an incomes policy *could* play in encouraging institutional changes. While we would not seek to claim that trade unions cause inflation, neither would we argue that the process by which money wages are determined is totally irrelevant to the general rate of inflation.

It was argued above that the fragmented structure of wage bargaining in Britain enables negotiators to ignore the macro-economic implications of agreements they make. The historical *rationale* of free collective bargaining was that the private decisions of employers and trade unions would by definition reflect their own needs and thus the needs of the national economy. However valid this assumption may have been in an era when the impact of market forces on wage bargaining was relatively sharp and immediate, it is extremely questionable in the context of a 'managed' economy. The growing importance of bargaining at the level of the enterprise and the workplace since 1945 has underlined the dichotomy which exists between the decisions of private negotiators and the objectives of policy-makers at national level. The problem is one of conflicting rationalities and, as Blackaby has pointed out:

> The requirement for policy is to try to find institutional changes which, as it were, bring the two rationalities closer together. The changes have to make more transparent the macro-economic consequences of the sum total of individual negotiating decisions, in such a way that those individual decisions are themselves affected.[27]

Blackaby has therefore suggested three reforms which should help to achieve this objective. First, he has proposed that each year the government, the TUC and the CBI should try to reach an agreement not only on what the level of pay settlements ought to be, but also (in the spirit of a 'social contract') on broader economic and social priorities. Second, he has advocated that all major negotiations in both the public and the private sector should be brought towards a common settlement date. Third, he has proposed that a national arbitral body should be established, possibly along the lines of the former Prices and Incomes Board, so that claims for exceptional treatment could be properly evaluated.

The idea of an annual tripartite agreement has been canvassed many times in recent years and was openly favoured by the last Labour government in its closing days. Such an agreement could not be limited to a simple norm for pay settlements, whatever political difficulties an enlargement in its scope might cause. As we noted above, the living standards of union members (and all employees) are now more dependent on the government's policy towards direct and indirect taxation than on changes in money wages and prices. Discussions on the structure and incidence of taxation will also call into question the volume and growth of public spending, and this is an issue on which the trade union movement and the employers' organizations are sharply divided. This division of opinion in turn rests on conflicting analyses of what has gone wrong with the British economy and on opposing strategies for increasing its rate of growth. It follows that the process of reaching a tripartite agreement is likely to be long and fraught with difficulties. It would be hard, for example, to imagine the powerful public sector lobby within the TUC accepting reductions in direct taxation as a *quid pro quo* for accepting relatively moderate pay settlements if such reductions were being financed by severe cuts in public employment. Nevertheless, without some kind of broad consensus it is difficult to see how the rate of inflation can be brought down to a more reasonable level and kept there.

The adoption of a common settlement date for major wage negotiations has also been mooted for several years. Obviously it would not only assist employers and governments in their annual budgeting but would also prevent some of the 'leap-frogging' which occurs when pay bargaining extends over most of the year. The problems involved in achieving this objective are, however, immense. The process of making comparisons would obviously be much more difficult for any union if all the groups with whom it wished to compare its own members' pay were simultaneously negotiating their own increases. Union officials who currently negotiate major wage increases in the latter part of the bargaining round may well feel that they enjoy a valuable tactical advantage over groups who settle earlier on, which they will no doubt be reluctant to lose. Above all, however, there is no practical way in which the total number of pay agreements can be synchronized at any one time in the year. The fragmented structure of wage bargaining in the manufacturing sector would enable private negotiators to adjust wage levels at any time if the need arose. Consequently, even if the government succeeded in persuading all public sector negotiators to move towards a common settlement date, with a common norm for settlements, difficulties would soon arise from the subsequent upward drift in earnings levels caused by informal and uncontrollable bargaining in the private sector.

The re-establishment of a national agency which would evaluate claims for special treatment seems more practicable, if only because there is an encouraging precedent. The TUC, however, has repeatedly voiced its objections to such a body, which are in essence based on the fear that it would limit the freedom of a trade union to get the best possible terms and conditions for its members through the use of its own bargaining power. In the public sector it is easy to see how references to such a body could become a very useful bargaining tactic for management negotiators. Third-party intervention would relieve the pressure on management to settle without in any way guaranteeing that an acceptable offer would eventually be made to the union negotiators. Nevertheless, the success which initially attended the work of the Comparability Commission suggests that even public sector unions will co-operate with a body which is seen to be independent of government influence and capable of making objective recommendations. The main deficiency in the current arrangements is that since 1971 there has been no national body empowered to examine wage agreements from the perspective of establishing a closer connection between money wages and productivity. In the absence of such a body, any future attempt to use incomes policy as a stimulus to improving the general level of efficiency, in either the public or the private sector, is unlikely to be effective.

Despite the shortcomings of Blackaby's proposals, there is little doubt that the principle on which they are based – the permanent regulation of collective bargaining – must be firmly grasped by governments, employers and trade unionists alike. One reason why incomes policies have sooner or later lost the support of negotiators is that they have all been introduced as a temporary expedient. Politicians have regularly assured negotiators that, when a given inflationary crisis has been resolved, incomes policy will be dismantled and free collective bargaining restored. The pretence was abandoned in 1978 when the Labour government announced its conversion to the principle of permanent regulation. Its successor, however, has rejected the concept of an incomes policy and has to date relied on a combination of monetary policy and cash limits. The difficulty with any policy which assumes the existence of a trade-off between inflation and unemployment is, quite simply, that no one seems to know exactly how far the Phillips curve has moved and how much unemployment will be needed before inflation begins to fall. Moreover, the imposition of stringent limits on public sector revenue expenditure implies that the government must have some kind of strategy, however rudimentary, for negotiating with its own employees. One can certainly sympathize with employers and union representatives who oppose a return to detailed statutory regulation of the kind which was imposed in 1972–4. A different approach, however, is needed in the circumstances of the early 1980s – one which will allow the parties enough flexibility to resolve their own particular problems and simultaneously encourage them to follow central guidelines, embracing the reform of plant pay structures and the negotiation of changes in working practices. Bearing in mind the problems of bringing customary unilateral controls over work under joint regulation, it cannot be claimed that this approach offers a magic formula for transforming workplace relations. It does, however, have the overriding advantage of focusing the attention of negotiators on the relationship between real incomes and efficiency and, given the deep seated problem of low productivity in British industry, this is a relationship which needs to be strengthened.

Conclusion

Devising blueprints for the reform of collective bargaining has been a favourite occupation among 'informed' observers of British industrial relations since the mid 1960s. Such strategies assume, however, that trade union representatives and their constituents can be induced to accept the normative principles on which the concept of bargaining *reform* is based. These include the desirability of formal joint regulation at plant and company level and the need for a more effective system of joint control over employee behaviour. The assumption is that extended joint regulation will help to legitimize managerial authority in an age when employees are less inclined to accept orders without question and passively tolerate arbitrary behaviour by their superiors. Without the active co-operation of the workforce, expressed through its shop floor representatives, managements will be unable to get on with the job of improving the efficiency and competitiveness of their enterprises. Unless British industry becomes more competitive, unemployment will continue to increase, living standards will decline and the *raison d'être* of trade unionism will in effect be challenged. The trade unions have, in short, acquired enough power to impose a veto on the future progress of the British economy but the more they use it, the more their own members will suffer. It follows that trade unionists must sooner or later accept both the logic of reform and the various changes that will inevitably follow. These include the general elimination of inefficient working practices, the acceptance of a measure of formal responsibility for the well-being of the enterprise and a recognition of the legitimacy of government regulation. All strategies for bargaining reform and worker participation are therefore based on the assumed need to integrate union representatives and their members into the framework of management control.

The analysis presented in this book suggests that this concept of reform and participation, however logical it may be in managerial terms, is likely to be viewed in a different light on the shop floor. Many factors influence the behaviour of employees, and in a book of this kind only their barest outline can be sketched. Clearly, however, they do not form a simple, one-dimensional pattern. Taking a broad retrospective view, the aspirations of employees have changed over the past two or three decades in terms of both the material rewards of work and the standard of treatment expected from management. To the extent that these changes have been reflected in either the growth of union membership, or the emergence of an articulate steward leadership in the workplace, or the spread of strike activity into hitherto strike-free areas, one can speak of a 'new militancy' among employees and those who represent them in collective bargaining. Yet these expectations have been mediated by union negotiators at all levels and tailored to fit the conventions of collective bargaining. The development of workplace organization and the spread of closed shops illustrates the crucial relationship between the power which union representatives seek to exert over their members and the power which they can wield in order to achieve certain objectives on their members' behalf. These objectives are, however, conditioned by the negotiators' view of what can in practice be achieved and, as such, are typically conservative in character.

Yet it would be a gross over-simplification to regard union officials and shop stewards purely as 'managers of discontent', helping to keep their members' demands within the framework of management control and the bargaining system. Employees' expectations of what can be achieved through collective action in the workplace are determined as much if not more by their experience outside the factory or office as by what they encounter in the work situation itself. From what we know of the principles of wage bargaining and the profound inequalities of status and security which are still apparent throughout British industry, it would seem that expectations change far more slowly than the more enthusiastic advocates of the 'new militancy' often imply. This does not mean that all the reported expressions of satisfaction with the *status quo* should be taken at their face value. Union officials and stewards alike have occasionally found themselves unable to control spontaneous outbreaks of discontent among hitherto quiescent workgroups. But it does suggest that in many work situations, even where union organization is relatively strong, grievances are often seen in personal or at most group terms. The larger the workplace, the more fragmented the sense of collective loyalty is likely to be. The growing obsession with wage and salary differentials, while partly the result of rapid inflation, also reflects the continuing strength of occupational consciousness. Indeed, one of the most difficult tests which union representatives in the workplace are likely to encounter is that of welding together disparate groups of employees in pursuit of *trade union* principles. Thus, in situations where union representatives are negotiating rule changes of some kind, their constituents are likely to view these changes from the perspective of their own immediate interests, which are not necessarily congruent with those of the representatives themselves let alone with those of the employer.

If trade unions pursued their bargaining objectives with the ruthless determination which popular reportage would sometimes have us believe and controlled their members with the iron-handed discipline which some critics have urged them to adopt, they would be a much more powerful force in industry than they in fact are. In reality, of course, most trade unions are pluralistic organizations in which conflicts of interest occur at every level. The larger the union and the more diverse the occupational characteristics of its membership, the more vulnerable it will be to internal conflict. There is always likely to be a dichotomy between formal and informal patterns of activity within every large union. On the one hand there is the formal system embodied in the union constitution, including the method of election to office and the pressure group activity of the contestants, the annual ritual of policy-making by conference and the administration of branch affairs. On the other hand there is the informal reality of workplace organization, including the strategic role of the shop steward, the negotiation of agreements which fit the circumstances of the workplace as distinct from union policy, the informal arrangements for inter-union co-operation and the taking of unofficial action. Some unions have attempted to bridge the gap by seeking to formalize the role of 'workplace democracy' within their constitutional systems of decision-making. The scope for conflict, however, will always be present and may in fact increase over the next few years.

For managements, the growth of quasi-autonomous workplace organizations presents a challenge and an opportunity. To the extent that a steward organization becomes less dependent on full-time officials and more inclined to interpret union policy in the light of local circumstances, there may well be more scope for managements to take initiatives on sensitive issues in the expectation of getting a positive response. But this view assumes that local union representatives are likely to adopt a more 'realistic' and 'responsible' approach to change and innovation that the official policy of their union would otherwise allow. While this may be the case in certain circumstances, much depends on the precise context in which managerial initiatives are launched and on the quality of management itself. It must always be remembered that for most employees, the behaviour of management is a much more salient feature of everyday life in the workplace than the activities of the union to which they may or may not belong. If rank and file members and their representatives have strong feelings on a given issue, any advice from their union official which runs contrary to their own objectives is likely to be ignored. In other words, the formal adoption by a trade union of a policy which is, for example, favourable to technological change or which advocates co-operation with an incomes policy may be repudiated by the leaders of a sophisticated workplace organization. Such non-compliance is usually ascribed to the influence of 'militants' and 'subversives' by the mass media, but seen from the perspective of the shop floor it may be a thoroughly rational response to a particular set of circumstances.

Yet whatever light has been or will be shed on the complexity of trade union behaviour – and much remains to be discovered – there is little doubt that trade union power will continue to be a major political issue in Britain in the foreseeable future. As long as workgroups who happen to be union members have the power to disrupt important services and supplies, as long as noisy and violent mass picketing is seen on television screens and as long as 'inflationary' wage claims are the staple diet of the mass media, the unions will continue to be regarded as a major problem. The problem for the unions themselves, however, is to continue to recruit new members, or maintain existing membership levels, at a time when their relative ineffectiveness is likely to be dramatically exposed. We may anticipate that in an era of high and rising unemployment, high inflation and stagnant or declining standards of living, the attraction of collective organization will be enhanced. The appeal of trade unionism is likely to be particularly strong for those employees who feel threatened by technological change, and it may be that many unions will be compelled to resist the introduction of what they see as job destroying technology. To the extent that this happens, the unions will only succeed in enhancing their reputation for unreasonable obstruction and short-sighted conservatism. The difficulty for the unions is that the whole weight of their history and tradition lies behind the principle of protecting and preserving their members' jobs and real incomes in a hostile environment. Their limited success in achieving these objectives does not seem to discourage employees from believing that they can in fact be achieved and the main task facing the unions over the next twenty years will be to continue to encourage this belief.

Notes and references

Preface

1 Ferdinand Zweig, *The British Worker* (Penguin 1952), pp. 181–2.

Chapter 1: History and tradition

1 Sidney Webb and Beatrice Webb, *Industrial Democracy* (London 1898), p. 173.
2 ibid., p. 562.
3 Eric Wigham, *The Power to Manage* (London: Macmillan 1973), p. 30.
4 Webb and Webb, *Industrial Democracy*, p. 572.
5 E. H. Phelps Brown, *The Growth of British Industrial Relations* (London: Macmillan 1959), pp. 132–6.
6 Webb and Webb, *Industrial Democracy*, p. 579.
7 Allan Flanders, *Management and Unions* (London: Faber 1970), p. 217.
8 Webb and Webb, *Industrial Democracy*, p. 591.
9 Eric Wigham, *Strikes and the Government, 1893–1974* (London: Macmillan 1976), p. 57
10 Webb and Webb, *Industrial Democracy*, p. 596.
11 ibid., p. 148.
12 ibid., p. 161.
13 ibid., p. 174.
14 Phelps Brown, *The Growth of British Industrial Relations*, p. 124.
15 Webb and Webb, *Industrial Democracy*, p. 219.
16 ibid., pp. 268–9.
17 ibid., p. 275.
18 Phelps Brown, *The Growth of British Industrial Relations*, p. 152.
19 Henry Pelling, *Popular Politics and Society in Late Victorian Britain* (London: Macmillan 1968), p. 71.
20 Webb and Webb, *Industrial Democracy*, p. 139.
21 ibid., p. 120.
22 John Lovell and B. C. Roberts, *A Short History of the TUC* (London: Macmillan 1968), pp. 20–1.
23 Webb and Webb, *Industrial Democracy*, pp. 268–9.

24 ibid., pp. 47–9.
25 Phelps Brown, *The Growth of British Industrial Relations*, pp. 231–2.
26 Webb and Webb, *Industrial Democracy*, p. 221.
27 Pelling, *Popular Politics and Society*, p. 150.
28 Margaret Morris, *The General Strike* (Penguin 1976), p. 254.
29 Phelps Brown, *The Growth of British Industrial Relations*, p. 194.
30 Pelling, *Popular Politics and Society*, p. 130.
31 V. L. Allen, *Trade Unions and the Government* (Longman 1960), pp. 235–7.

Chapter 2: Trade unions and the law

1 Otto Kahn-Freund, *Labour and the Law*, 2nd ed. (London: Stevens & Sons 1977), p. 3.
2 Richard Hyman, *Industrial Relations: A Marxist Introduction* (London: Macmillan 1975), p. 23.
3 ibid., pp. 131–48.
4 Kahn-Freund, *Labour and the Law*, pp. 163–6.
5 W. E. J. McCarthy, 'Principles and possibilities in British trade union law', in W. E. J. McCarthy (ed.), *Trade Unions* (Penguin 1972), pp. 346–8.
6 E. H. Phelps Brown, *The Growth of British Industrial Relations* (London: Macmillan 1959), pp. 183–4.
7 K. W. Wedderburn, *The Worker and the Law*, 2nd ed. (Penguin 1971), pp. 322–3.
8 ibid., p. 29. In this case the union concerned (the TGWU) was taking action in order to enforce a closed shop. A comparison with *Quinn* v. *Leathem* (1901) indicates how far the judges' attitudes had changed in forty years.
9 Allan Flanders, 'The future of voluntarism', *Personnel Management*, vol. 48, no. 278 (December 1966), p. 199.
10 *Royal Commission on Trade Unions and Employers' Associations, Report*, Cmnd 3623 (HMSO, June 1968), p. 288.
11 ibid., p. 302.
12 ibid., p. 136, para. 505.
13 ibid., p. 137, para. 508.
14 ibid., p. 65, para. 256.
15 'The agreement and institution of (satisfactory) procedures seems unlikely . . . to be a rapid process. . . . In the meantime if present trends continue, the number of unofficial and unconstitutional strikes, which we describe as a serious and urgent problem, will continue to grow. In these circumstances I have been reluctant to trust entirely to the expected benefits of better procedure agreements, and have sought some interim remedy which would be both workable and just. I have found it very elusive' (ibid., p. 279).

16 Peter Jenkins, *The Battle of Downing Street* (Tonbridge: Charles Knight 1970).

17 It was also contradicted by the Court of Appeal, which held that a union was *not* liable for the actions of its agents when the latter acted outside the scope of the authority delegated to them by the union.

18 Brian Weekes, Michael Mellish, Linda Dickens and John Lloyd, *Industrial Relations and the Limits of Law* (Oxford: Blackwell 1975), p. 63.

19 ibid., pp. 12–14.

20 ibid., p. 223.

21 When the case was ultimately decided by the House of Lords, the fine stood at £55,000.

22 Jim Mortimer, 'New series' *Personnel Management*, vol. 7, no. 1 January 1975), p. 30.

23 The Lords held that ACAS 'is not entitled to make a recommendation for recognition so long as it remains in ignorance of the opinions held by the majority of the workforce or of what may be conflicting opinions held by any group among them of significant size': *ACAS* v. *Grunwick Processing Laboratories Ltd* (1977). The fact that ACAS was, in this case, unable to ascertain the opinions of the majority because of the employer's refusal to co-operate made no difference.

24 *Earl* v. *Slater and Wheeler (Airlyne)* (1973).

25 *Grundy (Teddington)* v. *Willis* (1976).

26 Kevin Hawkins, *The Management of Industrial Relations* (Penguin 1978), pp. 161–2.

27 W. W. Daniel and Elizabeth Stilgoe, 'The impact of employment protection laws', *Policy Studies Institute*, no. 577 (June 1978), p. 84.

28 *Express Newspapers Ltd* v. *McShane and Ashton* (1979).

29 *Sarvant and others* v. *Central Electricity Generating Board* (1976).

30 *Royal Commission on Trade Unions and Employers' Associations*, p. 162.

31 John Gennard, Stephen Dunn and Michael Wright, 'The content of British closed shop agreements', *Department of Employment Gazette*, vol. 87, no. 11 (November 1979), pp. 1091–2.

32 McCarthy, *Principles and possibilities*, p. 365.

Chapter 3: Growth and structure

1 Michael Shanks, *The Stagnant Society* (Penguin Books 1961) p. 73.

2 Robert Price and G. S. Bain, 'Union growth revisited: 1948–74 in perspective', *British Journal of Industrial Relations*, November 1976. vol. 14, no. 3.

3 G. S. Bain, *The Growth of White Collar Unionism* (Oxford University Press 1970), pp. 51–2.

4 Price and Bain, 'Union growth revisited', pp. 350.

5 H. B. Davis, 'The theory of union growth' in W. E. J. McCarthy (ed.), *Trade Unions,* (Penguin 1972), pp. 215–17.
6 Price and Bain, 'Union growth revisited', pp. 349–50.
7 ibid.
8 G. S. Bain and Farouk Elsheikh, *Union Growth and the Business Cycle* (Oxford University Press 1976), ch. 4.
9 F. T. Blackaby, 'The reform of the wage bargaining system', *National Institute Economic Review,* no. 85 (August 1978), pp. 49–54.
10 G. S. Bain and Farouk Elsheikh, 'An inter-industry analysis of unionisation in Britain, *British Journal of Industrial Relations,* July 1979. vol. 18, no. 2, p. 142.
11 ibid., p. 153.
12 See, for example, James Morrell, 'Unions losing grounds', *Management Today* (February 1978), pp. 7–8.
13 Richard Hyman, *Industrial Relations: A Marxist Introduction* (London: Macmillan 1975), p. 52.
14 H. A. Turner, 'The morphology of trade unionism', in W. E. J. McCarthy (ed.), *Trade Unions* (Penguin 1972), p. 98.
15 ibid., p. 99.
16 Royal Commission on Trade Unions and Employers' Associations, *Report,* Cmnd 3623 (HMSO, June 1968), para. 679.
17 R. T. Buchanan, 'Merger waves in British trade unionism', *Industrial Relations Journal,* Summer 1974. vol. 5, no. 2, p. 39.
18 ibid., p. 40.
19 White collar unions have felt particularly aggrieved at a system of representation which seems weighted against them. As Clive Jenkins of ASTMS declared at the 1974 Annual Congress: 'The present groupings are a reflection of a ghostly membership of long-dead trade unionists. What we have is a middle based on ancient patterns of nineteenth century trade and organisation, a patter of industrial organisation.'
20 Peter J. Kalis, 'The effectiveness and utility of the disputes committee of the trades union congress', *British Journal of Industrial Relations,* vol. 16, no. 1, pp. 47–8.
21 Allan Flanders, *Trade Unions* (London: Hutchinson 1968), pp. 65–6.
22 Arthur Marsh, E. O. Evans and E. Garcia, *Workplace Industrial Relations in Engineering,* Engineering Employers' Federation, 1971, p. 63.

Chapter 4: Leaders and members

1 Richard Hyman, *Industrial Relations: A Marxist Introduction* (London: Macmillan 1975), p. 65.
2 Sidney Webb and Beatrice Webb *Industrial Democracy* (London: 1898), p. 58.

3 H. A. Clegg, *The System of Industrial Relations in Great Britain* (Oxford: Blackwell 1970), pp. 79–80.

4 B. C. Roberts, *Trade Union Government and Administration in Great Britain* (London: Bell & Sons 1956), p. 105.

5 Joseph Goldstein, *The Government of British Trade Unions* (London: Allen & Unwin 1952), pp. 270–1.

6 Clegg, *The System of Industrial Relations,* p. 86.

7 Webb and Webb, *Industrial Democracy,* p. 59.

8 R. Michels, *Political Parties,* (New York: Free Press 1962).

9 Tony Lane and Kenneth Roberts, *Strike at Pilkingtons* (London: Fontana/Collins 1971), pp. 215–22.

10 Michael Moran, *The Union of Post Office Workers* (London: Macmillan 1974), pp. 145–7.

11 R. Undy, 'The electoral influence of the opposition party in the AUEW engineering section, 1960–75' *British Journal of Industrial Relations,* vol. 17, no. 1 (March 1979), pp. 20–4.

12 Clegg, *The System of Industrial Relations,* p. 96.

13 ibid., p. 101.

14 Roger Undy, 'The devolution of bargaining levels and responsibilities in the Transport and General Workers' Union, 1965–75', *Industrial Relations Journal*, vol. 9 (1978).

15 Lane and Roberts, *Strike at Pilkingtons,* pp. 190–5.

16 Hyman, *Industrial Relations,* pp. 86–9.

17 John Hemingway, *Conflict and Democracy* (Oxford University Press 1978), pp. 14–17.

18 ibid., p. 24.

19 Allan Flanders, *Management and Unions* (London: Faber 1970), pp. 18–19.

20 Hyman, *Industrial Relations,* p. 91.

Chapter 5: Activity in the workplace

1 H. A. Clegg, *The Changing System of Industrial Relations in Great Britain* (Oxford: Blackwell 1979), p. 53.

2 John Purcell and Robin Smith (eds.) *The Control of Work* (London: Macmillan 1979), pp. 3–4.

3 Allan Flanders, *Management and Unions* (London: Faber 1979), p. 112.

4 Huw Benyon, *Working for Ford* (London: Allen Lane 1973), p. 138.

5 I. Boraston, H. A. Clegg and M. Rimmer, *Workplace and Union* (London: Heinemann 1975), p. 187.

6 William Brown, Robert Ebsworth and Michael Terry, 'Factors shaping shop steward organisation in Britain', *British Journal of Industrial Relations,* vol. 16, no. 2 (July 1978), pp. 141–3.

7 Eric Batstone, Ian Boraston and Stephen Frenkel, *Shop Stewards in Action* (Oxford: Blackwell 1977), pp. 137–53.

8 Royal Commission on Trade Unions and Employers' Associations, *Report,* Cmnd 3623, HMSO, June 1968, pp. 28–9.
9 John Gennard, Stephen Dunn and Michael Wright, 'The content of British closed shop agreements', *Department of Employment Gazette,* vol. 87, no. 11 (November 1979), pp. 1092–4.
10 W. E. J. McCarthy, *The Closed Shop in Britain* (Oxford: Blackwell 1964), pp. 28–37.
11 *Sarvant and others* v. *Central Electricity Generating Board* (1976).
12 Gennard, *et al,* 'The content of British closed shop agreements', pp. 1092–4.
13 H. A. Turner, G. Clack and G. Roberts, *Labour Relations in the Motor Industry,* (London: Allen & Unwin 1967), pp. 336–8.
14 Sidney Webb and Beatrice Webb, *Industrial Democracy* (London 1898), pp. 658–9.
15 Royal Commission on Trade Unions and Employers' Associations, p. 105.
16 Allan Flanders, *The Fawley Productivity Agreements* (London: Faber 1964), chs. 4, 5 and 6.
17 Allan Flanders, *Management and Unions* (London: Faber 1970), pp. 172–3.
18 William Brown, *Piecework Bargaining* (London: Heinemann 1973), p. 147.
19 ibid., p. 151.
20 Michael Terry, 'The inevitable growth of informality', *British Journal of Industrial Relations,* vol. 15, no. 1 (March 1977).
21 Harvie Ramsay, 'Participation: the shop floor view', *British Journal of Industrial Relations,* vol. 14, no. 2 (July 1976), pp. 130–3.
22 Peter Brannen, Eric Batstone, Derek Fatchett, Philip White, *The Worker Directors* (London: Hutchinson 1976), pp. 36–46.
23 M. Marchington, 'Shop-floor control and industrial relations', in John Purcell and Robin Smith (eds.), *The Control of Work* (London: Macmillan 1979), p. 150.
24 Alan Fox, *A Sociology of Work in Industry* (London: Collier Macmillan 1971), p. 149.
25 ibid., p. 150.
26 Richard Hyman, *Disputes Procedures in Action* (London: Heinemann 1972), p. 84.
27 Eric Batstone, Ian Boraston and Stephen Frenkel, *The Social Organisation of Strikes,* (Oxford: Blackwell 1978), p. 23.

Chapter 6: Collective bargaining

1 Royal Commission on Trade Unions and Employers' Associations, *Report,* Cmnd 3623, (HMSO, June 1968), p. 33, para. 129.

2 ibid.
3 ibid., p. 36, para. 149.
4 A. W. J. Thomson and V. V. Murray, *Grievance Procedures* (Farnborough: Saxon House 1976), pp. 128–30.
5 Richard Hyman, *Disputes Procedure in Action* (London: Heinemann 1972), p. 88.
6 Royal Commission on Trade Unions and Employers' Associations, p. 43, para. 176.
7 W. W. Daniel, 'Wage determination in industry', *Political and Economic Planning,* vol. 42, no. 563 (July 1976), pp. 26–30.
8 William Brown and Michael Terry, 'The changing nature of national wage agreements', *Scottish Journal of Political Economy,* vol. 25, no. 2 (June 1978), pp. 124–7.
9 ibid., p. 129.
10 A. W. J. Thomson and P. B. Beaumont, *Public Sector Bargaining: A Study of Relative Gain* (Farnborough: Saxon House 1978), p. 39.
11 Brown and Terry, 'The changing nature of national wage agreements', pp. 124–5.
12 R. F. Elliott and R. Steele, 'The importance of national wage agreements', *British Journal of Industrial Relations,* vol. 14, no. 1 (1976), p.51.
13 Daniel, 'Wage determination in industry', p. 29.
14 Royal Commission on Trade Unions and Employers' Associations, pp. 41–3, para. 170.
15 H. A. Clegg, *The Changing System of Industrial Relations in Great Britain* (Oxford: Blackwell 1979), p. 285.
16 Eric Batstone, Ian Boraston and Stephen Frenkel, *The Social Organisation of Strikes* (Oxford: Blackwell 1978), pp. 19–20.
17 Royal Commission on Trade Unions and Employers' Associations, p. 100, para. 377.
18 Approximately 10 per cent of the total number of working days lost through stoppages in 1977, for example, are attributable to one strike in the public sector – that of the firemen.
19 C. T. B. Smith, Richard Clifton, Peter Makeham, S. W. Creigh and R. V. Burn, 'Strikes in Britain', Department of Employment. Reported in *Department of Employment Gazette,* vol. 86, no. 11 (November 1978).
20 Royal Commission on Trade Unions and Employers' Associations, pp. 108–9, para. 401–2.
21 Richard Hyman, *Strikes* (London: Fontana 1971), p. 124.
22 H. A. Turner and Frank Wilkinson, 'The seventh pay policy, *New Society,* (17 July 1975).
23 R. J. Davies, 'Economic activity, incomes policy and strikes' *British Journal of Industrial Relations,* vol. 17, (July 1979) no. 2, pp. 215–20.
24 Clegg, *The Changing System of Industrial Relations,* p. 281.
25 John Gennard, *Financing Strikers* (London: Macmillan 1977), p. 65.

26 Daniel, 'Wage determination in industry', p. 113.
27 ibid., p. 114.
28 NBPI Report no. 123, 'Productivity agreements', Cmnd 4136 (HMSO, 1969), p. 39.
29 Daniel, 'Wage determination in industry', p. 118.
30 Derek Robinson, 'Differentials and incomes policy', *Industrial Relations Journal,* vol. 4, no. 1 (Spring 1973), pp. 6–7.
31 Daniel, 'Wage determination in industry', p. 119.
32 ibid., pp. 33–4.
33 Robinson, 'Differentials and incomes policy', p. 9.
34 Daniel, 'Wage determination in industry', p. 31.
35 Robinson, 'Differentials and incomes policy', p. 7.
36 Trades Union Congress, *Report,* 1975, p. 463.
37 ibid., p. 460.
38 Daniel, 'Wage determination in industry', p. 48
39 A. J. H. Dean, 'Earnings in the public and private sectors, 1950–75', *National Institute Economic Review,* no. 74 (November 1975), p. 64.
40 Thomson and Beaumont, *Public Sector Bargaining,* pp. 164–5.

Chapter 7: A giant's strength?

1 *The Sunday Times,* (23 April 1978).
2 Charles Mulvey, *The Economic Analysis of Trade Unions* (University of Glasgow 1979), p. 103.
3 J. E. King, *Labour Economics* (London: Macmillan 1972), pp. 45–7.
4 M. W. Reder, 'The theory of occupational wage differentials', *American Economic Review,* vol. 45, no. 5 (December 1955), pp. 833–52.
5 William Brown, *Piecework Bargaining* (London: Heinemann 1973), chs. 4 and 5.
6 William Brown, 'Engineering wages and the social contract, 1975–1977', *Oxford Bulletin of Economics and Statistics,* vol. 41, no. 1 (February 1979), pp. 51–61.
7 ibid., p. 59.
8 'Trends in earnings, 1948–77' *Department of Employment Gazette,* vol. 86, no. 5 (May 1978), pp. 520–30.
9 E. H. Phelps Brown, 'New wine in old bottles: reflections on the changed working of collective bargaining in Great Britain', *British Journal of Industrial Relations,* vol. 11 (July 1973).
10 A. W. Phillips, 'The relation between unemployment and the rate of change in money wages, 1861–1957', *Economica,* vol. 25, no. 4 (November 1958).
11 Milton Friedman, 'Unemployment versus inflation?'. Institute of Economic Affairs, Occasional Paper no. 44 (1975).

12 Robert Bacon and Walter Eltis, *Britain's Economic Problem: Two Few Producers,* (London: Macmillan 1976).

13 A. W. J. Thomson and P. B. Beaumont, *Public sector bargaining: A Study of Relative Gain,* (Farnborough: Saxon House 1973), p. 128.

14 Dudley Jackson, H. A. Turner and Frank Wilkinson, *Do Trade Unions Cause Inflation?*, 2nd ed. (Cambridge University Press 1975), pp. 113–4.

15 Lord Kahn, 'Thoughts on the behaviour of wages and monetarism', *Lloyds Bank Review,* no. 19 (January 1976), pp. 4–5.

16 W. W. Daniel, 'The PEP survey on inflation', PEP, vol. 41, no. 553 (July 1975), p. 11.

17 D. T. Jones, 'Output, employment and labour productivity in Europe since 1955', *National Institute Economic Review,* no. 77 (August 1976).

18 West Midlands Economic Planning Council, 'Industrial productivity – scope for improvement', *Midlands Tomorrow,* no. 8 (1975).

19 Brian Burkitt and David Bowers, *Trade Unions and the Economy* (London: Macmillan 1979), pp. 61–3.

20 Kenneth Roberts, *The Working Class* (London: Longman 1978), p. 27.

21 Peter Townshend, *New Society* (18 October 1979).

22 Roberts, *The Working Class,* p. 30.

23 ibid., p. 38.

24 W. W. Daniel, 'The PEP survey on inflation', *Political and Economic Planning,* vol. 41, no. 553 (July 1975), pp. 18–9.

25 Peter Brannen, Eric Batstone, Derek Fatchett and Philip White, *The Worker Directors* (London: Hutchinson 1976).

26 Eric Batstone and P. L. Davies, 'Industrial democracy: European experience', two reports prepared for the Bullock Committee on industrial democracy (London: HMSO 1977), p. 40.

27 Frank Blackaby, 'The reform of the wage bargaining system', *National Institute Economic Review,* no. 85 (August 1978), pp. 51 2.

Select Bibliography

Over the last ten years the literature on British industrial relations has increased rapidly. The following bibliography is intended to assist students who are unfamiliar with the subject and may feel somewhat daunted by the length of their reading lists.

Bain, George Sayers, *The Growth of White Collar Unionism* (Oxford University Press, 1970). The statistics quoted in the text are now out of date and should be supplemented by the articles which the author has written in the *British Journal of Industrial Relations* and which contain newer data. Nevertheless, this work is still by far the best analysis of British white collar unionism.

Batstone, Eric, Boraston, Ian and Frenkel, Stephen, *Shop Stewards in Action* (Blackwell, 1977). A well-written micro-analysis of shop steward behaviour and leadership styles. It should be read in conjunction with the appropriate sections of Clegg's *The Changing System of Industrial Relations in Great Britain.*

Batstone, Eric, Boraston, Ian and Frenkel, Stephen, *The Social Organisation of Strikes* (Blackwell, 1978). A book which is, in many ways, complimentary to the previous work by the same authors and throws valuable light on a subject of which too little is known.

Benyon, Hugh, *Working for Ford* (Penguin, 1973). An interesting combination of journalism and serious analysis. Reputed not to be popular with senior managers of the Ford Motor Co. Ltd.

Boraston, Ian, Clegg, Hugh and Rimmer, Malcolm, *Workplace and Union* (Heinemann, 1975). Useful study of a subject which was treated in a very superficial manner by the Donovan Report.

Brown, E. H. Phelps, *The Growth of British Industrial Relations* (Macmillan, 1959). Despite its age this is still the best general introduction to the development of the traditional institutions and procedural rules of British industrial relations between 1870 and 1914.

Berkitt, Brian and Bowers, David, *Trade Unions and the Economy* (Macmillan, 1979). Useful and lucid treatment of what, in the hands of some economists, can be excessively technical and tedious.

Clegg, Hugh, *The Changing System of Industrial Relations in Great Britain*

(Blackwell 1979). This book updates Clegg's earlier work published in 1970 but the basic approach remains the same. As a general reference book it is undoubtedly valuable.

Daniel, W. W., 'Wage determination in industry', *Political and Economic Planning,* vol. 42, no. 563 (July 1976). A lucid analysis of the principles and structures of wage bargaining in Britain. Invaluable to any student of incomes policies.

Flanders, Allan, *Management and Unions: The Theory and Reform of Industrial Relations* (Faber, 1970). A collection of articles and lectures delivered during the 1960s, some of which are now very dated but others are still worth reading.

Hawkins, Kevin, *The Management of Industrial Relations* (Penguin, 1978). A general introduction to the major talking points in British industrial relations in the mid to late 1970s.

Hawkins, Kevin, *A Handbook of Industrial Relations Practice* (Kogan Page, 1979). A textbook written for a managerial audience which contains some material of interest to students.

Hemingway, John, *Conflict and Democracy* (Oxford University Press, 1978). One of the very few books on trade union government which succeeds in making the subject interesting.

Hyman, Richard, *Industrial Relations: A Marxist Introduction* (Macmillan, 1974). Particularly interesting for Marxists.

Hyman, Richard, *Strikes* (Fontana/Collins, 1971). A collection of interesting essays which were particularly relevant in the context of the anti-strike hysteria of the late 1960s.

Lane, Tony and Roberts, Kenneth, *Strike at Pilkingtons* (Fontana/Collins, 1971). A very readable account of a major strike in 1970.

McCarthy, W. E. J. (ed.), *Trade Unions* (Penguin, 1972). A collection of useful, though in some cases dated, essays covering most aspects of the subject.

Thomson, A. W. J. and Beaumont, P. B., *Public Sector Bargaining: A Study of Relative Gain* (Saxon House, 1978). Good introductory account of the principles and procedures of bargaining in the public sector.

Webb, Sidney and Webb, Beatrice, *Industrial Democracy* (London, 1898). The classic work on collective bargaining. Still worth reading.

Wedderburn, K. W., *The Worker and the Law,* 2nd ed. (Penguin, 1971). An invaluable analysis of the development of British labour law, marred only by the lack (so far) of a third edition.

Index